Frommer's

Napa & Sonoma
day BY day®

4th Edition

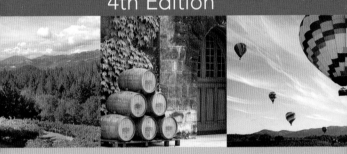

by Avital Andrews

FrommerMedia LLC

Contents

Published by:

Frommer Media LLC

ISBN: 978-1-628-87298-9 (paper); ISBN 978-1-628-87299-6 (ebk)

Editorial Director: Pauline Frommer
Editor: Michael Kelly
Production Editor: Erin Geile
Photo Editor: Meghan Lamb
Cartographer: Liz Puhl
Indexer: Maro RioFrancos

Front cover photos, left to right: View of vineyard in St. Helena © Meghan Lamb; Wine barrels stacked outside of the Château Montelena © Wollertz / Shutterstock.com; Hot air balloons © Meghan Lamb.

Back cover photo: Vineyards in Napa Valley © Meghan Lamb.

For information on our other products and services, please go to Frommers.com.

Frommer's also publishes its books in a variety of electronic formats. Some content that appears in print may not be available in electronic formats.

Manufactured in China

5 4 3 2 1

About this Guide

Organizing your time. That's what this guide is all about.

Other guides give you long lists of things to see and do and then expect you to fit the pieces together. The Day by Day guides are different. These guides tell you the best of everything, and then they show you how to see it *in the smartest, most time-efficient way*. Our authors have designed detailed itineraries organized by time, neighborhood, or special interest. And each tour comes with a bulleted map that takes you from stop to stop.

Hoping to taste the latest cabernet straight from the barrel at a boutique winery, learn about eco-friendly winemaking, or visit the Peanuts gang with your kids at the Charles Schulz Museum? Planning a walk through downtown Sonoma, or dinner and a bottle at one of the region's renowned restaurants? Whatever your interest or schedule, the Day by Days give you the smartest routes to follow. Not only do we take you to the top attractions, hotels, and restaurants, but we also help you access those special moments that locals get to experience—those "finds" that turn tourists into travelers.

The Day by Days are also your top choice if you're looking for one complete guide for all your travel needs. The best hotels and restaurants for every budget, the greatest shopping values, the wildest nightlife—it's all here.

Why should you trust our judgment? Because our authors personally visit each place they write about. They're an independent lot who say what they think and would never include places they wouldn't recommend to their best friends. They're also open to suggestions from readers. If you'd like to contact them, please send your comments our way at Support@FrommerMedia.com, and we'll pass them on.

Enjoy your Day by Day guide—the most helpful travel companion you can buy. And have the trip of a lifetime.

About the Author

Avital Andrews writes for dozens of national magazines, newspapers, and websites, including the *Los Angeles Times, USA Today, The Week, Pacific Standard,* Outside, Yahoo, Smarter Travel, and the Huffington Post. She is the lifestyle editor of *Sierra,* a magazine nominated for a 2016 Maggie in the category of "Lifestyles & Alternative Lifestyles." Avital's journalism is nationally recognized and has been covered by *The New York Times, The Atlantic, Time,* NPR, and MTV. She makes regular radio and TV appearances, has degrees from UCLA and Stanford, and lives in Northern California with her husband and young daughter. Follow her on Twitter @avitalb.

Rosie Spinks, who contributed to this book, is a freelance writer based in London. Originally from California, her work is featured in *The Guardian,* NPR, Slate, Fusion, *Outside, Marie Claire, Sierra, Good,* and others. A nomad at heart, she writes about travel, food, tech, feminism, sustainability, and global citizenship. Follow her on Twitter @rojospinks and find her at rojospinks.com.

Acknowledgments

Sincere thanks to Pauline Frommer for reaching out to commission this fourth edition, and for her generous attention throughout the process of producing it. Thanks also to Michael Kelly and Erin Geile, whose eagle-eyed edits make me look good; to Rosie Spinks, whose whip-smart editorial assistance was crucial; to Meghan Lamb, whose excellent photo editing and regional expertise improved this book immeasurably; and to cartographers Liz Puhl and Roberta Stockwell for their help on this edition's many maps. To my extended family (Arie, Ruth, Eyal, Leor, Sheindel, Cindy, Andy, Joe, and Claire): Thank you for being my rock, even when (especially when) times are tough. I am so grateful for each of you. This book is for Tim, and also for our little Hannah Eloise—my love for both of you is impossible to encapsulate in words.

An Additional Note

Please be advised that travel information is subject to change at any time—and this is especially true of prices. We therefore suggest that you write or call ahead for confirmation when making your travel plans. The authors, editors, and publisher cannot be held responsible for the experiences of readers while traveling. Your safety is important to us, however, so we encourage you to stay alert and be aware of your surroundings.

Star Ratings, Icons & Abbreviations

Every hotel, restaurant, and attraction listing in this guide has been ranked for quality, value, service, amenities, and special features using a **star-rating system.** Hotels, restaurants, attractions, shopping, and nightlife are rated on a scale of zero stars (recommended) to three stars (exceptional). In addition to the star-rating system, we also use a **kids icon** to point out the best bets for families. Within each tour, we recommend cafes, bars, or restaurants where you can take a break. Each of these stops appears in a shaded box marked with a coffee-cup-shaped bullet 🍵.

The following **abbreviations** are used for credit cards:

AE	American Express	DISC	Discover	V	Visa
DC	Diners Club	MC	MasterCard		

Travel Resources at Frommers.com

Frommer's travel resources don't end with this guide. Frommer's website, **www.frommers.com**, has travel information on more than 4,000 destinations. We update features regularly, giving you instant access to the most current trip-planning information available, and the best airfares, lodging rates, and car rental bargains. You can listen to podcasts, connect with other Frommers.com members through our active-reader forums, share your travel photos, read blogs from guidebook editors and fellow travelers, and much more.

A Note on Prices

In the "Take a Break" (coffee-cup icon) sections of this book, we have used a system of dollar signs to show the cost of an entree at a restaurant. Use the following table to decipher the dollar signs:

Cost	Restaurants
$	under $15
$$	$15–$20
$$$	$20–$30
$$$$	$30–$40
$$$$$	over $40

How to Contact Us

In researching this book, we discovered many wonderful places—hotels, restaurants, shops, and more. We're sure you'll find others. Please tell us about them, so we can share the information with your fellow travelers in upcoming editions. If you were disappointed with a recommendation, we'd love to know that, too. Please write to: Support@FrommerMedia.com

18 Favorite
Moments

18 Favorite Moments

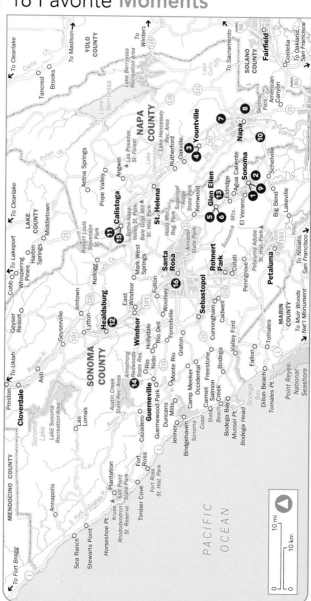

Previous page: A vineyard in Rutherford.

Sonoma town square.

❶ Relive the Bear Flag Revolt and other pivotal moments of California's history while wandering Sonoma's lovely town square. Mission San Francisco Solano, General Vallejo's home, and the Sonoma Barracks bring it all to life. *See p 74.*

❷ Take a romantic tandem-bike tour of Sonoma's wineries, then savor an intimate lunch for two on Gundlach Bundschu's bucolic picnic grounds. *See p 57.*

❸ Savor the tasting menu at one of Yountville's renowned eateries, such as Thomas Keller's French Laundry (p 92), hailed by many as America's best restaurant.

❹ Try to identify the 35 vintners in the John Michael Keating painting at the Napa Valley Museum's permanent exhibit, *The Land and the*

People of the Napa Valley. (Can you find Robert Mondavi, Joseph Phelps, or Louis P. Martini?) *See p 48.*

❺ Ride the tractor tram at Benziger Family Winery through the hills while learning about biodynamic winemaking. Your tour ("the most comprehensive in the wine industry," according to *Wine Spectator*) winds through estate vineyards, into caves, and ends with a memorable tasting. *See p 137.*

❻ Marvel at the beauty of spring wildflowers bursting forth from Audubon Canyon Ranch's well-guarded Bouverie Preserve in Glen Ellen. Keep an eye out for wild egrets or a bobcat.

❼ Enjoy an alfresco meal on the grounds of a Silverado Trail winery.

The Bakewell Tart dessert at the French Laundry.

4

⑧ Lose yourself in a foodie reverie at Spice Islands Marketplace, the Culinary Institute of America's abundant campus store. *See p 32.*

⑨ Embrace local flavor and music at one of the region's many farmers' markets. They happen almost every day of the week, and the most popular is the Sonoma Plaza Friday Farmers' Market. *See p 21.*

⑩ Get current on modern art—while enjoying a breath of fresh air—at Napa's 217-acre (87-hectare) di Rosa Preserve, where local artists' works are sprinkled into expansive meadows. *See p 51.*

⑪ Jump back in (anticipated) surprise at the eruption of Calistoga's famous Old Faithful Geyser. Sure, it happens every 30 minutes, but when was the last time you've seen water this hot shoot 60 feet (18m) high? *See p 38.*

⑫ Kayak or canoe down the Russian River on a lazy afternoon, looking for the perfect bank on which to break out your wine-infused picnic. *See p 118.*

⑬ Feel the exhilaration as you drive an open stretch of country

View the valley from a hot-air balloon.

Old Faithful Geyser in Calistoga.

highway like Route 12. Few moving-car views can match those countless rows of vines fanning by.

⑭ Quiet down for a contemplative moment in a grove of millennium-old trees at the Armstrong Redwoods State Reserve. *See p 112.*

⑮ Take a dip in mineral hot springs or indulge in a soothing mud bath at one of Calistoga's spas. Dr. Wilkinson's Hot Springs Resort in Calistoga is a good option. *See p 99.*

⑯ Chuckle at the antics of Snoopy, Lucy, Charlie Brown, and the rest of the Peanuts gang during a stroll through Santa Rosa's Charles M. Schulz Museum, which honors the cartoonist's whimsical contribution to American culture. *See p 37.*

⑰ Float aloft in a spectacularly colored hot-air balloon, serenely surveying miles of vineyards. *See p 60.*

⑱ Linger at a bustling tasting-room counter, quietly realizing that you've just found the wine you'd like to use to toast your child's wedding. ●

1 Strategies for Seeing Napa & Sonoma

Napa **&** Sonoma

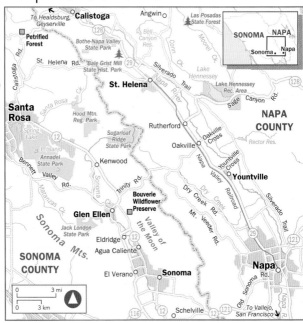

Napa and Sonoma have so much to see and do. That said, the first thing you should do is accept that you won't be able to do it all. It's easy to get overwhelmed by all there is to experience, but the best way to plan your trip to the two counties is to decide what type of vacation you want and develop a specific itinerary—with room for spontaneity, of course. Use this book to chart your course and choose the special-interest tours that appeal to you.

Rule #1: Decide where to focus: Napa, Sonoma, or both.

Once you know that, decide which parts of each seem to beckon most (perusing this book's "Charming Towns" chapter, p 67, will help). Napa Valley dwarfs Sonoma Valley in population, number of wineries, and sheer traffic. It's more commercial, boasting the bigger names (Mondavi, Beringer, Krug) and an intimidating selection of restaurants, hotels, and spas. Sonoma's catching up quickly, but many people prefer it because it's more low-key, less snobby, more backcountry—kind of like a Napa for insiders. Small, family-owned wineries are Sonoma's mainstay, tastings are less expensive (sometimes free), and winemakers themselves are often in the tasting room pouring your flight. Bottom line: Choose Napa if you want an active touring schedule, Sonoma for a restful, leisurely vacation.

Previous page: Signs point toward Sonoma's wineries.

Cabernet sauvignon grapes being harvested in September.

Rule #2: Don't drink and drive.

Those tiny tastes add up. Plenty of taxi and limo companies are more than happy to provide a chauffeur if you've had too much to drink. Uber started operating in the region in 2014, so that's an option too. Otherwise, designate a driver. Or walk.

Rule #3: Hit wineries early in the day.

Most tasting rooms open around 10am and, even on the busiest weekends, remain empty in the morning, leaving staff free to discuss the winery's goods. If you come after noon, expect a packed house (especially during high season) and a time-consuming line just to get a few sips, much less the employees' prolonged attention.

Rule #4: Visit during off-season (Nov–May) or midweek.

The region's optimum time, "crush," is when the wineries harvest their grapes—typically late summer and early fall—and the masses come in droves, especially on weekends. However, if you can only visit on a high-season Saturday and Sunday, there are ways to avoid the cattle drive. One is to skip the big names and head to the smaller, family-run wineries instead. Even those along

the Silverado Trail, which parallels Highway 29, get less traffic—locals use it as their main thoroughfare during high season. Another option is to stay in Sonoma—the western county gets congested too, but much less so than Napa.

Remember that most wineries are closed on major holidays, and many have restricted off-season hours, so call ahead if there's one you don't want to miss.

Rule #5: Be conscious of tasting fees.

Visitors didn't used to have to pay for sampling, but when Napa became a destination, wineries began collecting. To their credit, it wasn't so much to make a profit as to discourage visitors who, shall we say, prefer quantity over quality. Nowadays, the Napa norm is about $15 to $20 per flight (and much higher at certain places), though it is often applied toward a purchase and sometimes includes a souvenir glass. Sonoma's wineries are less likely to charge as much (or at all) for tasting.

Rule #6: Buying at the winery doesn't mean you're saving money.

In fact, you'll probably end up spending more at a winery than you would at stores (such as Bevmo) that buy cases in bulk. Exceptions to this strategy are wineries that offer big discounts on cases and those that sell their wines only from their tasting room (that is, they have no distribution). *Tip:* If you can ship your wine directly from the winery, you won't have to pay sales tax.

Rule #7: Don't let wine cook in your car.

Buy a cooler and a couple of ice packs, place them in your car's trunk, and *voilà*—your own portable wine cellar.

Wine shipping is an alternative to lugging around all those bottles you bought, but it can be confusing, because it's limited by regulations that vary by state. Complicating the matter further, mailing rules differ from winery to winery. Check the current legal situation as it pertains to your home before buying. Ask wineries and, if necessary, independent shipping companies, about their wine-transporting policies.

Rule #8: Keep a light attitude.

If you don't yet know everything about wine and it seems that

Mustards take over the vineyards in the spring.

Keep a light attitude while tasting wines.

everyone around you does (to an almost silly degree), don't feel bullied by those who deem themselves worthier simply because they're better versed in what's essentially just fermented grape juice. Wine country is about relaxing, having fun, learning, and taking in the scenery—not feeling intimidated. If you encounter a snoot pouring your taste, move on.

Rule #9: Make time to explore the area's natural splendor.

You can hike through a redwood forest, kayak the Russian River, stroll the rocky Pacific coast, and so much more. See "18 Favorite Moments" (p 1) and chapter 5, "The Great Outdoors," for ideas.

Rule #10: Get to know the wineries.

When at a winery, take the time to really get to know not only the wines but also the company's story: its history, its vineyards, and its employees. Most staffers are quite willing to regale you with tales and give you a tour. You can drink California wine just about anywhere in the world, but only by visiting a tasting room or touring a vineyard can you gain true appreciation for the painstaking processes that go into each bottle. ●

The Best Full-Day Tours of Napa & Sonoma

The Best of Napa in One Day

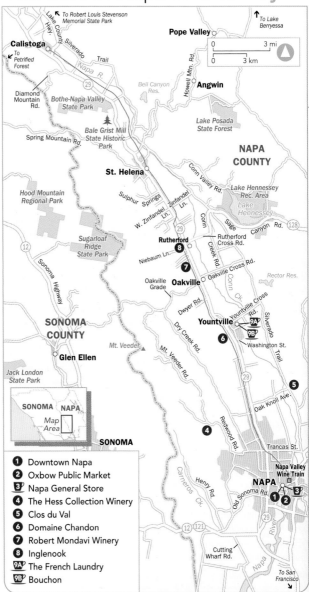

To Robert Louis Stevenson Memorial State Park

To Lake Berryessa

Pope Valley

Calistoga

To Petrified Forest

Lake County Hwy

Silverado Trail

Napa R.

Diamond Mountain Rd.

Bothe-Napa Valley State Park

Bell Canyon Res.

Angwin

Howell Mtn. Rd.

Bale Grist Mill State Historic Park

Spring Mountain Rd.

Lake Posada State Forest

NAPA COUNTY

St. Helena

Conn Valley Rd.

Lake Hennessey Rec. Area

Lake Hennessey

Sulphur Springs

W. Zinfandel Ln.

Zinfandel Ln.

Conn

Sage Canyon Rd.

128

Hood Mountain Regional Park

Rutherford
8

Rutherford Cross Rd.

Niebaum Ln.

7

Conn Creek Rd.

Sugarloaf Ridge State Park

Oakville Grade

Oakville

Oakville Cross Rd.

Conn Ck.

Rector Res.

12

Sonoma Highway

Dwyer Rd.

Dry Creek Rd.

Yountville
6

Yountville Cross Rd.

9A

9B

Silverado Trail

Washington St.

SONOMA COUNTY

Mt. Veeder

Mt. Veeder Rd.

Glen Ellen

Jack London State Park

5

Redwood Rd.

Oak Knoll Ave.

SONOMA | NAPA

Map Area

SONOMA

4

Trancas St.

Carneros Ck.

Henry Rd.

Napa Valley Wine Train

NAPA

1 2

3

1 Downtown Napa
2 Oxbow Public Market
3 Napa General Store
4 The Hess Collection Winery
5 Clos du Val
6 Domaine Chandon
7 Robert Mondavi Winery
8 Inglenook
9A The French Laundry
9B Bouchon

Old Sonoma Rd.

29

Napa River

12 121

Cutting Wharf Rd.

To San Francisco

0   3 mi
0   3 km

Previous page: Oxbow Public Market.

All you have is a day to make the most of Napa? That's a tall order because the valley is rich with worthwhile towns, wineries, sights, and activities, but it can be done—and done well. This full-day itinerary, manageable in a day by car, introduces you to the region's character. At the end of it, you can rest assured that you've experienced Napa's essence. But remember: Drinking-and-driving rules still apply, so designate a driver, don't swallow the wine, or limit your intake and eat heartily. START: **1st & Main sts. Tour distance: About 36 miles (68km).**

1 ★★ **Downtown Napa.** Not long ago, the actual town of Napa would never have been listed in a "best of Napa Valley" tour—but times have changed and the town's recent redevelopment merits it a spot right at the top. Hit First Street Napa to get a feel for everyday life here. Note the striking Italianate-style Opera House and how upscale this town's markets are. *Napa Tourist Information Center, 1331 First St., Napa.* ☎ *707/252-1000. www.napatouristinfo.com. Mon–Wed 10am–5pm; Thurs–Sun 10am–9pm.*

2 ★ **Oxbow Public Market.** This is a foodie's dream destination, showcasing the region's best comestibles under a single roof.

The Napa General Store in the Historic Napa Mill.

Walk through the marketplace to meet vendors selling artisanal cheeses, exotic spices, bottles from micro-wineries, and an impressive selection of other gourmet goodies. Free parking is available. *610 & 644 First St., Napa.* ☎ *707/226-6529. www.oxbowpublicmarket.com. Mon–Sat 9am–7pm; Sun 10am–6pm (closed Thanksgiving, Christmas & New Year's Day).*

3 ★ **Napa General Store.** End your downtown Napa visit at the Historic Napa Mill to pick up a box lunch ($15). Choose from a variety of fresh sandwiches and salads that come with a house-baked cookie and utensils. *Note:* Box lunches must be ordered at least a day in advance. If you didn't preorder, get something to go from the market's cafe (options include sandwiches, salads, Asian specialties, and hand-tossed pizzas) or sit and eat here—a cozy option if the weather's unsavory. *540 Main St., #100, Napa.* ☎ *707/259-0762. $$.*

Take Highway 29 north and exit at Trancas Street. Turn left on Redwood Road, a four-lane road that narrows into a two-lane road. Turn left at the Hess Collection's sign.

4 ★★★ **The Hess Collection Winery.** The drive up here provides a good example of the beautiful, rugged scenery that characterizes much of Northern

California. Once at the winery, avail yourself of art galleries, a garden that blooms in summer, and a stone-walled tasting room in the original 1903 structure, featuring a maple bar, barrel-lined walls, and the highlight: a full selection of Hess's current releases, including superb cabernet sauvignon and chardonnay. *4411 Redwood Rd., Napa.* ☎ *707/255-1144. See p 149.*

Wind back down Redwood Road and stay straight onto Trancas Street, then turn left on Silverado Trail.

5 ★ Clos du Val. You can't say you've done Napa's best without having seen at least one small, exclusive winery in the Stags Leap District along the scenic Silverado Trail. Marked with both French and American flags to properly convey this estate's thoroughly French heritage, Clos du Val's tasting room is behind ivy-covered walls. In it, try the flagship Stags Leap District cabernet sauvignon. Ask tasting-room staff for a tour of the demonstration vineyard, where you can learn about trellising techniques and how to identify different kinds of grapes. After trying the wines, settle into Clos du Val's beautiful olive grove and break out the food you bought earlier for a picnic lunch. *5330 Silverado Trail, Napa.* ☎ *707/261-5251. See p 142.*

Head southeast on Silverado Trail and turn right at Oak Knoll Avenue, then left onto Big Ranch Road. Turn right to get back onto Oak Knoll Avenue, and right again to get on Highway 29 N. Exit toward Yountville, then turn left on California Drive. Head up the long, vineyard-flanked driveway.

6 ★ Domaine Chandon. Cross a small footbridge over a life-filled pond (keep an eye out for egrets) and past some interesting

The Clos du Val winery.

sculptures to enter the educational visitor center, featuring interactive exhibits and a wall made entirely of bottles. Domaine Chandon specializes in "sparkling wine"—technically, it can't be called champagne because it's not produced in that proprietary French province. But since this winery is owned by the French company Moët Hennessy Louis Vuitton (LVMH), what you get is pretty similar to Moët et Chandon. The knowledgeable employees here will explain to you the nuances of effervescent wine. *1 California Dr. (at Hwy. 29), Yountville.* ☎ *888/242-6366. See p 145.*

Take California Drive northeast to merge onto Highway 29.

7 ★★ Robert Mondavi Winery. This mission-style venue gives the valley's most varied and comprehensive tours. Given today's time constraint, however, opt for the basic tour or just visit the art gallery before or after tasting on the Vineyard Tasting Room's patio overlooking rows of grapes, or, if you prefer, enjoy wines by the glass in the upscale To Kalon Room. *7801 St. Helena Hwy. (Hwy. 29), Oakville.* ☎ *707/226-1395. See p 156.*

Keep following Highway 29 northwest.

8 **★★★ Inglenook.** Formerly Niebaum-Coppola, then Rubicon Estate, in 2011, Inglenook at last acquired the rights to its original historic name. Film director Francis Ford Coppola's ivy-draped 1880s stone winery exudes grandeur. Inside, an impressive retail center promotes Coppola's wine products and, more subtly, his movies. The Centennial Museum chronicles the vineyard's rich history. Sample its estate-grown blends, all made from organic grapes, including the flagship Rubicon Cabernet Sauvignon, but note the caveat: Tasting fees start at $45 per person. Reservations recommended. *1991 St. Helena Hwy., Rutherford.* ☎ *707/968-1100. See p 150.*

Tasting sparkling wine at Domaine Chandon.

Patio of the Robert Mondavi Winery.

9A **★★★ The French Laundry.** If you want the best of Napa dining, there's only one place to go: a very, very famous little restaurant called The French Laundry. Chef Thomas Keller's intricate preparations, often finished tableside, are presented with extraordinary artistry. But when the check arrives, close your eyes and reassure yourself that this was a once-in-a-lifetime experience. Reservations are required and should be made at least 2 months in advance. *6640 Washington St., Yountville.* ☎ *707/944-2380. $$$$$. See p 92.*

If you've still got next month's mortgage to pay, dine at humbler **9B** **★★ Bouchon,** which also serves up Keller's inspired creations, but in toned-down bistro environs that are more friendly than froufrou. *6534 Washington St.* ☎ *707/944-8037. $$$$. See p 92.*

The Best of Sonoma in One Day

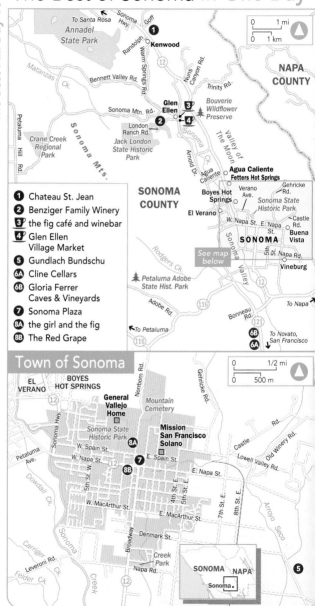

1 Chateau St. Jean
2 Benziger Family Winery
3 the fig café and winebar
4 Glen Ellen Village Market
5 Gundlach Bundschu
6A Cline Cellars
6B Gloria Ferrer Caves & Vineyards
7 Sonoma Plaza
8A the girl and the fig
8B The Red Grape

Town of Sonoma

Sonoma Valley is like Napa Valley's younger sibling. It's made up of the same kind of magic, but one gets the sense that it tries hard to match Napa's renown. The struggle to measure up has paid off, to the degree that many visitors profess that Sonoma has actually surpassed Napa in charm—and wine. This 1-day overview gives you a taste of the wineries, lets you experience the small-town feel, and takes you up bucolic stretches of highway. START: **Chateau St. Jean, 8555 Sonoma Hwy. (Hwy. 12), Kenwood. Trip Length: 26 miles (42km).**

❶ ★★ Chateau St. Jean. Notable for its grand buildings and expansive grounds, Chateau St. Jean is, in California, a pioneer in vineyard designation—making wine from, and naming it for, a single vineyard. A private drive takes you to a manicured picnic lawn overlooking meticulously maintained vineyards. In the large tasting room, where plenty of housewares are for sale, sample Chateau St. Jean's wide array of wines, including pinot noir, chardonnay, cabernet sauvignon, and the flagship Cinq Cépages, a Sonoma County bordeaux blend. *Sideways* notwithstanding, merlot is the winery's bestseller. *8555 Sonoma Hwy. (Hwy. 12), Kenwood.* ☎ *707/257-5784. See p 141.*

Continue southeast on Highway 12, turn right onto Arnold Drive, then make a slight right onto London Ranch Road.

❷ ★★ kids Benziger Family Winery. This is a true family estate. At any given time, two generations of Benzigers may be on site, and they make you feel like part of the clan. The property is known for its excellent 45-minute tractor-tram tour ($25, or $10 for ages 20 and younger), which takes off every 30 minutes between 11am and 3:30pm. It winds through the vineyards while providing a thorough explanation of why Benziger is a certified biodynamic winery, and what that means. The tram stops often so that you can examine exhibits and explore aromatic aging caves. The tour ends with an informative tasting. *Tip:* Tram tickets—a hot item especially in summer—are available on a first-come, first-served basis, but you can also book them online at www.benziger.com. *1883 London Ranch Rd., Glen Ellen.* ☎ *888/490-2739. See p 137.*

❸ ★★ the fig café and winebar. Call ahead and place a to-go order at this beloved Glen Ellen cafe, whose big-sister restaurant is Sonoma's famous girl and the fig (p 77). Sondra Bernstein's inspired lunch creations include pizzas, tarts, salads, and sandwiches. Pick up your meal and save it for the picnic

The expansive grounds of Chateau St. Jean in Sonoma.

The tram tour at Benziger.

grounds at the next stop. *13690 Arnold Dr., Glen Ellen.* ☎ *707/ 938-2130. $$$.* Alternatively, grab something from the deli counter at **④ ★ Glen Ellen Village Market,** where recommended options include panini, burgers, and burritos. *13751 Arnold Dr., Glen Ellen. 707/ 996-6728. $.*

From Glen Ellen, take Arnold Drive south (toward Holt), then turn left onto Leveroni Road. Two miles (3.2km) after Leveroni becomes Napa Road, make a left onto Denmark Street. You'll quickly see:

⑤ ★★ Gundlach Bundschu. If it looks like the people working here are enjoying themselves, that's because they are. Gundlach Bundschu is the quintessential Sonoma winery—nonchalant in appearance but obsessed with the craft. Members of this winemaking family are known for their mischievousness: They've pulled stunts like holding up Napa's Wine Train (p 63) on horseback and serving Sonoma wines to their "captives." The small, often crowded tasting room plays rock music as carefree—but attentive—staffers happily pour chardonnay, pinot noir, merlot, cabernet, and others. Now in its sixth generation, Gundlach Bundschu is California's oldest continually

family-owned and operated winery. This is the place to unfold your lunch feast: GB's picnic area is perched on the side of a small hill, giving it a sensational view of the Sonoma countryside. Work up an appetite by taking the short hike to the top of the knoll. *2000 Denmark St., Sonoma.* ☎ *707/ 938-5277. See p 148.*

Choose between visiting Gloria Ferrer or Cline, which are almost adjacent. Travel less than 2 miles (3.2km) north on Highway 121 and pull into either:

⑥A ★ kids Cline Cellars. If you're more interested in California history and tasting an array of unique wines, opt for this family-owned winery with a small, friendly tasting room and an intimate museum that showcases dollhouse-size dioramas of all 21 California missions. *24737 Arnold Dr. (Hwy. 121), Sonoma.* ☎ *707/940-4000. See p 142.*

OR:

⑥B Gloria Ferrer Caves & Vineyards. If you've had it up to here with chardonnays and pinots—or if you're just a big fan of champagne—choose Gloria Ferrer, which specializes in sparkling wine. It's a bit overrated as a tourist attraction—to see the eponymous caves, you stand at a railing and flip on a light switch, then wonder, "That's it?" But the bubbly's good, so come expecting just that, and you won't be disappointed. Or take a guided underground cave tour ($25; $15 for nondrinkers and children), which includes four tastings and starts at 11am, 1pm, or 3pm. *23555 Arnold Dr. (Hwy. 121), Sonoma.* ☎ *707/933-1917. See p 147.*

Continue northwest on Highway 121/Carneros Highway/Arnold Drive, then turn right onto W. Watmaugh Road. After about a mile (1.6km), turn left onto Broadway and stay on it until it ends on Napa Street. Turn left or right and look for parking.

⑦ ★★★ kids Sonoma Plaza.
The 8-acre (3.25-hectare) site of the 1846 Bear Flag Revolt is the pulse point of the entire county, and it hums with history and local culture. Despite the tense confrontation it commemorates, the plaza (California's oldest) is relaxing, with a cheery, parklike atmosphere. Well-preserved monuments—like the fascinating Mission San Francisco Solano, City Hall, General Vallejo's home, and old army barracks—add mystique. You'll be hard-pressed not to leave the plaza lugging shopping bags, because the boutiques, bakeries, tasting rooms, and galleries are irresistible. If your evening stroll is on a Tuesday in spring or summer, you'll

Sonoma Square park.

Cheese plate at the girl and the fig.

catch the farmers' market and its accompanying musical acts. (For more on farmers' markets, see p 21.) *Sonoma Valley Visitors Bureau, 453 1st St. E.* ☎ *707/996-1090. www.sonomavalley.com. Shop hours vary but many are open Mon–Sat 9am–5pm; Sun 10am–5pm.*

8A ★★★ the girl and the fig.
For dinner, go with this local favorite right on the plaza. From its refusal to use uppercase letters to its insistence on featuring figs in many of its recipes, this warmly decorated eatery serving inventive nouvelle French cuisine makes sure to defy convention, which works to its benefit. Sit outside if the weather's pleasant, and save room for dessert. *110 W. Spain St. (in the Sonoma Hotel), Sonoma.* ☎ *707/938-3634. www.thegirlandthefig.com. $$$. See p 77.*
If you're in the mood for great pizza, try **8B ★ kids The Red Grape,** a casual, artsy space a half-block off the plaza. Its unconventional selection of crispy thin-crust pies made with fresh, local ingredients in wood-stone ovens gratifies even the snobbiest of pizza connoisseurs. *529 1st St. W., Sonoma.* ☎ *707/996-4103. www.theredgrape.com. $$.*

The Best of Napa & Sonoma in Three Days—Day 3

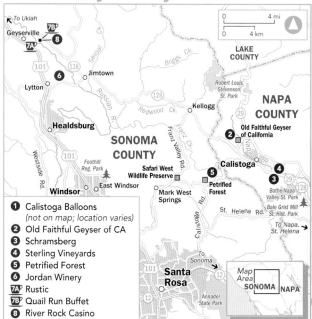

1 Calistoga Balloons
(not on map; location varies)
2 Old Faithful Geyser of CA
3 Schramsberg
4 Sterling Vineyards
5 Petrified Forest
6 Jordan Winery
7A Rustic
7B Quail Run Buffet
8 River Rock Casino

Follow the previous two itineraries for your first couple of days. On the third day, this full-day up-valley Napa and Sonoma tour gives you the lay of the land from above (balloons and aerial trams), below (from whence the geyser spews), and through. ***Tip:*** Plan ahead—advance reservations are required for ballooning and Jordan Winery. Also, know that ballooning requires getting up at around 5am. START: **Your hotel. Distance: 50 miles (81km), not including transport to, from, and during the hot-air balloon ride, or the drive from your hotel to Old Faithful.**

1 ★★★ **kids Calistoga Balloons.** If you've been in wine country this long, you've seen the colorful hot-air balloons floating above the vineyards. Sure, it means getting up at an ungodly hour, but once aloft, you'll know what sanctity means. Your expert pilot maneuvers the balloon into the clouds, creating a sublime

experience. A full champagne breakfast is served upon landing, in keeping with balloonist tradition. Reservations are required and should be made as far in advance as possible. *1458 Lincoln Ave., Calistoga.* ☎ *707/942-5758. www.calistoga-balloons.com. $239 per person, including transportation and brunch.*

Ballooning Tip

When the valley's foggy, companies drive passengers outside the valley to launch. Though they can't guarantee the flight path until hours before liftoff, they should refund your money if you decide not to partake.

If you're staying locally, Calistoga Balloons will deliver you back to your hotel. From there, drive to:

❷ ★★ kids **Old Faithful Geyser of California.** At this natural wonder (it's one of only three "old faithful" geysers in the world) surrounded by pleasant kitsch, you can dependably see 60-foot-high (18m) eruptions every 30 to 40 minutes. If you want, buy treats at the snack bar to munch on between spews. Or linger at the gift shop, where you can watch a video about the Golden State, get a penny stamped, or buy California-themed mugs, key chains, and wine glasses. *1299 Tubbs Lane, Calistoga.* ☎ *707/942-6463. See p 38.*

Take Tubbs Lane southwest and turn left on Foothill Boulevard/ Highway 128. Turn right on Peterson Drive, then right on Schramsberg Road.

❸ ★★ **Schramsberg.** This 200-acre (80-hectare) estate has a wonderful old-world feel—in his heyday, Robert Louis Stevenson was a regular. Schramsberg is the label presidents serve when toasting international dignitaries, and there's plenty of memorabilia in the front room to prove it. But the real mystique begins when you enter the 2½-mile (4km) aging caves—reputedly North America's longest—which were hand-carved by Chinese laborers in the 1800s. The free tour ends in a charming tasting room where you sit around a big table and sample varied selections of bubbly. *1400 Schramsberg Rd., Calistoga.* ☎ *707/942-4558. See p 157.*

Head northeast on Schramsberg Road to turn left on Peterson Drive. Turn left on Highway 29/128, then right on Dunaweal Lane.

❹ ★★ kids **Sterling Vineyards.** An aerial tram brings you to this dazzlingly white Mediterranean-style winery, perched atop a rocky, 300-foot-high (90m) hill. On your way up, marvel at the view, which spans many of Napa Valley's vineyards. When you land, follow the multimedia self-guided tour (one of wine country's most thorough), which details the winemaking process. This winery is a huge producer, churning out more than 500,000 cases per year. Admission includes a sit-down tasting. *1111 Dunaweal Lane, Calistoga.* ☎ *800/726-6136. See p 158.*

Go south on Dunaweal Lane to turn right onto Highway 29/128. Turn left on Petrified Forest Road.

Sparkling wine in Schramsberg caves.

5 ★★ **kids** **Petrified Forest.** Volcanic ash blanketed this area after Mount St. Helena erupted more than 3 million years ago. As a result, the redwoods in this mile-long (1.6km) forest have turned to stone through the slow infiltration of silica and other minerals. Look closely and you'll also see petrified seashells, clams, and other marine life, indicating that water covered this part of the planet long before the redwood forest grew. Take the ¼-mile (.4km) walking trail to see a collection of rock logs, plus the Pit Tree (a preserved pine in a 15-ft./4.5m-deep pit), a statue of Petrified Charlie (Charles Evans, this land's first owner), and other stiffened trees with names like The Giant (a redwood) and The Queen, who has a live oak growing out of her. *4100 Petrified Forest Rd., Calistoga.* ☎ *707/942-6667. See p 37.*

Take Petrified Forest Road west and turn right on Porter Creek Road/Mark West Springs Road. Merge onto Highway 101 N, exit on Lytton Springs Road and turn right, then left on Lytton Station Road, then left on Alexander Valley Road.

6 ★★ **Jordan Winery.** With ivy-covered buildings reminiscent of an 18th-century French château and hilltop views of Alexander Valley, Geyser Peak, and Mount St. Helena, Jordan Winery is a must-see in the Healdsburg area. Formal French gardens and a variety of trees (picnic tables are set under a massive oak) add to the experience. Tours of the winemaking facilities happen almost every day (though not on Sundays Dec–Mar), and conclude with sips of cab and chardonnay. Reservations required, and no one under the age of 21 is allowed in. *1474 Alexander Valley Rd., Healdsburg.* ☎ *800/654-1213. See p 150.*

7A ★★ **Rustic.** Have dinner at Francis Ford Coppola's winery's restaurant, formerly Chateau Souverain's Alexander Valley Grille. The menu lists pizzas, burgers, steaks, salads, seasonal soups, and a four-course tasting menu. On Tuesdays, trust the chef to send your dishes out a tavola style. *300 Via Archimedes, Geyserville.* ☎ *707/857-1400. $$$$.* For a more casual experience, head to **7B** **Quail Run Buffet** at the River Rock Casino (below), which is, well, a pretty typical casino buffet. But it's got a full late-night menu too. *3250 Hwy. 128, Geyserville.* ☎ *707/857-2777. $$$.*

Head east on Alexander Valley Road to turn left on Highway 128.

8 ★ **River Rock Casino.** Open 24 hours a day, 365 days a year, this bungalow-style casino owned and run by the Dry Creek Band of Pomo Indians stocks more than 1,200 slot machines, a variety of card tables, and frequent live-entertainment acts. Try your luck; if it runs out, gain perspective on the outside deck, which provides a view of the magnificent hills surrounding Alexander Valley. *3250 Hwy. 128, Geyserville.* ☎ *707/857-2777. www.riverrockcasino.com.*

Try your luck at River Rock Casino.

Local Farmers' Markets

Wine country is alive and colorful with free farmers' markets from Tuesday through Saturday. Here's when to go where:

TUESDAY: The **Napa Farmers' Market** happens from 8am to 12:30pm in the south parking lot across the street from Oxbow Public Market. Rollicking musical performances complement fresh, locally grown fruits and vegetables, baked goods, and coffee. *500 1st St. May–Oct (Tues & Sat).* The **Valley of the Moon Certified Farmers' Market** happens from 5:30pm to dusk, offering produce, food samples, flowers, crafts, nonprofit booths, and live entertainment. *Sonoma*

Local produce, flowers, and baked goods for sale at St. Helena's Farmers' Market

Plaza, 453 1st St. E., Sonoma. ☎ *707/529-0404. May–Oct.*

WEDNESDAY: **Santa Rosa** holds two Wednesday farmers' markets: One operates year-round in the Veterans' Building's east parking lot (at Maple St. and Hwy. 12) from 9am to 1pm (☎ 415/999-5635), and another downtown (May–Aug 5 to 8:30pm; 4th St. between B and D; ☎ 707/524-2123).

THURSDAY: The energy-filled **Guerneville Farmers' Market** happens on Guerneville Plaza (corner of River Rd./Hwy. 116 and Armstrong Woods Rd.) from 3 to 7pm. ☎ *707/865-4171. May–Oct.*

FRIDAY: **St. Helena's Farmers' Market** at Crane Park (on Crane St., off Hwy. 29) showcases fresh produce, flowers, baked goods, live entertainment, and arts and crafts from 7:30am to noon, rain or shine. ☎ *707/486-2662. May–Oct.* At **Sonoma Valley Certified Farmers' Market,** you might spot some of the valley's most prominent chefs eyeing the goods. It's open year-round 9am to 12:30pm. *241 W. 1st St.* ☎ *707/538-7023.*

SATURDAY: In addition to the **Napa Farmers' Market** (see above), Saturday also brings the **Calistoga Farmers' Market,** held at Sharpsteen Plaza year-round, rain or shine, from 9am to 1pm. *1235 Washington St.* ☎ *707/942-8892.* **Santa Rosa** holds another market in the Veterans' Building's east parking lot; see "Wednesday" (above) for details, though note that its Saturday hours are 8:30am to 1pm. In **Healdsburg,** from 9am to noon, the town's excellent (but sometimes crowded) farmers' market happens a block west of the Plaza (at North and Vine sts.). ☎ *707/694-9763. May–Nov.*

The Best of Napa & Sonoma in Five Days—Days 4 & 5

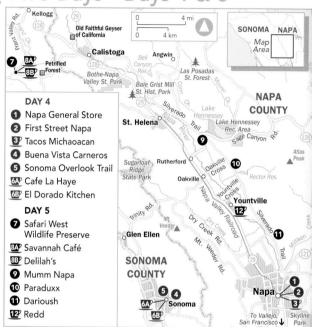

DAY 4

1. Napa General Store
2. First Street Napa
3. Tacos Michaoacan
4. Buena Vista Carneros
5. Sonoma Overlook Trail
6A. Cafe La Haye
6B. El Dorado Kitchen

DAY 5

7. Safari West Wildlife Preserve
8A. Savannah Café
8B. Delilah's
9. Mumm Napa
10. Paraduxx
11. Darioush
12. Redd

After conducting your first 3 days as outlined on the preceding pages, Days 4 and 5 will solidify your sense of the region, as well as expose you to more of both valleys' distinctive attractions. It's helpful if you spend the night of Day 4 in Sonoma County, so consider staying overnight at Safari West, the starting point of Day 5. (See p 130 for lodging details.) **DAY 4** START: **Napa Town Center, 1st & Main St., Napa. Distance: About 50 miles (80km). DAY 5** START: **Safari West Wildlife Preserve, 3115 Porter Creek Rd., Santa Rosa. Distance: About 32 miles (52 km).**

DAY 4

1 ★★★ Napa General Store. Start your day with a satisfying breakfast at the shop occupying the Historic Napa Mill—the store's homemade granola and chocolate beignets are worth trying. Eat outside for a view of the Napa River, or inside to cozy up near the fireplace.

While you're here, sniff the oils and soaps, all hand-crafted by local artisans. *540 Main St., Napa.* ☎ *707/259-0762. $$.*

2 ★ kids First Street Napa. At this writing, this retail complex (formerly the Napa Town Center) is less lively than it was before the 2014

Napa General Store.

earthquake, which shut down its anchor tenant, a major department store called McCaulou's. However, the center's new owners promise an inviting overhaul by 2017. Even right now, though, you can head here to sate a sweet tooth at **Anette's Chocolates** (1321 First St.; ☎ 707/252-4228). Look for the two huge oak trees that serve as town landmarks. Here you'll also find the **Napa Tourist Information Center** (see p 11). Stop in for local information, coupons, and pamphlets outlining self-guided walking tours of the town's historic buildings. *1290 Napa Town Center.* ☎ *707/255-9282.*

3 ★ **Tacos Michoacan.** Grab a bite at what used to be a well-known Napa taco truck but has since graduated into an enjoyable sit-down restaurant. *721 Lincoln Ave.* ☎ *707/256-0820. $$.*

Your scenic 25-minute drive from Napa Valley to Sonoma Valley starts westward on 1st Street, then merges onto Highway 29 S. Turn right onto Highway 12/121, then make a slight right onto Napa Road. Turn right on 8th Street E., then right again on E. Napa Street. Make a quick left on Old Winery Road.

4 ★★★ **Buena Vista Carneros.** America's oldest continuously operating winery was founded in 1857 and is worth a visit for its historical relevance alone. A restored stone press houses the tasting room—in it, try what the estate calls the "Carneros Quartet": a blend of its pinot noir, chardonnay, merlot, and cabernet sauvignon, all crafted via artisan methods. *18000 Old Winery Rd., Sonoma.* ☎ *800/926-1266. See p 138.*

Take Old Winery Road southwest, then turn right on E. Napa Street. Turn right on 1st Street E. Just beyond the Veterans' Memorial Building is a small lot adjacent to the Mountain Cemetery entrance. Park, then look for the trailhead sign.

5 ★ **Sonoma Overlook Trail.** Take in sweeping afternoon views from this well-maintained trail, an easy 2-mile-plus (3.2km) loop accented by interpretive signs, seasonal wildflowers, and manzanita trees. Not long ago, this hillside was doomed to be developed as a resort, but locals worked with the Sonoma Ecology Center to preserve the scenic area. See if you can spy San Pablo Bay or San Francisco's skyline—both should be visible on a clear day. If you want a workout, jog this instead of hiking it. If you're walking, though, allow about 2 hours. ☎ *707/996-0712. www.sonomaecologycenter.org.*

6A ★★ **Cafe La Haye.** You'll have worked up an appetite, so dine at this petite restaurant offering seasonal cuisine. *140 E. Napa St., Sonoma.* ☎ *707/935-5994. $$. See p 77.*

6B ★★ **El Dorado Kitchen,** a Mediterranean-inspired bistro, is more upscale. *405 1st St. W., Sonoma.* ☎ *707/996-3030. $$$. See p 77.*

DAY 5

7 ★★ **Safari West Wildlife Preserve.** Tours at this 400-acre (160-hectare) home of more than 800 exotic animals—zebras, giraffes, gazelles, cheetahs, and many, many more—start at 9 or 10am, depending on the season. Though the organization's primary mission is preserving wildlife and breeding endangered species, it also runs on the idea that in-person contact with animals raises awareness—and care—about the need to save species and protect their fragile lands. During the preserve's daily Classic Safari Adventures, guides drive you around the savannah-like property in open-air vehicles from which you'll see

Enjoy the views and sparkling wine at Mumm Napa in Rutherford.

wildebeest, oryx, ostrich, and many other freely roaming species. You'll want to take lots of pictures in the open-air aviary, and of all the lemurs and buffalo within view. If you're into zoology, pay extra ($225 for two people; $50 for each additional adult, $30 for each additional child) for a behind-the-scenes tour and chat with the keepers. Advance reservations are required for all tours, which are about 3 hours long. *3115 Porter Creek Rd., Santa Rosa.* ☎ *707/579-2551 or 800/616-2695. www.safariwest.com. Spring–fall tours daily at 9 and 10am, 1 and 4pm; winter tours daily at 10am and 2pm. Safari tours start at $83 for adults, children 3–12 $40 (not recommended for children under 3).*

8A ★ **Savannah Café.** Power up before leaving Safari West at its sit-down restaurant. ☎ *800/616-2695. $$$.* Reservations are required, but if you haven't made them, and it's summer, grab a bite from **8B** **Delilah's,** Safari West's deli, where you can get sandwiches, sides, and wines. ☎ *800/616-2695. $.*

Drive about 30 minutes to cross valleys again: Going east on Porter Creek, turn left on Petrified Forest Road, then right on Highway 28. Turn left on Deer Park Road, then right on Silverado Trail. Once on Silverado, this portion of the tour can be done by either bicycle or car.

9 ★★ **Mumm Napa.** This winery in a big redwood barn looks almost humble at first glance. Once through the door, however, you'll understand that Mumm means big business. Just beyond the extensive gift shop is the tasting room, which serves all manner of sparkling wines. Appreciate vineyard and mountain views from the open patio—and don't miss the permanent Ansel Adams collection, a timeless staple amid the winery's ever-changing photography exhibits. *8445 Silverado Trail, Rutherford.* ☎ *707/967-7700. See p 153.*

⑩ ★ Paraduxx. Rows of vineyards fan by as you travel farther south on Silverado Trail to reach this chic, airy tasting room. Try flavorful reds served in stemless Riedel alongside small plates of spiced almonds. *7257 Silverado Trail, Napa.* ☎ *707/945-0890. See p 155.*

⑪ ★★ Darioush. Even farther south on the Silverado Trail is Darioush, a winery distinctive for its Persian-themed architecture. Wines worth trying here include the shiraz, merlot, cabernet sauvignon, viognier, and chardonnay, all served with pistachios. Opt for the appointment-only private tasting with cheese pairing ($75) to taste local artisan *fromage* with your wine, plus get a tour of the stunning facilities. *4240 Silverado Trail, Napa.* ☎ *707/257-2345. See p 143.*

The beautiful fall colors of vineyards along the Silverado Trail.

Paraduxx's chic tasting room.

⑫ ★★ Redd. For an impeccable dinner, make your way to Richard Reddington's global-inspired Yountville restaurant, where the chef puts together tantalizing seasonal California creations that well-trained servers present in a modern dining room. *6480 Washington St. Yountville.* ☎ *707/944-2222. $$$$. See p 93.*

The Best of Napa & Sonoma in One Week—Days 6 & 7

DAY 6

1. Healdsburg
2. HKG Estate Wines
3. Korbel Champagne Cellars
4. Guerneville
5. Fort Ross State Historic Park
6. Highway 1
7. The Tides Wharf Restaurant & Bar

DAY 7

8. Geyserville Grille
9. Locals
10. Russian River
11. Ferrari-Carano
12A. Dry Creek Kitchen
12B. Bear Republic Brewing Co.

If you've followed these daily tours until now, you've gotten a good sense for lower Sonoma. An extra 2 days gives you the luxury of being able to explore northeastern Sonoma, which you got a peek of at the end of Day 3. This itinerary expands on the 5-day tour to include posh Healdsburg, quirky Guerneville, and the majestic scenery that typifies much of California. (Frankly, it'd be close to a crime to be this near the Pacific and ignore the rocky coast.) You'll also learn more about California history at Fort Ross and taste wines from the Dry Creek and Russian River Valley appellations. ***Tip:*** If you're staying in the area for a week or more, consider renting a vacation home instead of staying at a hotel. Consult chapter 6 for ideas, or check sites like www.airbnb.com and www.riverhomes.com. **DAY 6 START:** Plaza St. & Healdsburg Ave., Healdsburg. Distance: About 62 miles (100km). **DAY 7 START:** Hoffman House Café, 21712 Geyserville Ave., Geyserville. Distance: About 21 miles (34km) not including kayaking and shuttling.

Downtown Healdsburg.

DAY 6

❶ ★★★ Healdsburg. This ritzy town gets much of the credit for putting northern Sonoma on the tourist map. Until not even 2 decades ago, it didn't produce a blip on travelers' radar, but it's now a huge draw for those seeking true Sonoma refinement. You'll find a plethora of tasting rooms (a couple of the best are **La Crema** and **Gallo Family Vineyards**), excellent restaurants, fancy hotels, unique shops and galleries—and, surprisingly, a small-town vibe. Learn about the town's history at the **Healdsburg Museum** (p 84), then, for a wonderful cup of joe, head to **Flying Goat Coffee**. See p 84 for a detailed walking tour.

Head south on Healdsburg Avenue to turn right on Mill Street. Stay straight to go onto Westside Road.

❷ ★ HKG Estate Wines. Get your first taste of the Russian River Valley appellation at this California Historical Landmark, formerly called Hop Kiln Winery. As its commemorative plaque says, this 1905 structure "represents the finest existing example of its type, consisting of three stone kilns for drying hops, a wooden cooler, and a two-story press for bailing hops for shipment." Indeed, this is a superb example of a stone hop kiln. In the rustic tasting room, sample the award-winning pinot noirs, as well as the pinot grigio, chardonnay, and sparkling rosé. Also on site: a duck pond and the rose garden, perfect for picnics. *6050 Westside Rd., Healdsburg.* ☎ *707/433-6491. See p 149.*

Head southwest on Westside Road. When you get to River Road, make a slight right.

❸ ★★ Korbel Champagne Cellars. Korbel, too, is within the Russian River Valley appellation and has been specializing in bubbly since 1882. The winery's colorful rose garden and free tastings make for a delightful visit. If you're getting hungry for lunch, a tasty sandwich from the gourmet deli should do the trick. *13250 River Rd., Guerneville.* ☎ *707/824-7000. See p 151.*

Take the short but beautiful drive southwest on River Road, which becomes Main Street.

❹ ★★ Guerneville. This off-the-beaten-path village is perfect for a walking tour (see p 88). The town's

Brandy tower at Korbel.

gay-friendly population is progressive and proud.

Drive toward the ocean by heading southwest on Main Street (Hwy. 116) and veering slightly right onto Highway 1.

⑤ ★★ kids Fort Ross State Historic Park. What's now a historic park was the Russians' southernmost settlement in their failed attempt to colonize North America. Don't miss the Call Ranch House and its gardens or the Russian Cemetery. Fort Ross's natural wonders will surround you. *19005 Hwy. 1, Jenner.* ☎ *707/847-3286. www. parks.ca.gov. Park grounds open daily at sunrise and close at sunset ($8 per vehicle, $7 per vehicle for seniors). Hours for the historical buildings, the visitor center, and the bookstore vary by season (so call first) but are most likely to be open Fri–Sun 10am–4:30pm. See p 115.*

⑥ ★★ Highway 1. Yes, this 21-mile (34km) stretch of road is spectacular enough to merit its own bullet point—especially during sunset. You'll pass Goat Rock Beach, the Russian River headwaters, the seaside towns of Jenner and Bridge Haven, and a natural cutout called Duncan Cove. End in the resort town of Bodega Bay for a dinner overlooking the water. (See p 115 in chapter 5 for a more detailed description of this drive.)

⑦ kids The Tides Wharf Restaurant & Bar. All 150 seats at the restaurant at the Inn at the Tides afford at least a decent view of the bay. Surroundings look familiar? You're perceptive: This dining room was the set for a raucous scene in Alfred Hitchcock's *The Birds*. Menu options include seafood, pasta, and house-made desserts. *835 Hwy. 1, Bodega Bay.* ☎ *707/875-3652. $$$.*

Playing in the waves on the beach off Highway 1.

DAY 7

⑧ ★★ Geyserville Grille. Have a hot breakfast in the Geyserville Inn's homey dining room, made more so by a brick fireplace and stained-glass windows. When you're done, buy a boxed lunch (about $10) from this family-owned restaurant specializing in California-style gourmet food. You'll want it later. *21712 Geyserville Ave. (at Geyserville Inn), Geyserville.* ☎ *707/857-3264. $$.*

Take Geyserville Avenue southeast.

⑨ Locals. Taste Russian River–produced wines at this small, modern tasting room, which stocks more than 60 options from about 10 tiny wineries. The educational—and free—tasting experience lines up varietal flights, which means you get to taste, say, five cabs or seven zins (served in Riedel crystal), to determine how different producers interpret the same type of grape. Buy a bottle of your favorite to complement that to-go lunch you bought at Geyserville Grille, or pop

How to Taste Wine Like a Pro

Stopping at tasting rooms to sample the goods is one of wine country's top rituals. Wine tasting provides pleasure and a lesson in why the products Sonoma and Napa turn out rank so highly among the wines of the world.

Precautionary notes would say "taste moderately," as there are some 200 tasting rooms, and wine's virtues take time to notice. Because we're all on a very enjoyable learning curve, you can discover wine at many levels. If you should encounter a staffer with attitude (unfortunately, it happens), don't buy anything. Just move on to your next stop.

The time-honored techniques for tasting wine involve three steps: a good look, a good smell, and a good sip. You'll learn most quickly if you compare wines side by side. This will reveal differences and features you might not discern by tasting one wine at a time. Think of it as the wines talking to each other ("I'm smoother than you are," "I'm more puckery than all of you"). By listening to these little conversations, you can discover just how you want your wines to be.

Tasting rooms have their own rituals, usually offering a series of sips. When it seems appropriate, and when the tasting room isn't too busy, ask your host whether you can do some comparisons.

—John Thoreen, "The Wine Tutor"

over to Diavola next door for another bite to eat. *21023 Geyserville Ave., Geyserville.* 707/857-4900. www.tastelocalwines.com. Daily 11am–6pm.

Follow Geyserville Avenue southeast and get on Highway 101 S. Exit on Westside Road and turn left on Westside Road. Stay straight to go onto Mill Street, then turn right on Healdsburg Avenue. Across the street from the state-beach entrance (before the bridge) is the:

⓾ ★★★ kids Russian River.
Rent a canoe or kayak from an excellent company called River's Edge and float 15 miles (24km) from the Alexander Valley Campground to River's Edge Beach in Healdsburg. Watch as the biome

becomes wooded, and keep an eye out for swimming holes, vineyards, and a good riverbank on which to enjoy your food and wine. The beach at Rio Lindo, 11 miles (18km) down, is a good option, but part of the fun is choosing a spot and making it your own. To experience the river at a leisurely pace, allow about 6 hours. Guided trips are available upon request. Reservations recommended. See chapter 5 (p 116) for more details. *13840 Healdsburg Ave., Healdsburg.* 707/433-7247. www.riversedgekayakandcanoe.com. $60; $25 for ages 12 and younger; $10 for dogs. Rentals include paddles, life vests, coolers, dry bags, and shuttle rides.

Head south on Healdsburg Avenue to get on Highway 101 N. Exit on

Enjoying the beach at Rio Lindo on the Russian River.

Dry Creek Road and turn left on Dry Creek Road. Turn left on Yoakim Bridge Road and right on Dry Creek Road.

⑪ ★★ Ferrari-Carano. One of Sonoma's more beautiful wineries has an Italian château–style hospitality center. A highlight here, aside from tasting the chardonnay and other varietals, is walking through the wonderland of colorful flowers in the formal garden. Ponds, waterfalls, and walkways make your visit all the more magical. *8761 Dry Creek Rd., Healdsburg.* ☎ *707/433-6700. See p 145.*

12A ★★★ Dry Creek Kitchen. Healdsburg has no shortage of dining options, but celeb chef Charlie Palmer's place may be your top fine-dining option, especially now that Cyrus has closed. Palmer melds splendid seasonal cuisine, excellent service, and an elegant garden setting within the hip Hotel Healdsburg. *317 Healdsburg Ave.* ☎ *707/431-0330. $$$$. See p 86.* A more laid-back Healdsburg option is **12B ★ kids Bear Republic Brewing Co.** This high-energy American brewery with kitschy but fun decor is a great place for trying house-made beer and a greasy appetizer, burger, or pasta. *345 Healdsburg Ave.* ☎ *707/433-2337. $$. See p 85.* ●

Wine Country **for Foodies**

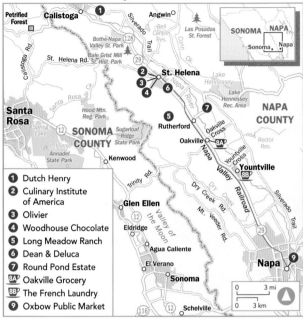

1 Dutch Henry
2 Culinary Institute of America
3 Olivier
4 Woodhouse Chocolate
5 Long Meadow Ranch
6 Dean & Deluca
7 Round Pond Estate
8A Oakville Grocery
8B The French Laundry
9 Oxbow Public Market

If you're a gourmand, Napa's your Disneyland. Oodles of specialty-food stores, farms, and culinary institutes are here to pique your senses. And to whet your appetite further, there's a farmers' market almost every day of the week (see p 21). The endless food-and-wine pairings—mixed in with a smattering of some of the world's best restaurants and chefs—are the icing on the cake.
START: In Calistoga, at Dutch Henry. Distance: About 30 miles (48km), doable in a full day.

1 ★ **Dutch Henry.** This small family-owned winery produces no more than 2,500 cases of wine each year, and even fewer cases of its acclaimed olive oil, which is so distinctive that it has its own tasting notes. At $34 per bottle, the expertly blended extract of Italian, Spanish, and Mexican olives isn't cheap, though you can taste it for free. Reservations recommended. *4310 Silverado Trail, Calistoga.*

☎ 707/942-5771. www.dutchhenry. com. Wine tasting $20 for six wines, refundable with a two-bottle purchase. Olive-oil tasting is free. Daily 10am–4:30pm.

Head east on Silverado Trail. Turn right on Larkmead Lane, then left on Highway 29.

2 ★★★ **The Culinary Institute of America.** The West Coast arm of the New York heavyweight of

Previous page: Preparing for takeoff for a balloon ride over Napa Valley.

Cooking classroom at the Culinary Institute of America in St. Helena.

food education (CIA, to insiders) is an imposing stone château to which wannabe chefs flock to sharpen their skills. Not an enrolled student? No worries: There's lots for visitors to do, including watching cooking demos ($20 each, 1:30pm on weekends, reservations required), marveling over displays of ancient food-making artifacts, and shopping at an extensive marketplace that stocks every kind of specialty ingredient, cooking tool, and utensil you can imagine—and more cookbooks than you could get through in a long lifetime. There's also a wonderful restaurant on site. *2555 Hwy. 29, St. Helena.* ☎ *707/967-1100. www. ciachef.org. Spice Islands Marketplace is open daily 10am–6pm; Wine Spectator Greystone Restaurant entrees $18–$42. Tues–Sat 11:30am–2pm for lunch & 5:30–8:30pm for dinner.*

Keep heading south on Highway 29. When it becomes St. Helena's Main Street, park your car.

❸ ★★ **Olivier.** Sample, sample, sample at this French-inspired purveyor of epicurean delights. Big, copper olive-oil dispensers line the walls, so try mixing your own—or shop for beautiful kitchenware from Provence. *1375 Main St., St. Helena.* ☎ *707/967-8777. See p 78.*

❹ ★★ **Woodhouse Chocolate.** The gourmet handmade confections here cost a pretty penny—but

to a true palate, they're worth the price. Try the fan-shaped Thai ginger tidbit or the brown-butter ganache ($1.85 each). *1367 Main St., St. Helena.* ☎ *800/966-3468. www. woodhousechocolate.com. Daily 11am–6pm (Fri–Sat 'til 6:30).*

Head south a half-mile on Main Street/Highway 29.

❺ ★★ **Long Meadow Ranch.** This innovative, organic farming operation is a winery known for its reds—but it's also an environmentally responsible ranch that, depending on season and supply, supplies Napa's best restaurants with extra-virgin olive oil, eggs, and heirloom fruits and vegetables. To experience more than just the wine flights ($20), consider the Chef's Table experience ($125; reservations required), which gets you a garden tour and a three-course meal plucked from the land. If you want to come back when you've got the morning and afternoon free, you can combine the Chef's Table experience with the Mayacamas Estate Experience ($75; reservations required) for a visit to the home ranch, the wine cave, and the valley's oldest olive orchards (planted

Sample olive oils at Olivier.

Tasting chocolates at Woodhouse.

in the 1870s) before your meal. *738 Main St., St. Helena.* ☎ *707/963-4555. www.longmeadowranch.com. Tasting room open daily 11am–6pm (some require reservations).*

Head south a mile on Main Street/Highway 29.

❻ ★★ Dean & Deluca. California's only D&D outlet stocks fresh local produce, cheeses, and a fantastic array of international food products and gifts, plus 1,400 California wines. There's an espresso bar too, in case you need a pick-me-up after all of today's grazing. *607 St. Helena Hwy. (Hwy. 29), St. Helena.* ☎ *707/967-9980. www.deandeluca.com. Sun–Thurs 7am–7pm, Fri–Sat 7am–8pm.*

Head south 2⅔ miles on Highway 29, then turn left onto Rutherford Road. After about a mile, you'll see:

❼ ★★ Round Pond Estate. If you don't have time for Long Meadow's tour, make an appointment at Round Pond, which also makes artisan olive oil and premium red wine. During the 30-minute "Splash and Dash Tasting" ($20), you'll sample olive oils, red-wine vinegars, and artisan syrups. Opt for Round Pond's tour ($65), though, and you'll see the olive

orchards, learn about harvesting techniques and oil-extraction processes, and taste the Italian and Spanish olive-oil varieties paired with estate-grown vegetables while an expert teaches you the oils' many culinary uses. *886 Rutherford Rd., Napa.* ☎ *707/302-2575. www.roundpond.com. Tastings and tours (starting at $20) are available daily; reservations required.*

🅱🅰 ★★ Oakville Grocery. If you didn't already picnic at Long Meadow, Napa's two true foodie options for lunch are on opposite ends of the fanciness scale. The 130-year-old, recently renovated Oakville Grocery is a casual, crowded little store selling gourmet foodstuff, much of it locally made and available for sampling, and offering a nice wine selection in the back. Buy ready-made sandwiches and entrees, and at the espresso bar, pick up coffee drinks to go. There's an ice cream counter, too. If you're lucky, you'll spot Martha Stewart, a regular here, shopping for flavored salts. *7856 St. Helena Hwy. (Hwy. 29), Oakville.* ☎ *707/944-8802. $. Daily 6:30am–5pm ('til 6pm Fri & Sun).*

Oakville Grocery.

A Foodie Tour of Sonoma County

If you're a foodie visiting Sonoma, spend as much time as possible on **Sonoma County Farm Trails** (☎ 707/837-8896; www.farmtrails. org), a network of local, sustainable farms that encourages visitors to come and not only buy, but also interact by picking berries, touring apiaries, taking hayrides, and petting farm animals. Visit the website to order a free map and guide. Up in Healdsburg, **Relish Culinary Adventures** (14 Matheson St.; ☎ 707/431-9999; www.relishculinary. com) offers cooking classes and tours of local farms. You'll also find a buffet of gourmet dining options around Healdsburg's plaza, including the wonderful **Barndiva** (p 85); it wins everyone over with its rustic outdoor dining area, which is strung with lights, and its local fare, whose preparation and presentation is obviously thoroughly thought through. In the town of Sonoma, try the seasonal menu at **El Dorado Kitchen** (p 77). Its chef, Ryan Fancher, was trained by Thomas Keller, who taught him to use French techniques to showcase wine country's regional bounty. Fancher takes familiar classics, like grilled cheese, and gives them a modern tweak. His prices are reasonable, too. If you're a pasta lover, try **Della Santina's ★★** (133 E. Napa St., Sonoma; ☎ 707/935-0576; www.dellasantinas.com), a family-owned trattoria just off Sonoma's town square. Its northern Italian fare has been a Sonoma staple for more than 25 years—a tried-and-true local favorite. Visit **The Olive Press** (24724 Hwy. 121, Sonoma; ☎ 707/939-8900; www.theolivepress.com), an exceptional olive-pressing facility dedicated to making extra-virgin California oils, which are sold alongside culinary delights like tapenades, specialty crackers, and distinctive balsamic vinegars. To satisfy your sweet tooth, milk the **Chocolate Cow** (452 1st St. E., Ste. F.; ☎ 707/935-3564; www.thechocolatecow sonoma.com), tucked into a Sonoma alleyway, for all it's worth. Choose from a variety of fudges and chocolates, or on a hot day, get your favorite ice cream flavor topped with shaved ice ($6).

The second option? **8B²** **★★★ The French Laundry,** a culinary experience that should be on every gourmand's bucket list. Reservations are required. Even if you can't get in, wander through Thomas Keller's expansive herb garden across the street. *6640 Washington St., Yountville.* ☎ *707/944-2380. $$$$$. See p 92.*

From Round Pond Estate, go north on Rutherford Road/Highway 128, which becomes the Silverado Trail.

Turn left on Trancas Street, then right back onto the Silverado Trail. Turn right on 1st Street.

❾ ★ Oxbow Public Market. Finish the day by sampling the best in local wines and artisanal foods. A veritable farmers' market that's open daily, Oxbow sits in the heart of downtown Napa. Dessert sounding good right about now? Go for one of the spiced ice creams at Three Twins. *610 & 644 1st St.* ☎ *707/226-6529. www.oxbow publicmarket.com. See p 11.*

Wine Country with Kids

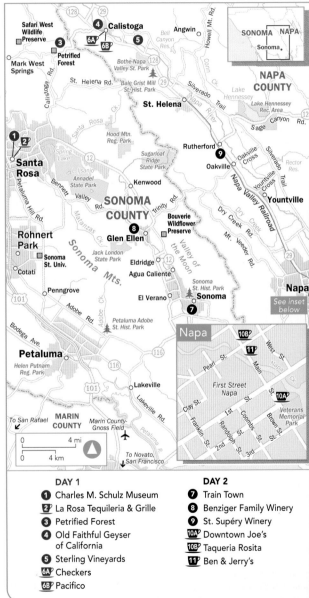

DAY 1

1. Charles M. Schulz Museum
2. La Rosa Tequileria & Grille
3. Petrified Forest
4. Old Faithful Geyser of California
5. Sterling Vineyards
6A. Checkers
6B. Pacifico

DAY 2

7. Train Town
8. Benziger Family Winery
9. St. Supéry Winery
10A. Downtown Joe's
10B. Taqueria Rosita
11. Ben & Jerry's

True, Napa and Sonoma are no Anaheim or Orlando, but that doesn't mean there isn't lots to do here for families wanting to spend quality time together. Some local attractions were actually designed with kids in mind. Others, while not specifically aimed at entertaining children, can definitely accommodate youngsters while educating, perhaps even enthralling, them. *Tip:* Flip through this book to find attractions marked with the **kids** symbol. START: **Charles M. Schulz Museum. Time: Two full days. Distance: About 20 miles (32km) on Day 1; 40 miles (64km) on Day 2.**

DAY 1

❶ ★★ Charles M. Schulz Museum. Charlie Brown is practically Santa Rosa's logo: Charles "Sparky" Schulz, though originally from Minnesota, lived here most of his adult life. In his honor, town residents opened this museum in 2002, less than 2 years after he died. An introductory video, narrated by Schulz's widow, Jean, reveals the local rituals that were a part of the cartoonist's daily life, including his involvement with the **Redwood Empire Ice Arena** adjacent to the museum. Exhibits include a faithful replica of Schulz's studio, featuring his original drawing board, books, and photos; the *Morphing Snoopy Sculpture,* a huge artwork portraying Snoopy's many personas; and a mural that, at first glance, looks like Lucy holding the football for Charlie Brown. Look closer, though, and you'll see that the image is actually made of 3,588 comic images printed on small ceramic tiles. You can buy just about any *Peanuts*-themed product you can think of in the massive gift shop. Outside, a Snoopy-shaped labyrinth adds dimension. *2301 Hardies Lane, Santa Rosa. ☎ 707/579-4452. www.schulzmuseum.org. Admission $10 adults, $5 seniors 62+, students & kids. Sept–May Mon & Wed–Fri 11am–5pm, Sat–Sun 10am–5pm; May–Sept daily 11am–5pm (Sat–Sun opens at 10am).*

Charles M. Schulz Museum.

❷ kids La Rosa Tequileria & Grille, a big, festive Mexican restaurant, is rowdy enough that no one will mind loud youngsters in the mix. Kids love the taquitos and guacamole; adults love the margaritas. *500 4th St. ☎ 707/523-3663. $$.*

From Hardies Lane, turn left on W. Steele Lane, left on Guerneville Road, then left on Highway 101 N. Exit at River Road and turn right on Mark Springs Road (it turns to the right and becomes Porter Creek Road). Turn left at Petrified Forest Road.

❸ ★★ Petrified Forest. Children can find plenty of petrified specimens at this 3.4-million-year-old grove. Volcanic ash blanketed this area after the same eruptions that caused Mount St. Helena to burst forth. The giant redwoods here have since turned to stone through the slow infiltration of silicates and other minerals. Take your kids on the ¼-mile (.4km) walking trail and tell them to keep an eye out for the park's many marine fossils, hard evidence that this piece of the planet was once a sea before it was a forest. There's an interesting museum, as well as a discovery shop and picnic grounds. *4100 Petrified Forest Rd., Calistoga.* ☎ *707/942-6667. www. petrifiedforest.org. Admission $10 adults, $9 seniors 62+, $9 kids 12–17, $5 kids 6–11, free for kids younger than 6 (docent-led tours cost more and take off at 11am and 1 and 3pm). Daily 10am–7pm ('til 5pm in winter, 6pm in spring & fall).*

Head northeast on Petrified Forest Road for nearly 4 miles (6.4km), then turn left on Foothill Boulevard/Highway 128. Turn right on Tubbs Lane.

❹ ★★ **Old Faithful Geyser of California.** One of the world's three "old faithful" geysers is named for its dependable eruptions every 30 to 40 minutes, spewing 350°F (177°C) water as high as 60 feet (18m). Kids get delighted during the 3-minute performance. While waiting, they can check out the educational exhibits about seismic activity and California history in the exhibit hall, which also houses a gift shop and a snack bar. The site also keeps fainting goats, which look like regular goats until they're slightly startled. Then they stiffen up and fall over. *1299 Tubbs Lane, Calistoga.* ☎ *707/942-6463. www.oldfaithfulgeyser.com. Admission $14 adults, $12 seniors 55+, $8 kids 4–12, free for kids younger than 4. Daily 8:30am–8pm ('til 7pm in winter).*

From Tubbs Lane, turn right onto Highway 29, then left on Silverado Trail. Turn right on Dunaweal Lane.

Take a tram at Sterling Vineyards to enjoy this great view.

❺ ★★ **Sterling Vineyards.** Now that your kids have developed an affinity for the area, take them along for wine tasting. What's that? You can't do wineries with children? Think again. At Sterling, kids will love the aerial gondola that brings you in. The $15 kids' admission fee includes a goodie bag (adults pay $39 for a tour and wine tasting; kids under 3 get in free), and young ones might enjoy seeing the artifacts and videos along the multimedia self-guided tour. Parents will enjoy the four wines poured in the panoramic tasting room. *1111 Dunaweal Lane, Calistoga.* ☎ *707/942-3300. See p 158.*

Go south on Dunaweal Lane to turn right on Highway 29/128. Turn left on Petrified Forest Road.

6A **Checkers.** Kids love the pizza and calzones at this cheerful eatery. *1414 Lincoln Ave.* ☎ *707/942-9300. $$. See p 101.* Or treat them to Mexican fare at colorful **6B** ★ **Pacifico.** *1237 Lincoln Ave.* ☎ *707/942-4400. $$. See p 102.*

DAY 2

❼ ★★ **Train Town.** This mini-amusement park located a mile south of Sonoma's town square has been here since 1968, but the charm has not worn off. The theme is locomotion, and a 20-minute train ride on a scaled-down railroad traverses the wooded property, going over bridges and through tunnels. Other attractions include a petting zoo, a Ferris wheel, and a merry-go-round. *20264 Broadway, Sonoma.* ☎ *707/938-3912. www.traintown.com. Admission is free but tickets cost $6.25 per train ride; $2.75 per amusement ride (a book of 6 tickets costs $12.75). Daily 10am–5pm in summer, Fri–Sun only in winter (closed holidays).*

Take Broadway south to turn left on Leveroni Road, then right on Arnold Drive. Turn left on London Ranch Road.

❽ ★★ Benziger Family Winery. Founded as a family estate, Benziger's 45-minute tractor-drawn tram tour entertains kids and educates them about the agricultural processes that make wine. Tours are available either by reservation or on a first-come, first-served basis, so if it's high season, come in the morning to buy tickets for later. *1883 London Ranch Rd., Glen Ellen.* ☎ *800/726-6136. See p 137.*

Go northeast on London Ranch Road and turn left on Arnold Drive. Turn left on Sonoma Highway/Highway 12, then right on

Train Town in Sonoma.

Trinity Road, which becomes Dry Creek Road. Stay straight onto Oakville Grade Road, then turn left on Highway 29.

❾ St. Supéry Winery. The emphasis here is on education. During the self-guided tour, kids can wander through a demonstration vineyard and learn about growing techniques. Inside, they'll gravitate toward coloring books and interactive displays. *8440 St. Helena Hwy. (Hwy. 29), Rutherford.* ☎ *800/942-0809. See p 157.*

Take Highway 29 south and make a slight right on Solano Avenue, then right onto W. Lincoln Avenue. Turn right on Main Street.

⓾ₐ ★ Downtown Joe's. This American grill and brewery is child-friendly and pet-friendly. *902 Main St., Napa.* ☎ *707/258-2337. $$. See p 73.* If the family's more in the mood for Mexican, popular **⓾ʙ ★ Taqueria Rosita** is inexpensive but manages to maintain a Napa feel. *1214 Main St., Napa.* ☎ *707/253-9208. $.*

Afterward, stop at **⓫ Ben & Jerry's** for a big scoop of the Vermont company's latest quirky flavor. *1136 Main St., Napa.* ☎ *707/696-9683. $.*

Wine Country for First-Timers

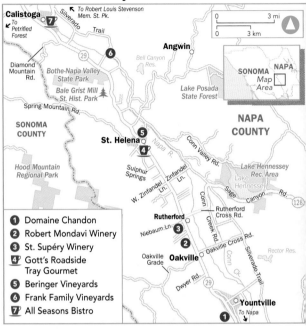

1 Domaine Chandon
2 Robert Mondavi Winery
3 St. Supéry Winery
4 Gott's Roadside Tray Gourmet
5 Beringer Vineyards
6 Frank Family Vineyards
7 All Seasons Bistro

Are you a Napa novice? Not to worry: Highway 29 will show you the way. Following the path outlined below will up your wine-knowledge quotient and ensure that you leave wine country closer to "connoisseur." Plus, you'll be able to go home knowing that you've really gotten a sense for Napa Valley and its wineries. START: **Domaine Chandon, 1 California Dr. (at Hwy. 29), Yountville. Distance: About 17 miles (27km), doable in a full day.**

1 ★ Domaine Chandon. The comprehensive tour and tasting ($40) walks you through the entire bubbly-making process, from the cellars to the riddling room and the bottling line. You'll also learn about the winery's history, including how the French champagne house Moët et Chandon founded it in 1973. *1 California Dr. (at Hwy. 29), Yountville.* ☎ 888/242-6366. *See p 145.*

Drive northeast on California Drive, then merge onto Highway 29 N.

2 ★★ Robert Mondavi Winery. The basic, hour-long production tour covers all aspects of the winemaking process and gives you a look at the destemmer-crusher, the tank room, the bottling room, and the vineyard. Top-notch guides make sure you know what you're looking at. Most tour options require reservations. *7801 St. Helena Hwy. (Hwy. 29), Oakville.* ☎ 707/226-1395. *See p 156.*

Keep heading north on Highway 29.

3 St. Supéry Winery. This straightforward winery is a great place for first-timers to learn more about oenology in a relaxed atmosphere. Its emphasis is education—while here, take the "Vineyard to Glass Tour," which provides an insider's look at winemaking and includes a barrel tasting, or take the "Aromatherapy with a Corkscrew" workshop, which will teach you how to identify wine aromas and attributes. There's also a demonstration vineyard where you can learn about growing techniques. Reservations recommended. *8440 St. Helena Hwy. (Hwy. 29), Rutherford.* ☎ *800/942-0809. See p 157.*

Beringer Winery.

Keep heading north on Highway 29 for about 4 miles (6.4km), then turn left on Larkmead Lane.

4 ★ Gott's Roadside Tray Gourmet. For a quick bite, stop at this burger shack with an impressive wine selection. *933 Main St., St. Helena.* ☎ *707/963-3486. $. See p 80.*

Keep heading north on Highway 29.

5 ★★ Beringer Vineyards. This winery pioneered the idea of public tours in 1934, and it's obvious that Beringer has since perfected that brainchild. Today, Napa's oldest continually operating winery offers two informative tours, plus a bunch of tasting options. *2000 Main St., St. Helena.* ☎ *866/708-9463. See p 137.*

6 Frank Family Vineyards. Napa's least intimidating winery is staffed with exceptionally attentive employees who take the time to explain anything you want to know about wine. *1091 Larkmead Lane, Calistoga.* ☎ *800/574-9463. See p 146.*

7 ★★ All Seasons Bistro. The California-cuisine menu (fresh, local ingredients) matches wines to dishes, so you'll know what's just right for the entree you choose. *1400 Lincoln Ave., Calistoga.* ☎ *707/942-9111. $$$. See p 101.*

Gott's Roadside.

Wine Country for Nondrinkers

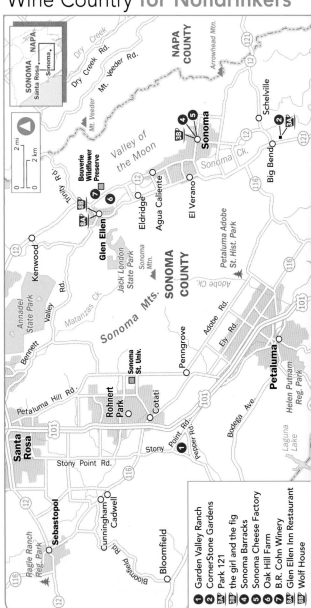

1. Garden Valley Ranch
2. CornerStone Gardens
2A Park 121
3B the girl and the fig
4. Sonoma Barracks
5. Sonoma Cheese Factory
6. Oak Hill Farm
7. B.R. Cohn Winery
3A Glen Ellen Inn Restaurant
3B Wolf House

Want to visit wine country but are put off because you don't drink alcohol? Come anyway. Though wine put this region on the map, the tourism and agriculture industries have kept it there, making sure that visitors are kept interested both before and after the tasting room. As a result, there's now a plethora of activities for those who just want to take a relaxing trip to the California countryside to do some wine-free sampling and seeing. Here's how to get the wine-country experience without the wine. *Note:* For nonalcoholic attractions in addition to these, also see the itineraries for foodies (p 32), history buffs (p 46), art aficionados (p 50), and outdoor enthusiasts (p 109). START: **Twin Hill Ranch, 1689 Pleasant Hill Rd., Sebastopol. Distance: About 40 miles (64km), doable in a day.**

❶ ★★ Garden Valley Ranch.

This 9-acre (3.6-hectare) Victorian ranch blooms with more than 8,000 rosebushes. From May to October, self-guided tours are available for $5 per person. If you've brought along lunch or snacks, enjoy them in the fragrance garden, which overlooks thousands of flowers. There's also a nursery that sells 600 varieties of roses. *498 Pepper Rd., Petaluma.* ☎ *707/795-0919. www. gardenvalley.com. Nursery open Wed–Sun 10am–4pm (closed Nov– Jan). Self-guided tours ($5, including a descriptive booklet) Wed–Sun by appointment only. Docent-led tours cost $10 (including a descriptive booklet) and are available by appointment but require a minimum of 20 people and include lunch.*

From Pepper Road, get on Highway 101 S. Take Highway 116 E., then turn left on Frates Road, which becomes Adobe Road, which becomes Highway 116 again, then becomes Highway 121.

❷ ★★ CornerStone Gardens.

Prominent landscape architects designed these 9 acres (3.6 hectares) of 20 gardens, whose walk-through outdoor spaces are aimed at those interested in high-concept gardening. On-site shops worth visiting include **Chateau Sonoma** (☎ 707/935-8553), with its nicely curated selection of French antiques and vintage decor; **Country by Eurasian Interiors** (☎ 415/775-1610), which deals in restored antiques and a worldly selection of home accessories; and **Artefact Design & Salvage** (☎ 707/933-0660), offering lovely garden pieces and found objects. *23570 Arnold Dr. (Hwy. 121), Sonoma.* ☎ *707/933-3010. www. cornerstonegardens.com. Daily 10am–5pm (gardens close at 4pm; may close at 3pm for special events). Free admission, though docent tours for groups of 10 or more cost $6 per person (reservations required).*

❸ᴬᴾ ★ Park 121,

adjacent to Cornerstone, has menu highlights that include "adult grilled cheese" (Bellwether farms carmody, bacon, and quince paste on wheat), Blue Bottle coffee, and a good selection of local wines. *23584 Arnold Dr. (Hwy. 121), Sonoma.* ☎ *707/938-8579. $$.*

Take Highway 121 northwest, then turn right on Watmaugh Road and left on Broadway. Turn right on E. Napa Street.

For a more comprehensive sit-down meal, head to the beloved **3B** ★★★ **the girl and the fig,** just off Sonoma Plaza. Cheese sampling at the restaurant's well-stocked *salon de fromage* is a great alternative to wine tasting. *110 W. Spain St. (in the Sonoma Hotel), Sonoma. ☎ 707/938-3634. $$$. See p 77.*

4 ★★ **kids Sonoma Barracks.** Cross 1st Street again to get to this landmark, part of Sonoma State Historic Park. General Vallejo, whose assignment it was to secularize the mission, kept his Mexican troops here to guard against Native American tribes and rebuff possible threats from Russian settlers, though none ever developed. During and after the revolt, these barracks were the Bear Flag Party's headquarters. When the U.S. took over, American soldiers moved in for a spell. Since then, it's been a winery, a law office, and a private residence, among other things. It became state property in 1958, and today there are two museum rooms

Sonoma Barracks.

and a theater where you can catch the 22-minute video about Vallejo. History buffs will especially appreciate the gift-shop merchandise. *Tip:* If possible, coincide your visit with the every-other-Saturday 2pm firing of the cannon. *E. Spain St. & 1st St. E., Sonoma. ☎ 707/939-9420. www. parks.ca.gov. Daily 10am–5pm. Admission $3 for adults, $2 for children. Admission also includes Mission San Francisco Solano (see p 75).*

5 ★ **Sonoma Cheese Factory.** Walk across the plaza to this third-generation family enterprise, the first cheese producer west of the Mississippi to win a gold medal from the authoritative Wisconsin Cheese Makers Association. Here, you can sample cheeses to your heart's content. *2 E. Spain St., Sonoma. ☎ 800/535-2855. See p 76.*

From Spain Street, turn left on 1st Street, then right on Napa Street. Make a slight right on Sonoma Highway/Highway 12.

6 ★★ **Oak Hill Farm.** This 45-acre (18-hectare) farm and its **Red Barn Store** has existed since

Vineyards at B.R. Cohn Winery.

the 1950s and still grows its remarkable heirloom vegetables entirely sustainably. The real highlight here is the century-old dairy barn housing the store. More than just an old-fashioned farm stand (though it's that, too), it's a unique place to buy organic produce, fresh flowers (also grown here), beautiful wreaths, and handmade gifts. The farm's bountiful fields serve as a beautiful backdrop. Unfortunately, it's open only on Saturdays. *15101 Sonoma Hwy. (Hwy. 12), Glen Ellen.* ☎ *707/996-6643. www.oakhillfarm. net. May–Dec Sat 9am–3pm.*

7 B.R. Cohn Winery. Yes, this is a winery, but the estate also specializes in gourmet olive oils and handcrafted vinegars. Sample them in the small tasting room, which is filled with framed platinum albums from vintner Bruce Cohn's other job as manager of the Doobie Brothers. His property is graced with groves

of rare olive trees, terraced hills of plush lawn, and several picnic tables. As you'd expect from a connected fellow like Cohn, many musical events happen here. Check the website to see what's coming soon. *15000 Sonoma Hwy. (Hwy. 12), Glen Ellen.* ☎ *800/330-4064. See p 138.*

8A ★ Glen Ellen Inn Restaurant. This homey dining room serves seasonal cuisine. Reservations recommended. *13670 Arnold Dr., Glen Ellen.* ☎ *707/996-6409. $$$. See p 96.* Another local option is **8B ★ Wolf House,** a classy but relaxed joint with local food and warm service. It's connected to the Jack London Lodge. *13740 Arnold Dr., Glen Ellen.* ☎ *707/996-4401. Reservations recommended. $$$. See p 97.*

Wine Country **for History Buffs**

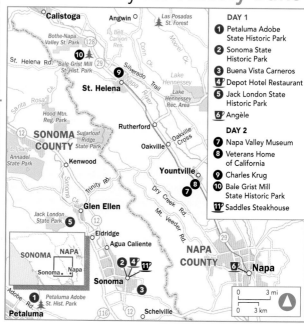

DAY 1
1. Petaluma Adobe State Historic Park
2. Sonoma State Historic Park
3. Buena Vista Carneros
4. Depot Hotel Restaurant
5. Jack London State Historic Park
6. Angèle

DAY 2
7. Napa Valley Museum
8. Veterans Home of California
9. Charles Krug
10. Bale Grist Mill State Historic Park
11. Saddles Steakhouse

To get to the real roots of the land, beyond tasting rooms and the newer tourist attractions—and to find out why so many from so far away came here with dreams of paradise so many years ago—follow this northwest-bound, county-crossing itinerary. It'll give you an overview of wine country's rich cultural, political, and agricultural history, and will help you get to know the region's most colorful historical characters, including Jack London, General Mariano G. Vallejo (California's last Mexican governor), the members of the Bear Flag Party, Agoston Haraszthy, and American veterans.
START: **Petaluma Adobe State Historic Park, 3325 Adobe Rd., Petaluma.**
Distance: About 40 miles (64km), doable in 2 days.

1 ★★ KIDS Petaluma Adobe State Historic Park. What's now a state-owned site was, in the mid-1800s, General Vallejo's working *rancho*, which he used for commercial ventures such as growing crops, rearing cattle, raising sheep, and breeding horses. After Vallejo was taken captive during the 1846 Bear Flag Revolt, squatters took over. In the early 1900s, the state acquired the land and made it a historic park, refurnishing many of the rooms in the adobe-and-redwood main building with authentic artifacts to bring history back to life. Start at the **Visitor Center** to see exhibits portraying some of the agricultural and domestic activities that happened here. Then get maps to tour the historic Petaluma Adobe house. *3325 Adobe Rd. (off Hwy. 116), Petaluma.* ☎ *707/762-4871. www.parks.ca.gov. Tues–Sun 10am–5pm. Admission $3 adults, $2 children (also good at the mission, barracks, and Lachryma Montis).*

Take Highway 116 east and turn left onto Watmaugh Road. Turn left onto Broadway/Highway 12 and continue 1 mile (1.6km) until you hit Sonoma. Park at the Plaza.

❷ ★★★ kids Sonoma State Historic Park. Less a park than a series of historic attractions throughout town, a thorough visit should include **Mission San Francisco Solano** (p 75), the **Bear Flag Monument**, the **Sonoma Barracks** (p 44), the **Blue Wing Inn** (p 75), and, if you're in town at the right time, a tour of **Toscano Hotel** (p 76). *Main office: 363 W. 3rd St. (at W. Spain St.), Sonoma.* ☎ *707/938-9560. www.parks.ca.gov. Admission $3 adults, $2 children (includes all SHP sites). Hours vary; call ahead.*

Also part of the park is **Lachryma Montis**, where Vallejo lived with his wife after the Bear Flag Party deposed him in 1846. In 1933, the state acquired the property and opened it to the public. Today, it (and an adjacent museum) continues

to educate visitors. *W. Spain St., near E. 3rd St., Sonoma.* ☎ *707/938-9559. Admission $3 adults, $2 children (includes all SHP sites). Daily 10am–5pm. Occasional free docent-led weekend tours; call ahead for schedule.*

From 1st Street, turn left on W. Spain Street, then right on E. 2nd Street. A left on E. Napa Street will bring you to Old Winery Road. Turn left to get to:

❸ ★★★ Buena Vista Carneros. The nation's oldest continuously operating winery, its historical significance is that this is the birthplace of California wine: In 1851, a Hungarian colonel named Agoston Haraszthy planted a few vines here. A decade later, he bolstered the local winemaking culture by returning from a trip to Europe with thousands of cuttings of hundreds of varieties, many of which he planted at this winery that he founded. *18000 Old Winery Rd., Sonoma.* ☎ *800/926-1266. See p 138.*

Enjoy lunch at **❹ ★★ Depot Hotel Restaurant,** which serves northern Italian cuisine. Its historic stone building, 2 blocks off the plaza, was once a destination for 19th-century train passengers. *241 W. 1st St., Sonoma.* ☎ *707/938-2980. $$$.*

Sonoma State Historic Park in Sonoma.

From Old Winery Road, turn right on E. Napa Street, then right onto Sonoma Highway/Highway 12. Turn left onto W. Verano Avenue, then right onto Arnold Drive, then left on London Ranch Road.

⑤ ★★ kids Jack London State Historic Park. This is where the famous writer of *The Call of the Wild, White Fang,* and more than 50 other stories lived from 1905 until his death in 1916. In addition to 29 miles (47km) of hiking trails (many of them eucalyptus-lined), the 1,400-acre (567-hectare) park features a number of historic sites, including London's gravesite—his ashes rest in a small copper urn—plus the remains of his burned-down dream house, the wood-framed cottage where he penned many of his later books; the stone "House of Happy Walls," a museum dedicated to London's life (with a visitor center selling his books); an old distillery building; and more. To commemorate the 2016 centennial of London's death, the park is presenting an escalated calendar of events; check the website for details. *Tip:* Pick up the $1 self-guided tour map upon arrival to get oriented. Picnic tables are available. *2400 London Ranch Rd., Glen Ellen. ☎ 707/938-5216. www.parks.ca.gov and www.jack londonpark.com. Park admission $10 per car, $5 walk-in or bicycle. Park grounds daily 9:30am–5pm; London's cottage daily 12pm–4pm (cottage admission is $4 for adults, $2 for seniors 62+ and children age 13–18, free for children 12 and under).*

⑥ ★★ Angèle. Finish the day at this rustic but upscale restaurant serving French country cuisine in the boathouse of the Historic Napa Mill, built in 1884. Interior wood gives the restaurant a long-ago feeling, as do beam ceilings and concrete floors. *540 Main St., Napa. ☎ 707/252-8115. $$$$. See p 72.*

DAY 2

⑦ ★ Napa Valley Museum. Though it's housed in a modern building, this museum gives an excellent overview of Napa history.

Hiking through Jack London State Park.

Its mission is to promote the valley's cultural and environmental heritage. You'll learn how Chinese people, Jews, and other ethnic groups contributed to valley life. Downstairs is a permanent multimedia exhibit demonstrating the winemaking process. Before you leave, check out the painting by John Michael Keating and see how many winemakers you can spot; among them are Robert Mondavi and Joe Heitz. *55 Presidents Circle, Yountville.* ☎ *707/944-0500. www. napavalleymuseum.org. Admission $7 adults, $3.50 seniors, $2.50 kids under 17. Wed–Sun 10am–4pm.*

❽ Veterans Home of California. Napa Valley Museum is actually on the grounds of America's largest veterans' home, founded in 1884. It's the home of 1,100 ex-soldiers, most of them age 62 or older. Also on site is the 1,200-seat Lincoln Theater (☎ 707/944-9900), a 9-hole golf course, a 35,000-volume library, a baseball stadium, bowling lanes, and many other amenities. *260 California Dr., Yountville.* ☎ *707/944-4600.*

Continue north on Highway 29.

❾ ★ Charles Krug. This is the valley's oldest working winery; it was founded in 1861 but ceased operation during Prohibition. *2800 Main St. (Hwy. 29), St. Helena.* ☎ *707/967-2229. See p 140.*

Continue north on Highway 29.

❿ ★ Kids Bale Grist Mill State Historic Park. This park is worth a short stop to see the massive wooden water-powered gristmill that was built in 1846 and ran until the early 1900s. On weekends, watch the mill in action as a miller performs demonstrations, and then buy the grain you just saw being ground. *3369 Hwy. 29, St. Helena.*

Milling day at the Bale Grist Mill State Historic Park.

☎ *707/942-4575. www.parks.ca.gov. Free admission to park; mill admission $5 adults, $2 kids. Sat–Sun 10am–5pm.*

A mile-long (1.6km) History Trail links this park to ★ **Bothe-Napa Valley State Park** (☎ 707/942-4575); if you're motivated and have time, take it to see ★★ **Pioneer Cemetery,** a typical mid-1800s graveyard where many Napa settlers, including **George C. Yount** (p 90), are buried.

Now hop back in the car and head back to Sonoma for dinner. Follow Highway 29 southeast, turn right on Highway 12/Fremont Road, then make a slight right on Napa Road, turn right on 8th Street E., and turn left on E. MacArthur Street.

Distinguished **⓫ ★★ Saddles Steakhouse** is at lovely MacArthur Place (p 130), the former Burris-Good estate whose two-story Victorian was built in the mid-1800s—it's still got its original white picket fence. *29 E. MacArthur St.* ☎ *707/ 938-2929. $$$$.*

A Day for **Arts Aficionados**

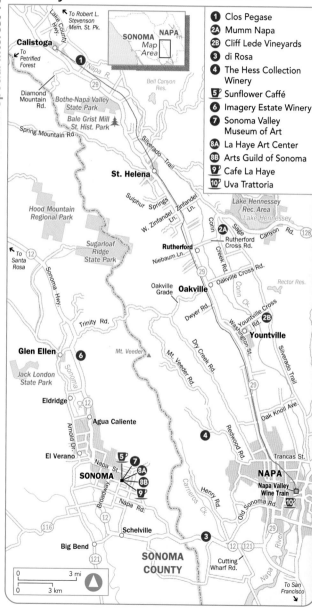

1 Clos Pegase
2A Mumm Napa
2B Cliff Lede Vineyards
3 di Rosa
4 The Hess Collection Winery
5 Sunflower Caffé
6 Imagery Estate Winery
7 Sonoma Valley Museum of Art
8A La Haye Art Center
8B Arts Guild of Sonoma
9 Cafe La Haye
10 Uva Trattoria

Robert Mondavi wrote, "Wine is art. It's culture. It's the essence of civilization and the art of living." Naturally, then, the land of viticulture abounds with art forms, from the visual to the audible to the experiential. There's a reason why creative luminaries like Pixar's John Lasseter, *Peanuts* creator Charles Schulz, and film director Francis Ford Coppola decided to move here. Though there's no way to list every art attraction in the Napa-Sonoma region—that's a whole other book—this tour should give you a taste, at least, of the talent that abounds here. START: **Clos Pegase, 1060 Dunaweal Lane, Calistoga. Distance: about 90 miles (145km), doable in a day.**

① ★★ Clos Pegase. Named for the mythological winged horse-god, this winery's winning design is the result of an architects' competition. Its stunning structures house a world-class fine-art collection, including a huge painting behind the tasting bar. There's also a remarkable sculpture garden. *1060 Dunaweal Lane, Calistoga.* ☎ *707/942-4981.* See p 142.

Take Dunaweal Lane south to turn left on Highway 128/29. Turn left on Deer Park Road, then right on Silverado Trail.

②A ★★ Mumm Napa. Explore Mumm's photography gallery, which displays original Ansel Adams works in long Spanish-style hallways. Then enjoy sparkling wine in the glass-enclosed tasting room. *8445 Silverado Trail, Rutherford.* ☎ *707/967-7700.* See p 153.

OR:

From Silverado Trail, turn right on Oak Knoll Avenue, then left on Big Ranch Road, then right back on Oak Knoll Avenue. Turn left on Highway 29, then right on Highway 12/121 (Carneros Highway).

②B ★★ Cliff Lede Vineyards. This winery's (the surname is pronounced "lady") rose gardens showcase pieces by famous sculptors including Keith Haring, Jim Dine, and Lynn Chadwick. A new winemaking facility opened back in 2005, and the

Clos Pegase.

former one now serves as a modern-art gallery displaying rotating 6-month shows spotlighting the works of renowned artists and rising stars. *1473 Yountville Cross Rd., Yountville.* ☎ *800/428-2259.* See p 141.

From Mumm, head south on the Silverado Trail, turn right onto Yountville Cross Road, and follow the directions from Cliff Lede. From Cliff Lede, take Yountville Cross Road, then turn left on Yount Street and right on Madison Street. Turn left onto Highway 29 S. At Carneros Highway/Highway 12/121, turn right.

③ ★★★ di Rosa. Rene di Rosa, who died in 2010 at age 91, lived here, on the impressive preserve he created, sharing his iconoclastic personal art collection with the public in a confluence of contemporary art and bucolic nature. He started buying works by young up-and-comers in the 1960s and, by the end of his life, had amassed 1,800 avant-garde pieces by some 800 Bay Area artists, spanning media from canvas to fiber to porcelain—even to old cars. The art spreads over three galleries (one houses a photography hall) and spills out into the 217-acre (87-hectare) preserve, whose sculpture-laden meadows are set against vineyards and a palm-tree-lined lake. Don't miss the former di Rosa residence, where art is so pervasive that paintings are even hung on the ceiling. *5200 Carneros Hwy. (Hwy. 12/Carneros Hwy.), Napa.* ☎ *707/226-5991. www.dirosaart.org. Gatehouse Gallery admission: $5 suggested donation if full tour of grounds ($12–$15) is not purchased. Wed–Sun 10am–4pm year-round.*

Head east on Sonoma Highway (12/121). Turn left onto Old Sonoma Road, left onto Buhman Avenue, left onto Browns Valley Road, and again left onto Redwood Road.

❹ ★★★ **The Hess Collection Winery.** The architectural design

di Rosa's courtyard featuring Robert Hudson's Figure of Speech *(1984).*

Hess Collection.

here is contemporary to match Donald Hess's museum-quality art collection, acquired over more than 30 years, on the upper levels of the 1903 stone winery. Works on display include paintings and sculptures by modern-era American and European artists. *4411 Redwood Rd., Napa.* ☎ *707/255-1144. See p 149.*

Take Redwood Road southeast and turn right on Browns Valley Road. Turn right on Buhman Avenue, then right on Old Sonoma Road. Turn right on Highway 12/121 and make a slight right on Napa Road, then right again onto Broadway/Highway 12.

❺ **Sunflower Caffé.** Fill up on an organic salad or sandwich (or just grab a coffee drink) at this cheerful little cafe. Its owners curate their wall space each month with an eye toward new works by local artists. *412 1st St. W., Sonoma.* ☎ *707/996-6645. $$.*

❻ ★ **Imagery Estate Winery.** Each Imagery bottle label is a tiny version of an original painting commissioned specifically for the wine it hugs. Each must somehow incorporate a replica of Benziger's Parthenon. (Imagery is Benziger's sister winery.) And a curated collection of more than 175 artworks hangs in Imagery's gallery. *14335 Hwy. 12, Glen Ellen.* ☎ *707/935-4500. See p 149.*

Take Highway 12 southeast and turn right on Broadway.

❼ ★★ Sonoma Valley Museum of Art. Walking distance from the plaza, this excellent institution borrows local, international, and ethnic art of all media from private collections and other museums to create its themed exhibits. Showings have ranged from the somewhat frivolous ("The Art of the Wine Label") to the deeply emotional, like "Faces of the Fallen," portraits of the thousands of soldiers killed in Iraq. The museum has also brought in works by Rodin as well as textiles from Bali. However, SVMA prides itself

The "Contemplative Elements" exhibit at the Sonoma Valley Art Museum.

most on bringing to light lesser-known regional artists. After you've gotten your fill of the art, you can head to the museum's cafe for hot coffee and a pastry. *551 Broadway, Sonoma.* ☎ *707/939-7862. www. svma.org. Admission $5, free for students 18 and younger (free for everyone every Wed). Occasional lectures, workshops, and music performances; check website for schedule. Wed–Sun 11am–5pm.*

❽Ⓐ La Haye Art Center. Walking distance from the museum is this nonprofit gallery cooperative that's open when artists are working in their studios, or by advance appointment. If the door's locked, though, you might try ringing the bell for admittance. *148 E. Napa St.* ☎ *707/996-2253. www.lahaye artcenter.com.*

OR:

❽Ⓑ Arts Guild of Sonoma. This small, no-frills gallery features mixed-media works by local artists. *140 E. Napa St.* ☎ *707/996-3115. www.artsguildofsonoma.com. Thurs–Mon 11am–5pm.*

❾ ★★ Cafe La Haye. This self-appointed "place for food and art" is a small but smartly designed restaurant that enhances your dining experience with big, ever-changing works of modern art. Reservations recommended. *140 E. Napa St., Sonoma.* ☎ *707/935-5994. $$. See p 77.* If you're headed back to Napa for your lodging, head to

❿ ★ Uva Trattoria for after-dinner drinks and live music (usually jazz). Performances happen Wednesday to Sunday nights. *1040 Clinton St., Napa.* ☎ *707/ 255-6646. $$. See p 73.*

Wine Country for Health & Wellness

1 Bikram Yoga Petaluma
2 Lucy Restaurant & Bar
3A Bardessono Hotel & Spa
3B Osmosis Day Spa
4A Farmstead
4B Farm at the Carneros Inn

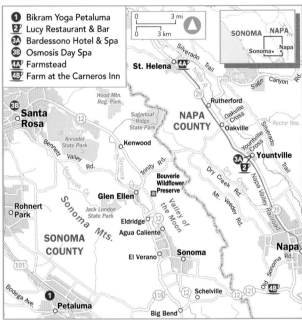

This region's calming scenery makes it perfect for a day focused on mind, body, and soul. Get pampered at a spa, eat for health, and expand your physical and spiritual horizons with yoga and meditation. Follow this itinerary to leave Napa and Sonoma feeling rested and reinvigorated. START: Bikram Yoga Petaluma, 1484 Petaluma Blvd. N. Distance: about 60 miles (95km), doable in a day.

1 ★ Bikram Yoga Petaluma.
Start your day with a session at this popular studio staffed by well-liked instructors (beginners are welcome). Sweat out your toxins during a refreshing workout in a bright, clean space, then enjoy the private outdoor showers. Classes start at 6am and run throughout the day; drop-in rates start at $18. *1484 Petaluma Blvd. N.* ☎ *707/775-2400. www.bikramyogapetaluma.com.*

From Petaluma, take Highway 101 south to Highway 116 east and left onto Highway 22, then exit toward Yountville.

Lunch in Yountville at **2 ★★ Lucy Restaurant & Bar** in the Bardessono Hotel (see below), much of whose "garden-first" cuisine comes straight from the property's vegetable-and-herb beds. *6526 Yount St.* ☎ *707/204-6000. $$$$.* See p 93.

Take a class at Bikram Yoga Petaluma.

③A ★★★ **Bardessono Hotel & Spa.** This shrine to modern luxury is one of only three LEED Platinum hotels in the United States, so everything is extraordinarily eco-friendly. It's also home to one of wine country's best spas. Release tension with a massage customized to your preferences, or try reflexology. Treatments are 60, 90, or 120 minutes, and cost between $85 and $360, while packages run $235 to $630. The spa also offers skin treatments, from ones that incorporate LED lights, to champagne baths ($60–$350). You'll have to travel about 40 minutes from Petaluma to get here, so arrange your day accordingly. *6526 Yount St.* ☎ *707/204-6000. See p 120.*

Or if you'd rather stay in Sonoma County, consider:

③B ★★ **Osmosis Day Spa.** This is the only place in America where you can experience a cedar enzyme bath, a Japanese heat treatment that's said to miraculously dissolve aches and pains. You can also sip tea in the lush Japanese garden or indulge in a customized facial or Swedish massage. Single treatments start at $89 but packages cost up to $459 (some include lunch). *209 Bohemian Hwy., Freestone.* ☎ *707/823-8231. www.osmosis.com.*

From Yountville, get back on Highway 29, heading north toward St. Helena.

④A ★ **Farmstead.** Finish your day with wine and dinner at Long Meadow Ranch's excellent restaurant in St. Helena. The chefs here are committed to using organic, local ingredients in their upscale farm-to-table cuisine. *738 Main St.* ☎ *707/963-9181. $$$.* To dine closer to the towns of Napa and Sonoma, consider **④B** ★ **Farm at the Carneros Inn,** whose menu also highlights organic, local produce. *4048 Sonoma Hwy.* ☎ *707/299-4880. $$$$.*

Wine Country **for Romance**

Driving Tour

BIKE TOUR

1. Sonoma Market
2. Sonoma Valley Bike Tours
3. Ravenswood
4. Sebastiani
5A. Gundlach-Bundschu Winery
5B. Della Santina's
6. Bartholomew Park Winery
7. Buena Vista Winery

DRIVING TOUR

8. Enterprise Rent-A-Car
9. Schug Carneros Estate Winery
10. Arrowood
11. Chateau St. Jean
12. Ledson Winery
13. La Toque

Bike Tour

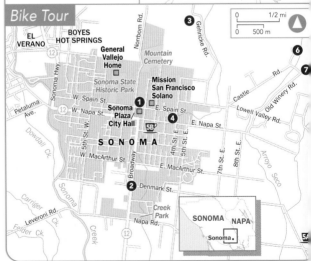

Whether you're trying to impress a new sweetie, aiming for the perfect proposal, celebrating your honeymoon, or vacationing for your 50th anniversary, wine country is a wonderful place for romance. This Sonoma-centric tour takes you to the wineries and restaurants best suited for lovebirds. *Note:* Before you start this itinerary, decide whether you want to make this a cycling or a driving tour. Then follow the appropriate travel plan below. (The biking path is leisurely, mostly flat, and not too strenuous.) START: **Sonoma Market, 500 W. Napa St., Sonoma. Distance: Biking: 13 miles (21km), doable in a day. Driving: 26 miles (42km), doable in a day.**

❶ ★★ Sonoma Market.
Whether you're biking or driving, stop here in the morning to assemble lunch for later from the deli and sandwich bar. If you order 24 hours in advance, the market can have a boxed picnic, including a sandwich, salad, and fruit ready and waiting (get two of the "signature box picnic for one," which cost $18 each). This market is locally loved for its selection of specialty foods, fresh breads, and reasonably priced wines. *500 W. Napa St., Ste. 550, Sonoma.* ☎ *707/ 996-3411. www.sonomamarket.com. Daily 6am–10pm.*

CYCLING TOUR
From the market, take Napa Street east and turn right on Broadway.

❷ Sonoma Valley Bike Tours.
Sonoma's the perfect place to attempt a bicycle built for two, so rent a tandem bicycle. The experience is even more fun if you've never tried this kind of riding before. As in any relationship, communication and listening are key to doing it successfully. *1254 Broadway, Sonoma.* ☎ *707/996-2453. www. sonomavalleybiketours.com. Tandem bikes $60 per day, return by 5pm, or $20 per hour. Daily 8:30am–5pm.*

From the cyclery, pedal north on Broadway and turn right on E. Napa Street, then left on E. 4th Street. Turn right at Brazil Street, then left on Gehricke Road (2½ miles/4km).

❸ ★ Ravenswood. If strong wine makes for strong love, this is the place to bolster your affection—the winery's motto, in fact, is "Zero wimpy wines." Tour the vineyards and cellar; a barrel tasting is included. *18701 Gehricke Rd., Sonoma.* ☎ *888/669-4679. See p 156.*

Head south on Gehricke Road, turn right on Brazil Street, then left on E. 4th Street (1⅓ miles/2.1km).

❹ ★★ Sebastiani. The big tasting room might be crowded, but that'll just push the two of you closer together. Besides, after tasting the cabernet and merlot, and strolling the historic grounds hand in hand, you'll both forget all about it. Or plan in advance to arrange for a customized private tasting (call for pricing). *389 E. 4th St., Sonoma.* ☎ *707/933-3230. See p 158.*

Take 4th Street south and turn left on Patten Street, then right on E. 5th Street. Turn left on Napa Road and left on Denmark Street (3 miles/4.8km).

5⓹ ★★ Gundlach Bundschu.
Unfold the picnic you bought from Sonoma Market at any of Gundlach Bundschu's many picnic grounds. The remote hillside tables and the olive grove near a pond both overlook the valley. If it's spring or summer, you might catch a music performance in the outdoor

amphitheater (check the website's event schedule). *2000 Denmark St., Sonoma.* ☎ *707/938-5277. See p 148.* If you prefer a restaurant lunch on the plaza, there's a romantic patio at 5B ★★ **Della Santina's.** *133 E. Napa St., Sonoma.* ☎ *707/935-0576. $$.*

From Gundlach Bundschu, take Denmark Street northwest and turn right on E. 7th Street. Turn right on Castle Road, which becomes Vineyard Lane (3 miles/4.8km).

⑥ Bartholomew Park Winery.
Share tastes of limited-production wines, then explore the historical museum, memorial park, and hiking trails. Or simply sit and enjoy the views—on a clear day, you can see to San Francisco. *1000 Vineyard Lane, Sonoma.* ☎ *707/939-3026. See p 135.*

Take Vineyard Lane, which becomes Castle Road, then turn left on Lovall Valley Road. Turn left on Old Winery Road (2 miles/3.2km).

⑦ ★★★ Buena Vista Carneros.
This estate inspires romance with its ivy-covered buildings,

Wines of Bartholomew Park Winery.

antique fountains, and restored 1862 press house, which houses the tasting room. *18000 Old Winery Rd., Sonoma.* ☎ *800/926-1266. See p 138.*

For where to have dinner, refer to the driving tour below.

DRIVING TOUR
From ① Sonoma Market (see above), take W. Napa Street west and turn right on Sonoma Highway 12.

⑧ Enterprise Rent-A-Car.
Evoke romance-movie scenes by renting a convertible. Enterprise offers pickup service, so if you don't already have a vehicle via which to get to the branch office, that won't be a problem. Additionally, all the gateway airports to wine country have many car-rental counters (see p 197). *18981 Sonoma Hwy., Sonoma.* ☎ *707/938-0200.*

In your open-top car, take Sonoma Highway southeast and turn right on W. Verano Avenue. Turn left on Arnold Drive, then right on Stage Gulch Road. Turn left on Highway 116, then right on Bonneau Road.

⑨ ★ Schug Carneros Estate Winery.
In the cozy tasting room, share sips of European-style wines, then stroll hand in hand to see the herb garden, the duck pond, and the spectacular view. If it's a clear day, you might be able to see Mt. Diablo in the distance. *602 Bonneau Rd., Sonoma.* ☎ *800/966-9365. See p 158.*

For where to have lunch, refer to the biking tour above.

Take Bonneau Road northeast and turn left on Highway 116/Arnold Drive. Turn right on Madrone Road, then left on Sonoma Highway/Highway 12.

⑩ ★ Arrowood.
More than 25 years ago, a married couple founded this winery on a hillside overlooking Sonoma. Today, their love for each

Tasting at Schug Carneros Estate Winery.

other and for wine is evident in the bright tasting room. After tasting, go out onto the veranda and gaze upon Sonoma Mountain, its valley—and each other. *14347 Sonoma Hwy. (Hwy. 12), Glen Ellen.* ☎ *800/938-5170. See p 135.*

Follow the highway northwest.

⓫ ★★ Chateau St. Jean. Romantic in the more academic sense of the word (it has a bit of a nationalistic French feel about it, though "Jean" is pronounced the American way), this château provides a nice setting for you and your loved one. It's got a fancy visitors' center, a small art gallery, and a formal garden with a pond. *8555 Sonoma Hwy. (Hwy. 12), Kenwood.* ☎ *707/257-5784. See p 141.*

Keep following the highway northwest.

⓬ ★ Ledson Winery. Fairy-tale-like architecture, complete with regal gates, a castle, and a hyper-pruned fountain courtyard, evokes scenes of prince-and-princess romance. If you're getting in the mood for an intimate dinner back at your hotel, pick up a to-go meal at this winery's gourmet market—and don't forget a bottle of pinot noir or chardonnay. If you'd rather

eat alfresco, though, Ledson has pretty picnic grounds. *7335 Sonoma Hwy. (Hwy. 12), Kenwood.* ☎ *707/537-3810. See p 152.*

Head to Napa to dine at 15-table **⓭ ★★ La Toque,** whose romantic setting complements Chef Ken Frank's excellent French cuisine. *1314 McKinstry St., Napa.* ☎ *707/257-5157. $$$$$. See p 73.*

Ledson Winery.

Wine Country **Without a Car**

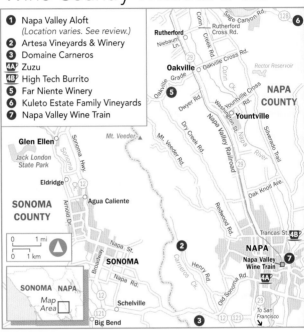

① Napa Valley Aloft
   (Location varies. See review.)
② Artesa Vineyards & Winery
③ Domaine Carneros
④A Zuzu
④B High Tech Burrito
⑤ Far Niente Winery
⑥ Kuleto Estate Family Vineyards
⑦ Napa Valley Wine Train

Traffic is an increasing problem in Napa, and you definitely didn't plan this getaway just to sit in gridlock. Besides, if you're planning to try all the wine you'd like to, getting behind the wheel just shouldn't factor in. So let others shuttle you around while you sip to your heart's content. Take this opportunity to see far-apart wineries that are off the main drag and experience some of Napa's best alternative ways to get around. *Note:* This itinerary requires advance planning to secure reservations. *Tip:* For other non-car transportation ideas (bikes, bus, and so on), refer to "Savvy Traveler" (p 193). For walking tours, flip to chapter 4 (p 67).

① ★★★ kids **Napa Valley Aloft.** Wine country's ultimate mode of transportation is the hot-air balloon. In fact, this is the world's busiest hot-air balloon flight corridor. Northern California's temperate weather allows for ballooning

year-round. On clear summer weekends in the valley, it's a rare day when you don't see at least one of the colorful airships floating above the vineyards. One of the best companies providing rides is Napa Valley Aloft. Though it's headquartered in

Yountville, employees will pick you up from your hotel as long as it's in Napa Valley south of Calistoga. (When you call to make your reservation, ask whether your lodging is within shuttling range.) You'll have to get up before the sun, but it'll be worth it for the breathtaking serenity you'll experience as you float 3,500 feet (1,050m) above spectacular scenery. Skilled pilots double as informative tour guides, creating a personalized adventure. You'll get pastries and coffee before the flight and a full champagne breakfast upon landing. Delivery back to your hotel is included to Yountville (but costs $10 per shuttle of 12 passengers to Napa, Rutherford, or Oakville). Reservations are required and should be made as far in advance as possible. Another reputable company is **Calistoga Balloons ★★★** (see p 18). ☎ *855/944-4408. www.nvaloft.com. $229 per person.*

Napa Valley Aloft Balloons in Napa.

Ballooning Tip

When the valley is foggy, balloon companies drive clients outside the valley to nearby areas. Though they can't guarantee the flight path until hours before liftoff, they should refund your money if you decide not to partake.

Plan in advance for a chauffeur to meet you back at your hotel after ballooning. **Beau Wine Tours and Limousine Service** (☎ 707/938-8001; www.beauwinetours.com) provides limos, SUVs, and even trolleys. **California Wine Tours** (☎ 800/294-6386; www.californiawinetours.com) puts together personalized winery trips in town cars, SUVs, limos, and minibuses. And **Pure Luxury Limousine** specializes in luxury limos and wine tours (☎ 800/626-5466; www.pureluxury.com). See p 199 for more options.

② **★★ Artesa Vineyards & Winery.** In a limo is a perfect way to visit the spread-out Carneros appellation, and Artesa is one of the few wineries directly east of downtown Napa. A dramatic, modern tasting room makes this Spanish-owned winery on a hilltop a Carneros region gem. Try the small-lot chardonnay and pinot noir, then explore the visitors' center, which includes an exhibit about the region's history, a winemaking museum, and art displays. *1345 Henry Rd., Napa.* ☎ *707/224-1668. See p 135.*

③ **★ Domaine Carneros.** You can see this French-owned château beckoning you from the highway. Have your driver stop and then ascend the grand staircase into the only tasting room to serve sparkling wines made exclusively with

Carneros grapes. *1240 Duhig Rd., Napa.* ☎ *800/716-BRUT [2788]. See p 144.*

Beautiful views of Carneros from Artesa.

4A ★★ **ZuZu.** For lunch, direct your chauffeur to this local favorite. Mini Mediterranean plates meant for sharing are served in a comfortable, warm, and not remotely corporate atmosphere. Since you're not driving, indulge at the small but friendly wine-and-beer bar. *829 Main St., Napa.* ☎ *707/224-8555. $. See p 73.* For a quick to-go alternative, tell your driver to shift gears toward **4B** ★ kids **High Tech Burrito,** a great fresh-Mex chain, then take your healthy, creatively concocted wrap in the limo with you as you head north. *641 Trancas St., Napa.* ☎ *707/224-8882. $.*

5 Far Niente Winery. Yes, this one's on the beaten path, but it has a faraway feel, created by its stone structure and Southern-style gardens with 8,000 azaleas and 100 ginkgo trees. Taste Far Niente's current releases and late-harvest Dolce dessert wine. Appointment required. *1350 Acacia Dr., Oakville.* ☎ *707/944-2861. www.farniente. com. Mon–Fri 8am–4:30pm. Tours and tastings with cheese pairing ($65) Mon–Sun 10am–3pm (by appointment).*

Transportation Tips

Limos are the most luxurious transportation option, but they're certainly not the only game in town. Uber (www.uber.com) started operating in the region in 2014, so you can now get a personal driver with a few taps on your smartphone. You can cab it too; see p 199 for a list of options. If you've got your own car, rented or otherwise, but don't want to risk driving it after a few tastings, a company called **BeeDriven** will provide a knowledgeable local driver to chauffeur you in your own car, following any path you choose, even customizing an itinerary for you, if you like. And it starts at $40 per hour, which is less expensive than a limo. Advance reservations are recommended (☎ 707/637-4115; www.napabee driven.com). Shuttles are another option, but only if you don't mind not being in charge of your own itinerary (☎ 707/257-1950; www.wineshuttle.com).

❻ Kuleto Estate Family Vineyards. Bordering the far-flung (for Napa) Chiles Valley District appellation is this lovely spot for touring and tasting. Few wineries offer this great a view of Lake Hennessey, such mountainous scenery, or quite the possibility to glimpse wildlife. Appointment required. *2470 Sage Canyon Rd. (Hwy. 128), St. Helena.* ☎ *866/485-7579. www.kuletoestate.com. Tours and tastings ($40 per person) 10:30 & 11:45am, 1 & 2:30pm, by appointment only.*

Hit Napa's McKinstry Street Depot for **❼ ★ kids Napa Valley Wine Train**'s 5:30pm check-in time (boarding is at 6pm and the train departs for St. Helena at 6:30pm). Get to the station even earlier if you want to partake in the pre-boarding wine tasting. This rolling restaurant is a leisurely way to see Napa. The nonstop

The restaurant on the Napa Valley Wine Train.

3-hour journey through the vineyards of Napa, Yountville, Oakville, Rutherford, and St. Helena is a lazy 36-mile (58km) cruise on vintage-style cars finished with polished mahogany paneling and etched-glass partitions. The windows are slightly dirt-stained, but staffers are attentive, if not overly enthusiastic. Dinner's served with all the finery—linen, china, silver, and crystal—but the food itself isn't as memorable. The point here is the ride, which means that this is a more interesting trip during daylight saving time (it's best May–Aug). *Tip:* Sit on the west side for the best views. *1275 McKinstry St., Napa.* ☎ *800/427-4124. www. winetrain.com. Dinner packages $109–$139. Lunch packages $99–$139. Boarding times Mon–Fri 11am & 6pm. Schedules are abbreviated in winter. Check the website for special events, menus & tour packages.*

Enjoy sparkling wine from Domaine Carneros.

Wine Country **on a Budget**

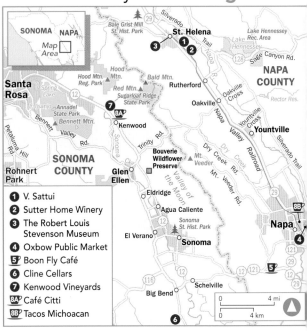

SONOMA NAPA

Map Area

Bale Grist Mill St. Hist. Park

Silverado Trail

St. Helena

Lake Hennessey Rec. Area

Lake Hennessey

Sage Canyon Rd.

❶ ❷ ❸

Hood Mtn. Reg. Park

Hood Mtn.

Bald Mtn.

NAPA COUNTY

Santa Rosa

Spring Lake

Red Mtn.

Sugarloaf Ridge State Park

Rutherford

Oakville Cross

Rector Res.

Annadel State Park

Bennett Mtn.

❼

8A

Oakville

Napa Valley

Yountville Cross

Yountville

Silverado Trail

Bennett Valley Rd.

Kenwood

Trinity Rd.

Bouverie Wildflower Preserve

Dry Creek Rd.

Mt. Veeder

Dry Creek Railroad

SONOMA COUNTY

Rohnert Park

Glen Ellen

Valley of the Moon

Mt. Veeder Rd.

Eldridge

Agua Caliente

Sonoma St. Hist. Park

Napa

8B

El Verano

❹

❶ V. Sattui
❷ Sutter Home Winery
❸ The Robert Louis Stevenson Museum
❹ Oxbow Public Market
5 Boon Fly Café
❻ Cline Cellars
❼ Kenwood Vineyards
8A Café Citti
8B Tacos Michoacan

Sonoma

5

Schelville

Big Bend

0 — 4 mi
0 — 4 km

❻

Abudget traveler might not choose a region characterized by splurging and expensive taste. Although Napa and Sonoma (especially Napa) are spendy destinations, the budget-conscious can still come here, indulge, and leave without breaking the bank. Here's how. START: **V. Sattui, 1111 White Lane, St. Helena. Distance: 53 miles (85km), doable in a full day.**

❶ ★★ **V. Sattui.** This historic winery offers free self-guided tours all day. Explore its aging cellars, museum, and outdoor spaces. At the deli and cheese shop, there are free food samples aplenty but a wine tasting will set you back $15. And no outside food is allowed. *Tip:* To fit everything in today, take advantage of V. Sattui's 9am opening time. *1111 White Lane, St. Helena.* ☎ *707/963-7774.* *See p 160.*

Take White Lane southwest and turn right on St. Helena Highway (easy walking distance).

❷ ★ **Sutter Home Winery.** Tastings here, which happen in the original 1874 winery, are free. Take a self-guided garden tour (also free) to see the estate's extensive grounds, which were modeled after Canada's Butchart Gardens. In the organic White Zinfandel garden, 125 rose species are available for viewing. *277 St. Helena Hwy. (Hwy.*

Enjoy a picnic at V. Sattui Winery.

29), St. Helena. ☎ 707/963-3104, ext. 4208. See p 159.

Take St. Helena Highway northwest and turn right on Adams Street. Turn left on Library Lane.

❸ **kids The Robert Louis Stevenson Museum.** Dedicated to the life of Robert Louis Stevenson, this one-room museum packs more than 8,000 writerly artifacts, including original manuscripts, photographs, and the author's copies of his own books. Admission is free. *1490 Library Lane, St. Helena. ☎ 707/963-3757. Tues–Sat noon–4pm (closed holidays). www.stevensonmuseum.org.*

Go southeast on Library Lane to turn right on Adams Street. Turn left on Highway 29 and take the ramp toward Lincoln Avenue. Turn right on Solano Avenue, then right onto Lincoln Avenue. Turn right on Soscol Avenue, then left on 1st Street.

❹ ★ **Oxbow Public Market.** Downtown Napa's main attraction

can be as cheap as you want it to be. Peruse the colorful stalls, people-watch, and pick up free samples: Try a bit of the gourmet ice cream at Three Twins, score free chocolate-caramel sauce at Anette's, savor slivers of cheese, and chomp on charcuterie at the Fatted Calf. *610 & 644 First St. ☎ 707/226-6529. www.oxbowpublicmarket.com. Open daily 9am–7pm, though some merchants stay open later (closed major holidays).*

From Oxbow Public Market, go west on 1st Street onto Highway 29 S. Turn right on Carneros Highway (Highway 121/12), and turn left to stay on it.

To feel as though you've gone to an expensive restaurant, head to ❺ ★★ **Boon Fly Café,** whose upscale interior, white-linen tables, and classy California cuisine belie the menu's affordable prices. *4048 Sonoma Hwy. (at the Carneros Inn), Napa. ☎ 707/299-4900. $$$. See p 72.*

Sutter Home Winery.

farmhouse, even though the winery's now a modern, high-production facility, most of it cleverly concealed in the original barnlike buildings. Though this place looks modest, its output is staggering: nearly 500,000 cases of wine per year. Alas, tours aren't available, but tastes are affordable (five wines start at $10) and include an array of varietals, including the popular sauvignon blanc, a crisp, light wine with hints of melon. You won't need reservations here, either for the tastings or the picnic grounds. *9592 Sonoma Hwy. (Hwy. 12), Kenwood.* ☎ *707/833-5891.* See p 151.

❻ ★ Cline Cellars. Get here in time to take the 1 or 3pm free tour, or walk around yourself to see the quaint grounds, which include ponds, rosebushes, and the highlight: a small, woodsy museum (free admission) housing dioramas of all 21 California missions. Tastings are free too, and they're poured in a rustic 1850s farmhouse. *24737 Arnold Dr. (Hwy. 121), Sonoma.* ☎ *707/940-4000.* See p 142.

From Cline, head east on Highway 121 and turn left (north) on Highway 12. From Audelssa, take Arnold Drive northeast and turn left on Sonoma Highway (Highway 12).

❼ ★ Kenwood Vineyards. The tasting room here is in a 1906

8A² ★ Café Citti. The high-quality northern Italian cuisine at Citti (pronounced "Cheat-ee"), a roadside trattoria, is delightfully inexpensive. Order from the huge menu board above the open kitchen, then grab a table—on warm evenings, the ones out on the patio are best—and a server delivers your hearty meal. Wine is available by the bottle, the espresso is strong, and everything can be packed to go. *9049 Sonoma Hwy., Kenwood.* ☎ *707/833-2690. $$.* If you're more in the mood for Mexican (or are headed back to lodgings in Napa), try **8B² Tacos Michoacan,** a sit-down version of a locally famous taco truck. Its offerings are fresh, tasty, and very affordable. *721 Lincoln Ave., Napa.* ☎ *707/256-0820. $.* ●

Napa

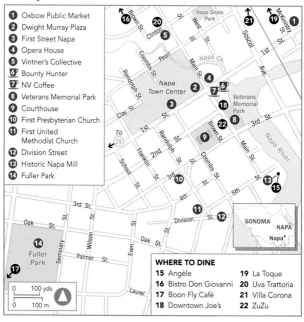

1. Oxbow Public Market
2. Dwight Murray Plaza
3. First Street Napa
4. Opera House
5. Vintner's Collective
6. Bounty Hunter
7. NV Coffee
8. Veterans Memorial Park
9. Courthouse
10. First Presbyterian Church
11. First United Methodist Church
12. Division Street
13. Historic Napa Mill
14. Fuller Park

WHERE TO DINE

15. Angèle
16. Bistro Don Giovanni
17. Boon Fly Café
18. Downtown Joe's
19. La Toque
20. Uva Trattoria
21. Villa Corona
22. ZuZu

This walking tour takes you through the city of Napa—the town, not the region, valley, or county. The southern bookend to the ritzier towns above it, Napa is the more lived-in, real-life community that caters more to its ever-growing residential population than to its tourists. But that's exactly its charm: Visitors feel invited in rather than pandered to. Plant yourself here for a day, sip a local cabernet, stroll along this riverside town's Victorian and Gothic landmarks, and mingle with locals ("Napkins," as they call themselves). For more information, contact Visit Napa Valley (☎ 707/251-5895; www.visitnapavalley.com). START: 1st & Main sts. **Distance: 1-mile (1.6km) of walking.**

❶ ★ Oxbow Public Market. Start your day at one of the town's newer attractions, a marketplace filled with artisan foods and wine sellers. Dine at one of the interesting eateries, buy specialty food items and souvenirs, and do dessert at **Kara's Cupcakes** ($3.50 each). *See p 11.*
Previous page: Main Street in St. Helena.

❷ Dwight Murray Plaza. Walk southwest on 1st Street, stopping just past Main, to this community gathering spot with various shops, a fountain, and picnic tables. Check out the mural depicting the Napa River waterfront in its early-1900s heyday. At press time, this

Shopping in Oxbow Public Market in Napa.

landmark was about to get treated to a major redevelopment, so there may be more there now than when this book was last updated—either way, it's worth a stop.

3 ★ kids First Street Napa.
Head to this retail complex to satisfy a sweet tooth at **Anette's Chocolates** or shop one of the stores, all of which are housed in historic buildings and connected by a pedestrian street. Look for the two huge oak trees that serve as town landmarks. Similar to Dwight Murray Plaza (see above), the shopping complex was

hit hard by the 2014 earthquake and is in the process of being redeveloped, possibly drastically, to become a more attractive destination. Here you'll also find the **Napa Tourist Information Center** (see p 11). Stop in for local information, coupons, and pamphlets outlining self-guided walking tours of the town's historic buildings. *1290 Napa Town Center.* ☎ *707/257-0332.*

4 ★ Napa Valley Opera House. Cross the street to Main to see this Italianate-style building. Even if you don't see a show, this performance venue is worth a look for its historic value alone. Listed on the National Historic Register, it was built in 1879. Some nights, Jack London read aloud to rapt audiences; others, traveling Vaudeville acts titillated patrons. Due to poor attendance, however, it closed in 1914 and sat quiet and dilapidating until local preservationists restored and reopened it—to the tune of $14 million. Today, operatic performances are still the minority at this 16-row venue, despite the establishment's name. Management prefers to bring in symphonies and musicals as well as jazz, comedy, and film classics

Stores and restaurants along Napa's waterfront.

(including sing-alongs). Occasionally, theater and dance troupes come through as well. Check the website for show times. *1030 Main St. ☎ 707/226-7372. www.nvoh.org. Box office open Mon–Sat noon–6pm (or until curtains close).*

⑤ ★★ Vintner's Collective.

Wine discoveries await at this 26-winery tasting room in the old Pfeiffer Building, which was built in 1875 and is Napa's first stone building (touch the native sandstone). After past lives as a brewery, saloon, brothel, and Chinese-owned laundry, in 2002 it became an outlet for small, virtually unknown wineries such as Judd's Hill, Melka, and Mi Sueno—in short, stuff you won't find at home. To boot, Keith Fergel (former sommelier of French Laundry, that is, the longtime wine expert at the region's most famous restaurant) named this tasting room his favorite stop for finding new wines. *1245 Main St. ☎ 707/255-7150. www. vintnerscollective.com. Daily 11am–6pm. Tastings start at $30.*

⑥ ★★ Bounty Hunter Wine Bar & Smokin' BBQ.

A combination wine bar/eating joint/retail shop/tasting room, Bounty Hunter has bottles that even devoted collectors would be hard-pressed to find elsewhere. With dozens of options available by the glass, and hundreds by the bottle, the thinking here is, "Find your own cult wine." Or just enjoy on-tap Guinness with a hearty sandwich. Before walking into this saloon-like space, admire its exterior: The brick Semorile Building, embellished with decorative cast-iron railing, was built in 1888 and is on the National Historic Register. *975 1st St. ☎ 707/ 226-3976. www.bountyhunterwinebar. com. Daily Sun–Thurs 11am–10pm (until midnight Fri–Sat). Tastings $2.50– $25 (2 oz. & 5 oz.); $9–$24 (flights).*

⑦ ★ Napa Valley Coffee Roasting Co.

For a sweet fix after Bounty Hunter, or if you just need a caffeinated pick-me-up, this roastery in the adjacent Winship Building (also on the Historic Register) sells small-batch custom roasts and a selection of pastries. *948 Main St. ☎ 707/ 224-2233. Mon–Sun 6:30am–7pm. $.*

⑧ Veterans Memorial Park.

Savor your coffee on the river's edge at this tranquil park. On holidays like Independence Day and Labor Day, the site comes alive with music and festivities. And when government officials come to town, this is where they hold press conferences. *Main & 3rd sts.*

⑨ ★ kids Courthouse.

Napa's Renaissance-style courthouse, built in 1878, is still very much a working court, complete with a law library, hall of records, and mediation center. It's on the National Register of Historic Places for its 19th-century architecture and history—in 1897, for example, this courthouse was the site of California's last public hanging. Explore the first-floor pictorial hall for a visual depiction of

Beer can chicken from Bounty Hunter.

Napa County's rich history. On the east lawn (2nd St.), look for the 1893 flagpole modeled after the Eiffel Tower, as well as a Wappo Indian grinding rock. *825 Brown St.*

❿ ★ First Presbyterian Church. Were it not for its protuberant steeple and ornamental doorway, this pyramidal church, built in 1874, would just look like a big rooftop sitting on the ground. It's one of the county's best examples of Victorian Gothic architecture—no surprise, then, that this California Registered Historical Landmark is also in the National Register of Historic Places. *1333 3rd St.* ☎ *707/224-8693. www.fpcnapa.org.*

Heading from downtown into the Napa Abajo District, you'll notice larger city blocks and a high concentration of residential architectural styles spanning the 1800s. This entire district is on the National Register of Historic Places.

⓫ First United Methodist Church. This mix of religious and secular architecture done in late-Gothic style is home to an elaborate sanctuary and gorgeous stained-glass windows. Try its small labyrinth. *625 Randolph St.* ☎ *707/253-1411. www.napamethodist.org. Labyrinth hours Mon–Fri 9am–4pm.*

Stroll riverward on **⓬ ★ Division Street,** so named because it divides Napa Abajo from downtown. All the turn-of-the-20th-century homes on this lane are historically significant, from the **Hayman House** (1227 Division St.) to the Greek Revival–style **Lamdin Cottage** (1236 Division St.).

⓭ ★★ Historic Napa Mill. Abutting the Napa River are this complex's Hatt buildings, also on the National Register of Historic

Rooms of the Napa River Inn and the Historic Napa Mill overlook the Napa River.

Places (sensing a theme here?). They're good examples of the industrial false-front brick buildings that used to cluster the river's once-bustling wharves. The 1884 building once housed a grain mill (the old tin silos are still attached) and a roller-skating rink. These days, it's a smart commercial center that includes the "haunted" **Napa River Inn** (see p 125) and a variety of shops: Stop at the upscale **Napa General Store, Amelia's Gifts,** and the **Vintage Sweet Shoppe** for locally made non-wine souvenirs or gifts. Notice the beautiful mosaic fountain—its scenes portray Napa Valley's history. *500 Main St.* ☎ *707/251-8500. www.historicnapamill.com.*

⓮ kids Fuller Park. Take a 15-minute stroll to Napa's first park. Of its 80-plus kinds of trees, many are marked with plaques commemorating important events. Named after Napa's 1905 mayor, John A. Fuller, the shaded park is a great place to relax; kids love its fountain and large playground. *Oak & Seminary sts.*

Where to Dine in Napa

★★ **Angèle** *FRENCH* This riverside spot has exciting food and surroundings to match. Its combination of wood beams, concrete walls and floors, bright yellow barstools, and heated patio works well for intimate dining. The culinary ante is way up there: Think crispy roast chicken with fresh corn and chanterelles, or King salmon with arugula salad and heirloom tomatoes, though the menu changes pretty often. If "chocolate soup" is on the dessert menu, it's a must. Reservations recommended. *540 Main St. (at Historic Napa Mill).* ☎ *707/252-8115. Entrees $28–$39. AE, MC, V. Lunch & dinner daily. Map p 68.*

★★★ **Bistro Don Giovanni** *ITALIAN* BDG is a bright, bustling restaurant highlighting quality ingredients and California flair. Entrees never disappoint, especially the thin-crust pizzas straight from the wood-burning oven and the house-made pastas. Start with the salad of beets and *haricots verts*. If the weather's nice, dine alfresco in the vineyard. Reservations recommended. *4110 Howard Lane.* ☎ *707/224-3300. Entrees $15–$45. AE, DC, DISC, MC, V. Lunch & dinner daily. Map p 68.*

★★ **Boon Fly Café** *AMERICAN* Along the rural Carneros Highway is a great bargain dining option: the gourmet roadhouse in front of the Carneros Inn. The inviting interior is done in modern barn style—there's a corrugated-metal watershed-like pizza oven and light, airy surroundings accented with dark wood. The food also balances rustic and chic with fancy renditions of comfort classics like beer-battered onion rings and flatbread

Riverside dining at Angèle.

pizzas. Breakfast options include satisfying omelets and pancakes. If you're passing by and in a hurry, try the tasty to-go items like donut holes and breakfast sandwiches. *4048 Sonoma Hwy.* ☎ *707/299-4870. Entrees $14–$26. AE, DC, DISC, MC, V. Breakfast, lunch & dinner daily. Map p 68.*

★ **kids Downtown Joe's** *AMERICAN* Foodies will want to steer clear, but those looking for a good, heavy breakfast, a down-home atmosphere, and live evening entertainment (Thurs–Sun) will appreciate this well-priced restaurant. Beers, such as the tart Golden Ribbon American, are made in-house, as are breads and desserts. If the sun's out, eat on the patio. Weekday happy hours feature specials such as $3 pints and half-priced appetizers. *902 Main St.* ☎ *707/258-2337. Entrees $13–$24. AE, DC, DISC, MC, V. Breakfast, lunch & dinner daily. Map p 68.*

★★ **La Toque** *AMERICAN/ FRENCH Wine Spectator* deemed this one of America's best restaurants. It's in the Westin Verasa Napa hotel (see p 126), and it's known for unrivaled cuisine, warm ambience, a long wine list, and accommodating waitstaff. The acclaimed chef, Ken Frank, uses fresh, organic ingredients in his culinary masterpieces. Try the truffle menu. *1314 McKinstry St.* ☎ *707/257-5157. Three-course tasting menu $80 per person, including dessert; add $52 for wine pairing. AE, DC, DISC, MC, V. Dinner daily.*

★ **Uva Trattoria** *ITALIAN* At this lively restaurant with a hopping music scene, jazz bands perform almost every evening, turning your reasonably priced meal into a special occasion. To start, order *arancini* (breaded, fried basil-risotto balls filled with Teleme cheese) and follow that with a gourmet pizza or house-made pasta. *1040 Clinton St.* ☎ *707/255-6646. Entrees $12–$33. AE, MC, V. Lunch Tues–Fri; dinner Tues–Sun. Map p 68.*

★ **Villa Corona** *MEXICAN* A funky, colorful local favorite hidden in the southwest corner of a strip mall. Order at the counter, then wait for the huge burritos, enchiladas, and chimichangas to arrive at your table. *3614 Bel Aire Plaza (on Trancas St.).* ☎ *707/257-8685. Entrees $6–$11. MC, V. Lunch & dinner daily. Map p 68.*

★★ **ZuZu** *TAPAS* If you've had it with French and Italian fare and wine-country-themed dining rooms, this neighborhood haunt will restore you. Enjoy affordable Mediterranean-inspired small plates, like tangy paella, paired with intriguing by-the-glass wines and a friendly attitude. Desserts aren't as interesting, but with a bottle of wine and more delicious plates than you could possibly devour, who cares? Reservations not accepted. *829 Main St., Napa.* ☎ *707/224-8555. Tapas $4–$15. MC, V. Lunch Mon–Fri; dinner daily. Map p 68.*

Sonoma

1. Terra Firma
2. Basque Boulangerie
3. Tiddle E. Winks
4. Vella Cheese Co.
5. City Hall
6. Bear Flag
7. Mission SF Solano
8. Blue Wing Inn
9. Sonoma Barracks
10. Toscano Hotel
11. Sonoma Cheese Factory
12. Swiss Hotel
13. Roche Winery Tasting Room

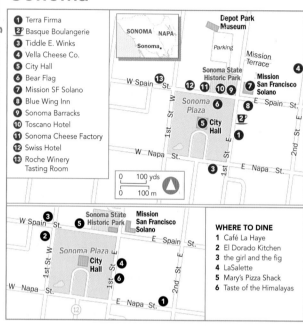

WHERE TO DINE
1. Café La Haye
2. El Dorado Kitchen
3. the girl and the fig
4. LaSalette
5. Mary's Pizza Shack
6. Taste of the Himalayas

At the northern boundary of the Carneros District, along Highway 12, is the centerpiece of Sonoma Valley: the actual town of Sonoma. It owes much of its appeal to Mexican general Mariano Guadalupe Vallejo, who fashioned this pleasant, slow-paced community after a typical Mexican village—right down to its central plaza, which is still Sonoma's geographical and commercial heartbeat. The plaza's Bear Flag Monument marks the spot where the crude Bear Flag was raised in 1846, signaling the end of Mexican rule. The symbol was later adopted by the state of California and placed on its flag. The 8-acre (3.2-hectare) park at the center of the plaza, with two duck-and-geese-filled ponds, might make you want to take an afternoon siesta—but don't. There's too much to see here. The plaza sits atop the "T" formed by Broadway (Hwy. 12) and Napa Street. Most of the surrounding roads form a grid pattern around this axis, making Sonoma easy to navigate. Depending on your pace, allow a half to a full day. START: **Sonoma Valley Visitors Bureau, 453 1st St. E. Distance: Less than a half-mile (.8km) of walking.**

1 ★ Terra Firma. Cross the street to get to this gallery selling African sculptures, paintings, baskets, and ethnic jewelry. It'll make you want to go to Kenya. *452 1st St. E.* ☎ *707/938-2200. www.terra firmagallery.com. Daily 10am–6pm.*

2 Basque Boulangerie. Grab lunch at this crowded little bakery with fresh sandwiches and good coffee. *460 1st St. E.* ☎ *707/935-7687. Daily 6am–6pm. $.*

3 ★★★ kids Tiddle E. Winks Vintage 5 & Dime. A treasure trove of nostalgic paraphernalia. Marvel at the meticulously kept tchotchkes, including authentic college pennants (some date back to the 1940s), vintage board games, and old-fashioned candies and sodas. This place is like a hands-on museum, and kids love it as much as adults do. *115 E. Napa St.* ☎ *707/939-6933. www.tiddleewinks. com. Mon–Sat 10:30am–5:30pm, Sun 11am–5pm.*

4 Vella Cheese Co. This store off the beaten path specializes in handmade cheeses. The friendly staffers are generous with the samples and always happy to educate. *315 2nd St. E.* ☎ *707/938-3232. www.vellacheese.com. Mon–Fri 9:30–6pm, Sat 9:30am–5pm, closed Sun.*

Walk past **5 City Hall,** which looks like something out of *Back to the Future,* and through a children's park, after which you'll see the **6 ★★ Bear Flag Monument,** representing the end of Mexico's rule.

7 ★★★ kids Mission San Francisco Solano. The plaza's crowning jewel, and its reason for being, is this must-see landmark, known also as the Sonoma Mission. For details, turn to p. 17. *114 E. Spain St.* ☎ *707/938-9560. www. parks.ca.gov. Daily 10am–5pm. $3 admission for adults, $2 for children. Admission also includes the Sonoma Barracks.*

8 ★ Blue Wing Inn. Across the street from the mission is this pleasantly dilapidated building, commissioned by Vallejo around 1840 to accommodate "emigrants and other travelers," as its inscription states. Notable guests included John C. Frémont (an explorer, general, senator, and presidential candidate) and Western legend Kit

Vella Cheese Co. in Sonoma.

Blue Wing Inn.

Carson, as well as members of the Bear Flag Party—not to mention a steady influx of outlaws and bandits. Admire it from the outside. *133 E. Spain St.*

⑨ ★★ kids Sonoma Barracks. Don't miss this historic landmark during your stroll through town. Turn to p 44 for details.

⑩ Toscano Hotel. Built in 1851 as a general store and library, this became a hotel in 1886. In 1972, the Sonoma League for Historic Preservation faithfully refurbished the building and opened it for public tours. *20 E. Spain St. ☎ 707/938-9560 (Sonoma State Historic Park). www.parks.ca.gov. Free tours Sat–Sun 1–4pm.*

⑪ ★ Sonoma Cheese Factory. This huge marketplace, a 75-year-old institution, has more cheese varieties than conceivably imaginable. Many are available for sampling, alongside other snacks and wine. There's also a small coffee and gelato bar. *2 Spain St. ☎ 800/535-2855. www.sonoma cheesefactory.com. Daily 9:30am–5:30pm ('til 6pm Sat).*

⑫ Swiss Hotel. Built in 1840, the Swiss Hotel was home to General Vallejo's brother, a vintner. Though it has nothing to do with Switzerland (the name was annexed from another local hotel that burned down), it's been a hotel and restaurant since 1909. Step into the bar to see many historic Sonoma photos. *18 W. Spain St. ☎ 707/938-2884. www.swisshotelsonoma.com.*

⑬ Roche Winery Tasting Room. Tastings of current releases cost $5, and snack plates are available. *122 W. Spain St. ☎ 707/935-7115. www.rochewinery.com. Daily 11am–7pm.*

Explore Sonoma.

Where to Dine in Sonoma

★★ **Cafe La Haye** *CALIFORNIA/ MEDITERRANEAN* Despite its limited hours and somewhat high prices, this tiny, artsy dining room is worth a visit for its top-notch food and wine. The baked almond-crusted goat cheese with roasted beets is a menu highlight. *140 E. Napa St.* ☎ *707/935-5994. Entrees $18–$42. MC, V. Dinner Tues–Sat. Map p 74.*

★★ **El Dorado Kitchen** *CALI-FORNIA* El Dorado Hotel's in-house establishment presents exquisite plates in a thoroughly comfortable space. The personalized six-course tasting menu is highly recommended. *405 1st St. W.* ☎ *707/996-3030. Entrees $22–$32. AE, DISC, MC, V. Lunch & dinner daily (bar after dusk). Map p 74.*

★★★ **the girl and the fig** *FRENCH* This cozy restaurant's gotten a lot of attention, and for good reason: The food's fantastic and imaginative. After dining, sample cheeses at the *salon de fromage*. *110 W. Spain St.* ☎ *707/938-3634. Entrees $13–$29. AE, DISC, MC, V. Lunch & dinner daily. Brunch Sun. Map p 74.*

★ **LaSalette** *PORTUGUESE* One of wine country's only Portuguese restaurants has a pleasant dining room decorated with hand-painted tiles. Choose from a large selection of cheeses and ports for a perfect ending to the inspired dishes. *452 1st St. E.* ☎ *707/938-1927. Entrees $25–$30. DISC, MC, V. Lunch & dinner daily. Map p 74.*

kids **Mary's Pizza Shack** *ITAL-IAN* Belying its name, this place actually has more pasta and sandwich choices than pizza options. Neither is it a shack; its bright, inviting interior is quite comfortable. *8 W. Spain St.* ☎ *707/938-8300. Entrees $7.95–$16. Pizzas $8.25–$26. AE, DISC, MC, V. Lunch & dinner daily. Map p 74.*

Taste of the Himalayas *INDIAN/NEPALI/TIBETAN* This friendly restaurant, whose founders are descendants of Nepali sherpas, is a good place to try *momos*, curry, or tandoori. *464 1st St. E.* ☎ *707/996-1161. Entrees $11–$23. AE, MC, V. Lunch & dinner Tues–Sun. Map p 74.*

St. Helena

1A Napa Valley Coffee Roasting Co.
1B Model Bakery
1 Olivier
2 Woodhouse Chocolate
3 Dennis Rae Fine Art
4 Market
5 St. Helena Wine Center
6 Hotel St. Helena
7 Findings
8 Jan de Luz
9 Vintage Home
10 Martin
11 Aerena Gallery

St. Helena
SONOMA NAPA

WHERE TO DINE

1 Archetype
2 Cindy's Backstreet Kitchen
3 Cook
4 Goose & Gander
5 Gott's Roadside Tray Gourmet
6 Press
7 The Restaurant at Meadowood
8 Terra
9 WF Giugni & Son Grocery Co.
10 Wine Spectator Greystone Restaurant

A first glance of St. Helena (say "Saint Hel-een-uh") gives the impression that this could be a pleasant Anytown, U.S.A. But a step into any of its myriad boutiques, galleries, and showrooms reveals otherwise; this level of posh couldn't be afforded many other places. Start this walking tour just off Main Street, and come expecting a foodie's dream itinerary. Cross the street to get a good taste of wine country's artsy side. Allow at least half a day. START: **Napa Valley Coffee Roasting Co., 1400 Oak Ave. Distance: Less than a half-mile (.8km) walk.**

1A ★ **Napa Valley Coffee Roasting Co.** Coffee and pastries fuel you in a relaxing and sunny ambience, bettered by an antique coffee press on display in the back and a communal book swap in the front. *1400 Oak Ave. ☎ 707/963-4491. Mon–Sun 7am–7pm. $.* Or you could opt for **1B** ★ **Model Bakery,** known for its great pastries and English muffins. *357 Main St. ☎ 707/963-8192. Daily 7am–5:30pm (5pm on Sun). $.*

2 ★★ **Olivier.** Sample a wide array of epicurean savories at this beautiful French-style store. The big copper vats lining the walls are olive oil dispensers; feel free to mix your own. Olivier also offers bath goods and upscale dishware imported from Provence. *1375 Main St. ☎ 707/967-8777. www.olivier napavalley.com. Daily 10am–6pm.*

3 ★★ **Woodhouse Chocolate.** Woodhouse is a salon that showcases

Napa Valley Coffee Roasting Co.

gorgeous handmade chocolates: Try the fan-shaped Thai ginger confection or the brown-butter ganache ($1.85 each). *Tip:* These decadent treats in delicate boxes can be shipped anywhere in America. *1367 Main St. ☎ 800/966-3468. www. woodhousechocolate.com. Daily 11am–6pm ('til 6:30pm Fri–Sat).*

❹ Dennis Rae Fine Art. A small gallery with striking art is a draw for fans of modern or wine-related works. *1359 Main St. ☎ 707-963-3350. www. dennisraefineart.com. Daily 10am–5pm.*

❺ ★ Market. This long restaurant with a wooden bar and stone walls has helpful waitstaff and playful American cuisine. Try "Our Favorite Mac and Cheese" and save room for desserts that'll take you back to childhood: homespun cotton candy (made tableside), s'mores, or butterscotch pudding. *1347 Main St. ☎ 707-963-3799. Entrees $13–$32. AE, MC, V. Lunch & dinner daily.*

❻ St. Helena Wine Center. More than your typical wine shop, this one has rare and high-end wines in the back (think Screaming Eagle), unique vodkas (like Charbay's green tea flavor), and tasty liqueurs. *1321 Main St. ☎ 707-963-1313. www.shwc. com. Daily 10am–6pm.*

Eclectic offerings at Findings.

❼ Hotel St. Helena. Step into this dark B&B to see the eccentric, almost creepy, decor (old dolls and mounted animal heads abound) and maybe to sip coffee at the small wine bar. *1309 Main St. ☎ 707-963-4388. www.hotelsthelena.net.*

❽ Findings. The eclectic offerings here combine the antique and the new; check out the jewelry, frames, and furniture. *1371 Main St. ☎ 707/963-6000. www.findings napavalley.com. Daily 10am–6pm.*

❾ ★ Jan de Luz. This impressive home-decor store features custom-embroidered table linens, upscale furnishings, even fountains and fireplaces. *1219 Main St. ☎ 707/963-1550. www.jandeluz.com. Mon–Sat 10am–5:30pm; Sun 11am–5:30pm.*

❿ ★ Napa Valley Vintage Home. An inspiring store with distinctive home goods such as pillows, linens, candles, and books. *1201 Main St. ☎ 707/963-7423. www.napavalleyvintagehome.com. Mon–Sun 10am–5:30pm.*

Now that you've walked the most interesting part of Main Street's south side, cross the street and slip into **⓫ ★★ Martin.** A true showroom, this lavish store displays everything from art books to large furnishings. *1350 Main St. ☎ 707/967-8787. www.martinshowroom. com. Tues–Sat 10am–6pm.*

⓬ ★ Aerena Gallery. Walk in to admire this sparse space with light-hearted art. *1354 Main St. ☎ 707/603-8787. www.iwolkgallery. com. Daily 10am–5:30pm.*

Where to Dine in St. Helena

★ Archetype NEW AMERICAN

This newish restaurant—it opened in 2014 to replace French Blue—partnered with the Michelin-starred team from Solbar (see p 102), and you can feel that pedigree in the food. Archetype is beloved especially for its hearty breakfasts and brunches—don't forgo the cinnamon walnut rolls with orange-cream-cheese frosting. Lunch or dinner might be petrale sole fish and chips or mushroom and ricotta crepes. The dining room, done in whites and neutrals, is relaxing and attractive. Reservations recommended. *1429 Main St.* ☎ *707/968-9200. Main courses $15–$32. AE, DISC, MC, V. Brunch, lunch & dinner Wed–Sun. Map p 78.*

★★ Cindy's Backstreet Kitchen CALIFORNIA/AMERICAN

An upscale, down-home kind of place, this darling dining room presents unfussy yet creative dishes made with local ingredients. *1327 Railroad Ave.* ☎ *707/963-1200. Entrees $15–$29. DC, DISC, MC, V. Lunch & dinner daily. Map p 78.*

★★ Cook ITALIAN

Cook's dining room is lovely, but it's the food that takes center stage. The simple, elegant northern Italian fare includes handmade pastas and ingredients that are as seasonal and local as it gets. The straightforward menu says things like "risotto. always different" and "soup. we'll let you know." The restaurant, which opened in 2005, has been honored with a Michelin Bib Gourmand for almost every year it has existed. New in 2016 is an adjacent gastropub, also from chef Jude Wilmoth, called **Cook Tavern** (in the former Armadillo's space). Head there if you prefer a more casual affair. *1310 Main St.* ☎ *707/963-7088. Main courses $18–$24. AE, DISC, MC, V. Lunch Mon–Sat; dinner daily. Map p 78.*

Goose & Gander NEW AMERICAN

Taking the place of the much-loved Martini House is this newish gastropub with sophisticated cuisine and swanky cocktails. Chef Jeff Larson specializes in things like culotte steaks with béarnaise butter and Gruyère burgers with a side of duck-fat-fried potatoes. The lodge-like setting includes black tufted-leather booths and a Prohibition-style lair of a bar. *1245 Spring St.* ☎ *707/967-8779. Entrees $12–$38. AE, DC, DISC, MC, V. Lunch, dinner & bar daily. Map p 78.*

★ Gott's Roadside Tray Gourmet DINER

It's not every day that a roadside burger shack gets a spread in *Food & Wine* magazine. But then, this outdoor diner—built in 1949—isn't your average fast-food stop. Its excellent hamburgers on soft but sturdy buns are known the valley over. And vegetarians need not sigh when their dining companions stop at Gott's: Even the veggie burger is great. *933 Main St.* ☎ *707/963-3486. Entrees $7–$17. AE, MC, V. Lunch & dinner daily. Map p 78.*

★ Press STEAKHOUSE

In 2014, Press got a new chef: Trevor Kunk, a Charlie Palmer mentee who previously cooked at New York's Beard-winning Blue Hill restaurant. Kunk is big into land stewardship, so he encourages his staff to spend time on the farms that supply his kitchen. The result is a modern steakhouse whose offerings are built from hyper-local produce, sustainably raised meats, and free-range eggs. The wine list is huge but doesn't stray past Napa Valley. Also new here: a renovated, family-friendly back patio with fire pits. *587 St. Helena Hwy.* ☎ *707/967-0550. Main courses $29–$120. AE, DISC, MC, V. Dinner Wed–Mon. Map p 78.*

★★★ The Restaurant at Meadowood *NEW AMERICAN*

Christopher Kostow's heartfelt New American cuisine has earned him three Michelin stars for 4 years running. In 2013, while he was still in his thirties, the James Beard Foundation named him the West's best chef. Meadowood's sincere approach to fine dining means that its staff personalizes a 10-course tasting experience for each guest ($330, not including wine pairing). There's no formal menu but rather a phone conversation, after you make a reservation, to learn about your preferences and restrictions. Then Kostow taps local farmers and foragers for ingredients that he turns into pure magic. Reservations are required well in advance, a dress code is enforced, and children younger than age 12 aren't permitted. *900 Meadowood Lane.* ☎ *877/963-3646. Tasting menu starts at $330, though less expensive options are available at the bar. AE, DISC, MC, V. Dinner Tues–Sat. Map p 78.*

★★ Terra *NEW AMERICAN*

Terra manages to be humble even though it serves some of northern California's most extraordinary food. The dining room is rustic-romantic with stone walls. And the menu, by James Beard Award–winning chef Hiro Sone, reflects the region's bounty while weaving in European and Japanese influences. Desserts are sublime, especially the orange risotto in brandy snap with passion fruit sauce. Reservations

Grab a sandwich and candy from W F Giugni & Son Grocery Co.

recommended. *1345 Railroad Ave.* ☎ *707/963-8931. Main courses $16–$38. AE, DC, MC, V. Dinner Thurs–Mon. Map p 78.*

W F Giugni & Son Grocery Co. *SANDWICHES* Locals come here for a satisfying bite and an escape from pretense—there's always a long line at the counter. Don't be surprised if you get hit by a touch of nostalgia here: Historical propaganda clutters the walls, and among the grocery items for sale are Cokes in glass bottles and old-time jawbreakers. *1227 Main St.* ☎ *707/963-3421. Sandwiches $5.45–$6.45. No credit cards. Daily 9am–4:30pm. Map p 78.*

★★ Wine Spectator Greystone Restaurant *CALI-FORNIA* You know a restaurant at the Culinary Institute of America (where students learn to become executive chefs) has got to be good—and is it ever. Watch as chefs prepare small plates, then try them with a new-to-you wine. *2555 Main St.* ☎ *707/967-1010. Entrees $18–$42. AE, DC, DISC, MC, V. Lunch & dinner Tues–Sat. Map p 78.*

Healdsburg

1 Moustache Baked Goods
2 La Crema
3 The Cheese Shop
4 Plaza Park
5 Hand Fan Museum
6A Thumbprint Cellars
6B Toad Hollow Vineyards
7A Costeaux French Bakery
7B Flying Goat Coffee
7C Downtown Bakery & Creamery
8 Healdsburg Museum
9 Hauck Cellars
10 Studio Barndiva
11 Windsor Vineyards Tasting Room

WHERE TO DINE

1 Baci Café & Wine Bar
2 Barndiva
3 Bear Republic
4 Bergamot Alley
5 Chalkboard
6 Dry Creek Kitchen
7 Healdsburg Bar & Grill
8 Oakville Grocery
9 Ralph's House
10 Raven Theater
11 Scopa
12 Shed Café
13 Spoonbar
14 Taqueria El Sombrero
15 Willi's Seafood & Raw Bar

Healdsburg is a town on the rise. Not long ago, it was just another agricultural Sonoma borough, content to quietly produce some of the world's best food and wine. But word got out about where all that refined alimentation was coming from, and entrepreneurs picked up on the excitement. Hence the recent arrival of fancy hotels and restaurants, big names, and big money, definitively stamping the town onto the jet-setter map. And Healdsburg's status just keeps rising, thanks to all the famous wineries that keep opening tasting rooms downtown, new shops targeting well-heeled travelers, and perennial attractions like the jazz festival each summer and the twice-weekly organic farmers' market (see p 21). Still, Healdsburg gracefully maintains a friendly small-town personality with reverence for the area's rich history—and just a touch of quirk. This full-day walking tour highlights the town's best tasting rooms and historical spots. START: **Moustache Baked Goods, 381 Healdsburg Ave. Distance: Less than a half-mile (.8km).**

Start your morning with San Francisco cult brand Four Barrel Coffee at 1 ★ **Moustache Baked Goods,** where you can also fuel up with cupcakes. *381 Healdsburg Ave. 707/395-4111. $.*

2 ★★ **La Crema.** Modern design sets this tasting room apart, as do its coastal artisan wines. The winery specializes in Burgundian varietals, so try the chardonnay and pinot noir. *235 Healdsburg Ave.*

Tasting room of Thumbprint.

📞 800/314-1762. www.lacrema.com. Daily 10:30am–5:30pm. Tastings $10–$30.

❸ **The Cheese Shop.** This intimate shop just off the plaza specializes in artisan cheeses from South America. There's also a variety of local *fromage* and a great olive selection. You can taste for free before purchasing. *423 Center St.* 📞 *707/433-4998. www.sharpandnutty.com. Mon–Sat 11am–6pm.*

❹ ★ **Plaza Park.** There are plenty of picnic benches in Healdsburg's acre-wide focal point. At this site of fairs, festivals, and concerts, find the Olympic flame statue honoring local athletes. On the other end of the park is the 1847 millstone from Cyrus Alexander's gristmill. In between, there's a fountain, plus palm, pine, and redwood trees.

❺ ★ **Hand Fan Museum.** Take a break from sampling wine and visit this tiny room, which displays a multicultural collection of beautiful hand fans, some dating back to the 1700s. *219 Healdsburg Ave.* 📞 *707/431-2500. www.handfanmuseum.com.*

Wed–Sun 11am–4pm, or by appointment, closed rainy days. Free.

❻Ⓐ ★ **Thumbprint Cellars.** This tasting lounge has sleek furnishings, a young vibe, and handcrafted small-lot wines. Thumbprint holds occasional events like blending seminars and winemakers' dinners, so call (or go online) to find out what's going on and whether you need a reservation. *102 Matheson St.* 📞 *707/433-2393. www.thumbprintcellars.com. Daily 11am–6pm. Tastings $5–$10.*

OR:

❻Ⓑ ★ **Toad Hollow Vineyards.** This tasting room is a playful place to start your day. Frog-themed everything is everywhere, but the wines served over a river-stone bar focus attention into your glass. This winery's founder, Todd Williams, died in 2007—he was Robin's brother. You can still feel the family's jovial, playful spirit here. *409A Healdsburg Ave.* 📞 *707/431-8667. www.toadhollow.com. Sun–Fri 11am–5pm; Sat 10:30am–5:30pm. Tastings $5–$10 (refunded with purchase).*

Frankie Williams, the owner of Toad Hollow.

7A ★★ **Costeaux French Bakery.** If the wine's leaving you in need of a midday coffee or pastry, head to Costeaux, a sunny spot beloved by locals. It's been a Healdsburg tradition since 1923, with its delicious breads, soups, salads, and desserts. *Fun fact:* This French-feeling place claims the record for having baked the world's largest pumpkin pie. Look for the 6-foot-3-inch (1.9m) pie tin on the wall. *417 Healdsburg Ave.* ☎ *707/433-1913. $.* Devotees consider **7B** ★ **Flying Goat Coffee,** with two locations in Healdsburg, California's best java; they'll drive miles for a cup. *324 Center St.* ☎ *707/433-9081, ext. 205. 419 Center St.* ☎ *707-433-8003. $.* Aromatic **7C** **Downtown Bakery & Creamery** sells fantastic sticky buns, fruity pastries, and fresh breads. *308A Center St.* ☎ *707/431-2719. $.*

8 ★★ **kids** **Healdsburg Museum.** From Center Street, turn right onto Matheson Street, and as you pass St. Paul's Episcopal Church, admire its stained-glass windows. A few steps farther and you're at Healdsburg's museum. Andrew Carnegie donated $10,000 in 1909 to make this Neoclassical Revival–style building a public library, so its entryway still bears his name. Inside, artifacts document local history, from Pomo Indian times to the town's former life as Rancho Sotoyome, to the squatter squabbles known as the "Westside Wars." One man who emerged victorious after the land conflicts became Healdsburg's founder in 1857: Ohio entrepreneur Harmon Heald. The museum also recounts the period after Healdsburg's incorporation with photos and period costumes. Because it's also a historical society, hands-on research facilities with microfilmed newspapers and official county records are available. *221 Matheson St.* ☎ *707/431-3325. www.healdsburgmuseum. org. Wed–Sun 11am–4pm. Free.*

9 ★ **Hauck Cellars.** This tasting room features Sonoma County Harvest Fair winners, including zinfandels and cabs. Enjoy wine on the patio, where you can also picnic. Call ahead and they'll have a cheese plate waiting for you. *999 Foreman Lane.* ☎ *707/486-0017. www.hauckcellars.com. Mon–Tues, Thurs & Sun 11:30am–5pm; Fri–Sat 11:30am–7pm.*

10 ★★ **Studio Barndiva.** If you dined at **Barndiva** (see below) and covet the art there—most a combination of modern and folk—stop by this lofty gallery space, which doubles as a nighttime event venue. *237 Center St.* ☎ *707/431-7404. www. barndiva.com/studio. Daily 10am–5pm, or until 4:30pm on event nights.*

Healdsburg's Best Shopping

Though they're not explicit stops on this tour, Healdsburg is packed with inspired shops; among the best are exotic **One World Fair Trade** (☎ 800/625-4183) and **Terra Firma** (☎ 707/723-1723), haven-like **Copperfield's Books** (☎ 707/433-9270), and sleek **Lime Stone** (☎ 707/433-3080). For specialty wines, try **The Wine Shop** (☎ 707/433-0433).

⓫ ★★ **Windsor Vineyards Tasting Room.** This spot, formerly called Souverain, is where you can taste the output of Windsor Vineyards. Drop in to taste a variety of varietals with views of the plaza, or shop for foodie accessories and country-living designs. *308 B Center St. ☎ 707/921-2893. www.windsorvineyards.com. Daily 12am–7pm. Tastings $10–$15, refunded with purchase of three bottles.*

Where to Dine in Healdsburg

Baci Café & Wine Bar ITALIAN Baci's menu stretches beyond its Italian focus (a good helping of pastas and wood-fired pizza) to Kobe beef, short ribs, and other unexpected delights. *336 Healdsburg Ave. ☎ 707/433-8111. Entrees $14–$32. AE, DISC, MC, V. Dinner Thurs–Mon. Map p 82.*

★★★ **Barndiva** NEW AMERICAN The philosophy here is "eat the view" because chef Ryan Fancher (formerly at French Laundry) insists on using only seasonal, local ingredients. The result is food that's remarkably creative and memorably delicious. The ambience, which might be called "barnhouse modern," is something special too. Whether you eat out back or in the art-filled dining space, the managers' detail-orientedness shines through, making a meal here an experience you'll be glad you traveled for. Reservations recommended. *231 Center St.*

☎ 707/431-0100. Entrees $26–$42. AE, MC, V. Lunch Wed–Sun; dinner Wed–Sat. Map p 82.*

★ **kids Bear Republic Brewing Co.** AMERICAN This lively, casual brewpub offers appetizers galore, creative sandwiches, and a huge selection of handcrafted ales. Decor includes old bikes hanging from the ceiling and a California-themed agricultural mural. *345 Healdsburg Ave. ☎ 707/433-2337. Entrees $10–$28. MC, V. Lunch & dinner daily. Map p 82.*

Before Dinner: Bergamot Alley

While waiting for your table, stop into this wine bar for its artsy, lofty space and rebellious wine list—European vintages only. Check out the old-timey pulley door system on the wine room in the back. *328A Healdsburg Ave. 707/433-8720. www.bergamotalley.com. Map p 82.*

Try the Racer 5 at The Bear Republic Brewery.

★★ Chalkboard *TAPAS* It was sad to see Cyrus—and its two Michelin stars—go, but locals perked up when it became clear that what took its place in **Hotel Les Mars** (see p 129) was itself no slouch of a restaurant. Chef Shane McAnelly, a Northern California native, sources ingredients from the restaurant's 3-acre (1.2-hectare) garden, a testament to his commitment to presenting ingredients that are organic, seasonal, and local on small plates meant for sharing. The menu is ever-changing, though heirloom tomatoes, beets, and fava beans tend to feature big. In addition to fresh cocktails, you can order a flight of local wines. Daily specials are scrawled on a big (yup) chalkboard. *29 North St.* ☎ *707/473-8030. Main courses $17–$26. AE, DISC, MC, V. Lunch Sat–Sun; dinner daily 5pm–close. Map p 82.*

★★★ Dry Creek Kitchen *CALI-FORNIA* Celeb chef Charlie Palmer's venture is a melding of splendid cuisine and excellent service. Within hip Hotel Healdsburg, the kitchen turns out inspired, well-presented dishes based on what's seasonally relevant. *317 Healdsburg Ave.* ☎ *707/431-0330. Entrees $28–$39; tasting menu $79. AE, MC, V. Dinner daily. Map p 82.*

kids Healdsburg Bar & Grill *AMERICAN* This all-American restaurant has a big menu for kids and a refreshing on-tap selection (Guinness and Sierra Nevada included) for parents. There's a strong do-it-yourself vibe too, from ordering at the kitchen to making your own Bloody Mary (Sat & Sun). Sporadic live music really gets the place going. *245 Healdsburg Ave.* ☎ *707/433-3333. Entrees $11–$22. MC, V. Lunch & dinner daily; breakfast Sat & Sun. Map p 82.*

★★ Oakville Grocery *CALIFOR-NIA* One of four stores bearing this name, Healdsburg's outpost has an alfresco eating area that's always packed on sunny days. Before settling on your order, browse the gamut of colorful gourmet options in this impressive market. Try a sandwich or pizza with wine from the tasting bar. *124 Matheson St.* ☎ *707/433-3200. Entrees $10–$18. AE, MC, V. Breakfast, lunch & dinner daily. Map p 82.*

★ **Ralph's House** FRENCH In this minimalist white restaurant, the menu focuses on globally influenced small plates—and a Healdsburg-centric wine list. Reservations recommended. *109 Plaza St.* ☎ *707/633-4499. Entrees $14–$36. MC, V. Dinner daily; lunch Sat–Sun. Map p 82.*

★★ **Scopa** ITALIAN This popular newcomer to the square serves pizza and pasta by candlelight in a cozy, brick-walled space. Friendly servers help you pair the proper wine with your grilled calamari with white bean, or ravioli stuffed with stinging nettles. *109 Plaza St.* ☎ *707/433-5282. Entrees $15–$19. AE, MC, V. Lunch & dinner daily. Map p 82.*

★★ **Shed Café** CALIFORNIA Cindy Daniel's open, glassy enclave debuted in 2013 as part of **Shed,** a greater food destination featuring a well-curated retail selection, a "fermentation bar" (wine, beer, kombucha, etc.), an upstairs beekeeping workshop, and more. In the cafe, the food is fresh, colorful, and creative—and whenever possible, sourced locally. Many of the entrees come hot from the wood-burning oven, and menus change daily—past hits have included "Mendocino sea urchin with local seaweeds" and "charred leek terrine with Nantucket scallops." ***Tip:*** Sit outside if you'd like to eat within view of the creek. *25 North St.* ☎ *707/471-7433. Main courses $13–$25. AE, DISC, MC, V. Breakfast, lunch & dinner Wed–Mon. Map p 82.*

★★ **Spoonbar** AMERICAN Located in the modern **h2hotel** (see p 128), this small, slick space feels urban compared to Healdsburg's small-town vibe. It's a reliable spot for a burger, some fancier snacks, a cocktail, and people-watching. *219 Healdsburg Ave.* ☎ *707/433-7222. Entrees $12–$23. AE, MC, V. Lunch & dinner daily. Map p 82.*

★ **Taqueria El Sombrero** MEXICAN This low-key joint, popular with locals, has all the expected Mexican fare, plus breakfast and seafood. *245 Center St.* ☎ *707/433-3818. Entrees $2–$10. DISC, MC, V. Breakfast, lunch & dinner daily. Map p 82.*

★ **Willi's Seafood & Raw Bar** SMALL PLATES An energetic vibe permeates Willi's dining room, bar, and outdoor patio. If you want to hunker down with your own big meal, this isn't the place—but if you're good swapping tastes of fancily prepared seafood like miso-glazed sturgeon, Willi's fits the bill. *403 Healdsburg Ave.* ☎ *707/433-9191. Small plates $10–$25. DISC, MC, V. Lunch & dinner daily. Map p 82.*

After Dinner: Raven Theater

The 500-seat pulse point of the town's performing arts scene stages uproarious theatrical and stirring music performances. Check the website for show times. *115 North St.* ☎ *707/433-6335. www.raven theater.org. Map p 82.*

Guerneville

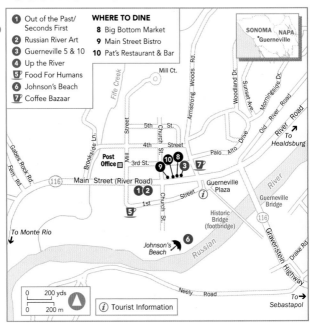

① Out of the Past/
Seconds First
② Russian River Art
③ Guerneville 5 & 10
④ Up the River
⑤ Food For Humans
⑥ Johnson's Beach
⑦ Coffee Bazaar

WHERE TO DINE

⑧ Big Bottom Market
⑨ Main Street Bistro
⑩ Pat's Restaurant & Bar

ⓘ Tourist Information

A mystical redwood forest will enchant you as you make the
winding drive into Guerneville. The town itself (say "Gurn-ville")
is a throwback to everything small-town America used to be—except
for its very progressive orientation. Rainbow flags and signs proclaim-
ing "This is a hate-free zone" adorn many businesses—a respectful
hat tip to the village's largely gay and lesbian population. Many store-
keepers keep pets beside them—dogs and cats, mainly—as they
regale travelers with obscure facts about the area. This half-day walking tour, rather than a hyper-structured itinerary, is more a leisurely
stroll down Main Street, so part of your fun should be wandering into
boutiques that appeal to you in addition to the ones listed here.
START: **Where Highway 116 becomes Main Street, just after the Safeway
grocery store. Walk east. Trip Length: Less than a half-mile (.8km).**

① Out of the Past and **Seconds
First** are two businesses housed in
one incense-scented storefront.
You'll find oddities like Betty Boop
lightswitch covers and hilarious
fridge magnets, plus peculiar posters
and vintage clothes. *16365 Main St.*
☎ *707/869-2211. Daily 11am–6pm.*

② Russian River Art Gallery.
Wares here include artsy jewelry
and decorative collectibles. Even if
you don't intend to buy, step inside
to see the mural depicting the
town. *16357 Main St.* ☎ *707/869-
9099. www.therussianriverartgallery.
com. Wed–Mon 11am–5pm.*

Enjoy the beach in Guerneville on the Russian River.

3 Guerneville 5 & 10. This shop, which has been here since 1949, has dubbed itself "the fun store," and it's true. The wide selection of novelties is sure to make you smile—from throwback toys to nostalgic candy to big balloons. There's also plenty of art gear, crochet supplies, greeting cards, and stuff (inflatable boats, river shoes, towels) to get you out on the Russian River. *16252 Main St. ☎ 707/869-3404. www. guerneville5and10.com. Daily 10am–6pm.*

Veer off Main Street to find:

4 Food For Humans, a natural-foods market that stocks organic produce, snacks, and eco-friendly merchandise. *16385 1st St. ☎ 707/869-3612. $.* Buy a sandwich or a wrap, crackers, cheese, and fruit, then tote your picnic down to **5 kids Johnson's Beach on the Russian River,** where you can take a dip or admire Guerneville Bridge. There's a kiddie pool, which little ones love. *16241 1st St. www. johnsonsbeach.com. Daily 10am–6pm, mid-May to early Oct.* For a pick-me-up after your riverside picnic, try the java or ice cream at eclectic **6 Coffee Bazaar.** *14045 Armstrong Woods Rd. ☎ 707/869-9706.*

Where to Dine **in Guerneville**

Big Bottom Market *AMERICAN* Pastries, cheeses, wines, chocolates, and other delicious morsels await at this popular establishment. Enjoy breakfast panini and biscuits or soups and sandwiches for lunch. If it's summer, attend the Thursday through Saturday "bistro nights," a dinner menu set by executive chef Tricia Brown. In winter, the Wednesday night "market dinners" are a steal. If you care for a more formal option, check out the market's sister restaurant, Boon, two doors down. *16228 Main St. ☎ 707/604-7295. Entrees $5–$12. AE, MC, V. Breakfast, lunch & takeout daily except Tues; dinner offered in summer only. Map p 88.*

Main Street Bistro *ITALIAN* This recently expanded corner restaurant is undeniably upbeat. Menu options include pizza, sandwiches, salads, and pasta. Don't miss the evening jazz performances. *16280 Main St. ☎ 707/869-0501. Entrees $9–$28. AE, MC, V. Lunch & dinner daily. Map p 88.*

Pat's Restaurant & Bar *AMERICAN/KOREAN* By day, this is your basic down-home diner with an adjoining woodsy bar. By night, Pat's turns into a Korean place that melds things like kalbi ribs with mac 'n' cheese. This has been a restaurant since 1945, and some of the tough-looking staff seem like they might have been here the entire time. (Don't let their gruff demeanor fool you; they're as sweet and professional as can be.) *16236 Main St. ☎ 707/869-9905. Entrees $4–$11. Cash only. Breakfast & lunch daily. Map p 88.*

Yountville

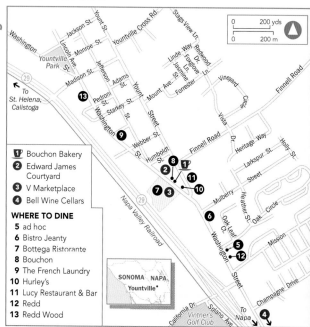

Bouchon Bakery
Edward James Courtyard
V Marketplace
Bell Wine Cellars

WHERE TO DINE
5 ad hoc
6 Bistro Jeanty
7 Bottega Ristorante
8 Bouchon
9 The French Laundry
10 Hurley's
11 Lucy Restaurant & Bar
12 Redd
13 Redd Wood

Pioneer George C. Yount, who planted Napa Valley's first grapevine, is this town's namesake and founder. Since before its 1855 inception, Yountville (say "Yont-ville") has been a premier winemaking spot. In 1973, prestigious French champagne house Moët et Chandon chose Yountville as the site for its U.S. expansion, and Domaine Chandon was born. About 20 years later, chef Thomas Keller bought a small restaurant called The French Laundry. Much of the sophistication that now defines Yountville sprang up around these two institutions—since their establishment, other prominent winemakers and chefs have moved in so that the mile-long walking town is now an unparalleled dining destination. When visiting, notice the locals—there are about 3,000 of them, and they range from world-famous chefs to immigrant grape pickers to young skateboarders to former soldiers who live at America's largest veterans' home. After dark, bars turn lively. This tour is relatively short because tiny Yountville's main attractions are unarguably its restaurants. (See "Where to Dine," below.) START: **Bouchon Bakery, 6528 Washington St. Distance: Less than a mile (1.6km) of walking.**

Grab a morning pastry at Thomas Keller's 🏆 ★ **Bouchon Bakery.** Buying from the small, usually packed boulangerie is an affordable way to sample the creations of one of America's most famous chefs. The confections here are as much a treat for the eyes as they are for the palate, so even if you don't partake, at least gaze at the perfectly laid out sweets in the glass case. There's no inside seating, so sit outside on a bench or stroll while savoring your buttery croissant, signature chocolate bouchon, or impossibly fresh bread. *6528 Washington St.* ☎ *707/944-2253. Daily 7am–7pm. $.*

As you walk out of Bouchon Bakery, turn right to explore:

❷ Edward James Courtyard. The myriad art galleries in this courtyard complex, formerly called Beard Plaza, were built in the late 1980s by the Beard family. The works for sale in these intimate exhibition spaces are the creations of talented glass artists, painters, sculptors, jewelers, and ceramicists. Much of the art is modern or wine-inspired, and there's a charming tasting room, worth a visit, called **Hope & Grace.** *6540 Washington St.*

Walk southward down Washington and on your left, you'll soon see:

❸ V Marketplace. This swap-meet-style shopping center is in a historic brick building. The onetime Groezinger Winery was built in 1870 and at its height was California's largest winery. Foodies will want to check out fabulous **Kollar Chocolates,** as well as **Napa Style,** a boutique selling cookware and home goods while offering food tastings, demos, and seasonal specialties.

Among the other shopping options: several art galleries, men's and women's fashions, a kids' clothing store, and, of course, a wine room. *6525 Washington St.,* ☎ *707/944-2451. www.vmarketplace.com. Daily 10am–5:30pm.*

Walk far down Washington and a bit off the beaten path (consider driving) to:

❹ ★ Bell Wine Cellars. This small artisanal winery has a tasting bar in a warehouse-like room among casks and barrels. But the wine's excellent, and so is the company: South African owner/winemaker Anthony Bell is liable to come out and tell you all about the ardent passion he has for crafting each wine he'll have you taste. Reservations recommended. *6200 Washington St.* ☎ *707/944-1673. www.bellwine.com. Daily 10am–4pm. Tours $50 (reservations required), tastings start at $20.*

The shops at V Marketplace.

Where to Dine in Yountville

★★ **ad hoc** *SOUTHERN* Waiting months to experience French Laundry prices not quite feasible? Then go for an ad hoc solution. With a four-course menu that changes daily, this originally temporary experiment drew in droves of foodies and racked up stellar reviews. Eventually, the talented Thomas Keller had to accept its permanence. Ad hoc also includes an **addendum** out back that packs boxed lunches to go (Thurs–Sat 11am–2pm) and offers a quiet picnic area by a lovely garden. *6476 Washington St.* ☎ *707/944-2487. Family-style prix fixe menu $50–$75. AE, MC, V. Thurs–Mon dinner; Sun brunch. Map p 90.*

★ **Bistro Jeanty** *FRENCH* This casual, warm bistro with muted buttercup walls and an inviting patio area serves seriously rich French comfort food, and is constantly converting first-time diners into lifelong fans. Menu highlights include tomato soup in a puff pastry, crème brûlée (made with a thin layer of chocolate cream), and rib-gripping free-for-alls including coq au vin, cassoulet, and a thick-cut pork chop au jus. *6510 Washington St.* ☎ *707/944-0103. Entrees $19–$40. AE, MC, V. Lunch & dinner daily. Map p 90.*

★★ **Bottega Ristorante** *ITAL-IAN* Celebrity chef Michael Chiarello showcases his signature bold flavors at Bottega, which has garnered an outrageously long list of accolades, and for good reason. There aren't many other places in the United States where Italian flavors shine brighter. *6525 Washington St.* ☎ *707/945-1050. Entrees*

The patio of Bistro Jeanty.

$16–$36. AE, DC, DISC, MC, V. Lunch Tues–Sun & dinner daily. Map p 90.

★★ **Bouchon** *FRENCH* Dark and rich surroundings complement attentive service and a refined menu developed by Thomas Keller. The *gnocchi a la parisienne*, made with wheat instead of potato, melt in your mouth. Don't neglect the excellent wine list. A bonus, especially for restless residents and off-duty restaurant staff, is the late hours, though the menu becomes more limited when crowds dwindle. *6534 Washington St.* ☎ *707/944-8037. Entrees $17–$59. AE, MC, V. Lunch & dinner daily. Map p 90.*

★★★ **The French Laundry** *AMERICAN/FRENCH* Not much has been left unsaid about what's often called one of the world's best restaurants. The interior is small and fancy, service is unparalleled, and the food—well, let's just say it can be described in two words: Thomas Keller. The chef's signature nine-course degustation tasting menu (there's a vegetarian option too) changes daily based on his ingenious whims. Book this once-in-a-lifetime experience well in advance—the waiting list to dine here is months long. *6640 Washington St.* ☎ *707/944-2380. Prix fixe dinner $295 per person, not including wine. AE, MC, V. Dinner daily. Lunch Fri–Sun. Dress code enforced. Map p 90.*

★★ **Hurley's Restaurant and Bar** *CALIFORNIA* Chef Bob Hurley is passionate about presenting balanced cuisine that pairs well with wine. Here you get elite food without the matching attitude. The bar,

The patio at Bottega.

which serves cocktails and snacks until midnight, is a local favorite. *6518 Washington St.* ☎ *707/944-2345. Entrees $21–$31. AE, DISC, MC, V. Lunch & dinner daily. Map p 90.*

★★ **Lucy Restaurant & Bar** *NEW AMERICAN* Like everything else at Bardessono Hotel, Lucy is not only exquisite but lots of fun. The servers are carefully chosen and are some of the best at what they do. The food they bring out is expertly crafted—you'll remember it for days to come. Try a house-made pasta, one of the sustainably raised meats, or treat yourself to the tasting menu with paired wines. *6526 Yount St.* ☎ *707/204-6030. Entrees $15–$39. AE, DC, DISC, MC, V. Breakfast & dinner daily; lunch Mon–Fri. Map p 90.*

★★ **Redd** *NEW AMERICAN* Richard Reddington, an alumnus of Daniel in New York and Spago in Beverly Hills, incorporates ethnic influences into his regionally inspired seasonal menu. The dining space is clean and modern with chic accoutrements. *6480 Washington St.* ☎ *707/944-2222. Entrees $14–$36. Tasting menus $80. AE, DC, DISC, MC, V. Lunch Mon–Sat, dinner daily & Sun brunch. Bar opens daily at 11:30am. Map p 90.*

★★ **Redd Wood** *ITALIAN* A casual spinoff of Richard Reddington's original restaurant (see above), this fun new spot in North Block Hotel features sassy waitstaff, intriguing decor, and a menu of oven-baked pizzas that puts Chicago to shame. *6755 Washington St.* ☎ *707/299-5030. Entrees $14–$35. AE, DC, DISC, MC, V. Lunch & dinner daily; breakfast Fri–Sat. Map p 90.*

Glen Ellen

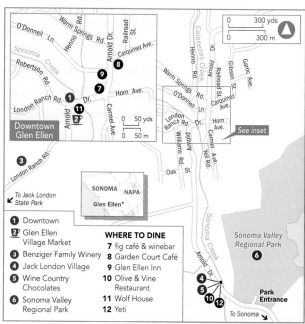

0 Downtown
2 Glen Ellen
Village Market
3 Benziger Family Winery
4 Jack London Village
5 Wine Country
Chocolates
6 Sonoma Valley
Regional Park

WHERE TO DINE
7 fig café & winebar
8 Garden Court Café
9 Glen Ellen Inn
10 Olive & Vine
Restaurant
11 Wolf House
12 Yeti

Glen Ellen, a small and sweet unincorporated Sonoma town,
is home to fewer than 5,000 people, which makes it a tight-knit
community. Local characters are many, from Pixar's John Lasseter (flip
to p 152 to read about his winery) to earthquake predictor Jim Berk-
land to Jack London's relatives—and indeed, Jack London himself.
Yes, the man is dead and gone (you can see his gravesite at the state
park dedicated to him), but he's still very much present, in the form of
extreme local reverence bordering on obsession. Though some
would argue that Glen Ellen is too spread out for a proper walking
tour (unlike other Sonoma County towns, there's no true town center),
it's doable if you're not averse to occasionally walking about a mile
along scenic byways. Otherwise, consider driving. This tour, depending on your pace, can be done in a half or a full day. **Tip:** There's not
much in the way of streetlights, so if you're going out after dark,
know that several local inns supply flashlights to guests upon request.
START: Arnold Dr. Distance: About 1½ miles (2.4km).

1 ★ **"Downtown."** What locals
call "downtown" is really just a
2-block stretch of Arnold Drive that
runs from Warm Springs Road to

London Ranch Road. It has about 20
buildings (many of them historic), a
few old bridges, a Civil War cannon,
and the convergence of the Sonoma

Tour of Benziger Vineyards.

and Calabasas creeks. The heyday here was about a century ago when trains brought in tourists. Still, the town hasn't changed much since the days when Jack London lived, wrote, and farmed nearby—it got its first traffic light in 2006 and still has virtually no sidewalks.

2 ★ **Glen Ellen Village Market.** This is a gourmet market without the gourmet attitude. Check out the hot and cold cases, the fabulous salad bar alongside an impressive produce section, and the excellent wine and cheese selection. Grab a snack here—the panini are delicious—or stock up on supplies for a picnic at Sonoma Valley Regional Park. *13751 Arnold Dr.* ☎ *707/996-6728. Daily 5am–9pm. $$.*

Walk or drive about a mile (1.6km) uphill on London Ranch Road.

3 ★★ **kids Benziger Family Winery.** Known for having the valley's best tour—it draws tourists around vineyards by tractor—this bio-dynamic winery is one of the region's most welcoming. *1883 London Ranch Rd.* ☎ *888/490-2739. See p 137.*

Walk or drive another half-mile (.8km) up London Ranch Road.

4 ★ **Jack London Village.** This quaint little shopping spot houses an eclectic selection of restaurants and boutique stores, including a cheese monger, the **Eric Ross Winery** tasting room, and a chocolate salon (see below). *14301 Arnold Dr. (For information about Jack London State Park in Glen Ellen, see p 48.)*

5 **Wine Country Chocolates.** Wine tastings abound in Napa and Sonoma, but chocolate tastings offer a new twist. Stop in to sample a variety of truffle flavors or to try

The Jack London Saloon in Glen Ellen's Jack London Village.

different percentages of cacao content. You can also peek through the kitchen window to marvel at the chocolatiers as they mix their magic. *14301 Arnold Dr., No. 1. ☎ 707/996-1010. www.winecountry chocolates.com. Free tasting bar, daily 10am–5pm.*

Just past the Jack London Village and across Calabasas Creek is an entrance to:

❻ KIDS Sonoma Valley Regional Park. This 162-acre

(65-hectare) park has beautiful biking and walking paths, easy hiking trails (some paved and some dirt), and a fenced dog park. It's most beautiful in spring, when wildflowers bloom, but fall's magnificent colors, just before the oaks shed their leaves, rank a close second. There's a pretty picnic and lawn area at the trail head. *13630 Sonoma Hwy. ☎ 707/565-2041. www.sonoma-county.org/parks. Open daily 8am–sunset. Parking $7.*

Where to Dine **in Glen Ellen**

★★ the fig café and winebar
CALIFORNIA/MEDITERRANEAN
The sister restaurant of the girl and the fig (see p 77)—which also refuses to capitalize its name—is more casual than its Sonoma Plaza sibling, but don't let the rustic neighborhood vibe fool you. The plates that come out of the open kitchen represent the kind of sophistication more commonly associated with upscale urban restaurants. Start with a thin-crust pizza, a cheese plate, or the signature fig and arugula salad, and finish things off with the lavender crème brûlée. A huge perk here is the lack of a corkage fee, so bring along your favorite wine—though wine's also available by the flight, glass, or bottle, and there's a nice list to choose from. Reservations not accepted. *13690 Arnold Dr. ☎ 707/938-2130. Entrees $14–$24. AE, DISC, MC, V. Dinner daily; brunch Sat & Sun only. Map p 94.*

KIDS Garden Court Café *AMERICAN* This sunny, genial place offers savory breakfasts and

lunches, Sonoma wines, and occasional special Friday-night dinners. At breakfast, order eggs done any which way. Lunch options consist mostly of sandwiches and salads. There's a pet-friendly umbrella-shaded terrace outside, and you can order your dog a meal off a three-option menu. *13647 Arnold Dr. ☎ 707/935-1565. Entrees $8–$13. MC, V. Breakfast & lunch Wed–Mon. Map p 94.*

★ Glen Ellen Inn Restaurant
CALIFORNIA/FRENCH A local favorite for its warm, romantic atmosphere. The beautiful presentations that emerge from the open kitchen change with the seasons. Garden seating is the favorable choice on sunny days, but the covered patio is also welcoming. The 550-selection wine list includes more than a dozen wines by the glass. For dessert, try the fabulous house-made sundae: Coconut-encrusted French-vanilla ice cream floats in bittersweet caramel sauce. Reservations recommended. *Tip:* There's a small parking lot behind the restaurant. *13670 Arnold Dr. ☎ 707/996-6409. Main*

Glen Ellen's fig café & winebar is the casual version of the famous Sonoma restaurant, the girl and the fig (see p 77).

courses $14–$25. AE, DISC, MC, V. Lunch & dinner Thurs–Tues. Map p 94.

Olive & Vine CALIFORNIA This dinner spot has a romantic sit-down area and creative menu options that do a good job of highlighting local produce and flavors. In Jack London Village. 14301 Arnold Dr. ☎ 707/996-9152. Entrees $23–$37. MC, V. Dinner Wed–Sun. Map p 94.

★ **Wolf House** NEW AMERICAN One of Glen Ellen's most famous establishments is in Jack London Lodge. Food is served either in the historic saloon or out on the terrace, overlooking a serene creek. The lunch menu adds fancy flourishes to old American favorites, while dinners emphasize locally procured ingredients, some even

culled from the lodge's garden. A reasonably priced Sonoma-centric wine list offers many by-the-glass options. After dinner, head to the Lodge's fun bar, which is filled with colorful folks, TVs broadcasting sports games, and Jack London photos and memorabilia. 13740 Arnold Dr. ☎ 707/996-4401. Entrees $15–$27. AE, MC, V. Lunch & dinner daily. Reservations recommended. Map p 94.

Yeti INDIAN/PAKISTANI For a taste of the Himalayas in one of wine country's tinier towns, Yeti doesn't disappoint. Sit indoors to watch Chef Narayan Somname prepare succulent, authentic appetizers and entrees behind the long bar, or enjoy a view of Sonoma Creek from the large outdoor patio. 14301 Arnold Dr. ☎ 707/996-9930. Entrees $16–$29. AE, DISC, MC, V. Lunch & dinner daily. Map p 94.

At Glen Ellen Inn, a burger is tiered and speared.

Calistoga

① Napa Valley
  Railroad Depot

② Dr. Wilkinson's
  Hot Springs Resort

③ Calistoga Pottery

④ Sharpsteen Museum

⑤ Napa River

⑥ Holy Assumption
  Monastery

⑦ Lee Youngman
  Fine Art

⑧ Vermeil Wines

⑨ Ca'toga Galleria
  d'Arte

10A Calistoga Roastery

10B Village Bakery

WHERE TO DINE

11 All Seasons Bistro

12 Bosko's

13 Brannan's

14 Checkers

15 Hydro Grill

16 Pacifico

17 Solbar

18 Sushi Mambo

Calistoga is an Old West–style town with more than a touch of California eccentricity. Its people are still obsessed with Sam Brannan, a Maine-born pioneer who became California's first millionaire by selling gold-mining tools after stoking frenzy for the precious metal: He ran through San Francisco shouting of its discovery. When he came to this formerly Wappo, then Spanish, area, he was so taken with its hot springs that he bought thousands of acres on which to develop a spa resort town similar to what already existed in Saratoga, New York. In 1885, meaning to say that he would transform this into the Saratoga of California, he instead (probably due to his demising penchant for alcohol) proclaimed, "I will make this the Calistoga of Sarafornia!" The name stuck, and more than 120 years later, pleasure seekers still come to enjoy the tiny town's therapeutic mineral water and mud baths. The waters here are so coveted that they're bottled and sold—the next time you see Crystal Geyser or Calistoga Water at your local market, remember your visit here. This tour highlights downtown Calistoga's history and cultural diversity, with stops at the town's best stores and galleries.
START: **The Historic Calistoga Depot, 1458 Lincoln Ave. Distance: Less than a half-mile (.8km) of walking, doable in a half to a full day.**

Lincoln Avenue is Calistoga's main drag.

① ★ kids **Napa Valley Railroad Depot.** In 1868, it became possible to take the train to Calistoga, making it a gateway destination for wine country. This depot, California's second oldest, is on the National Register of Historic Places. Its site now supports six restored rail cars that still look as though they've just docked at the station. Inside the cars is a variety of quirky businesses, including a psychic from India, a florist, and a decades-old wine store. *1458 Lincoln Ave.* ☎ *707/942-6333.*

② ★★ **Dr. Wilkinson's Hot Springs Resort.** You can get a massage at any old spa, but only at Dr. Wilkinson's, one of Calistoga's many hot-spring resorts, can you detoxify in a volcanic-ash mud bath with a facial mask and cucumbers over your eyes, then soak in a roiling mineral bath, then get wrapped in a blanket, *then* have a muscle-melting hour-long massage. It's called "The Works," and it's not for everyone (refrain if you're sensitive to heat or think you might not like being surrounded in mud—though it's better than it sounds), but those who like it *love* it. The spa might not win any awards for its bland decor but it gets first prize for its ability to relax

clients. Named for the late Dr. John Wilkinson, a chiropractor who provided alternative therapies in the 1940s, the resort is now co-managed by his children, Mark and Carolynne. *1507 Lincoln Ave.* ☎ *707/942-4102. www.drwilkinson.com. "The Works" $139 with a 30-minute massage or $179 for a mud bath with a 60-minute massage.*

③ **Calistoga Pottery.** A block south of Lincoln Avenue, this shop showcases a colorful array of ceramic pieces that you'll find in use at restaurants and wineries all over the valley. *1001 Foothill Blvd.* ☎ *707/942-0216. www.calistogapottery.com. Daily 9am–5pm (opens at 11am on Sun).*

④ kids ★★ **Sharpsteen Museum.** The Sharpsteen Museum chronicles northern Napa County's natural and cultural history. The definite highlight is the painstakingly created diorama depicting Brannan's resort as it was in 1868. The 32-foot-long (9.6m) town replica took nearly 3 years to build and sits under the panoramic photo on which it's based. Other exhibits display Wappo artifacts, Robert Louis Stevenson paraphernalia, a geothermal demonstration, and a restored stagecoach. Ben Sharpsteen, the museum's founder, was an Academy Award–winning Disney filmmaker (he directed *Dumbo* and others), so the museum also contains one of his Academy Awards, plus some fun Disney paraphernalia. *1311 Washington St.* ☎ *707/942-5911. www.sharpsteen museum.org. Daily 11am–4pm. Suggested donation: $3+ for adults.*

Just to the left of the museum is the beautiful:

❺ **Napa River,** home to a threatened population of steelhead and Chinook salmon. Right here, you can actually cross the river on foot—there's a shallow barrier across which adults and kids can easily wade to get to the playground on the other side.

Back out on Washington Street, pass the mint-green Community Presbyterian Church (3rd and Washington St.) to find the fairy-tale-like:

❻ ★★ **Holy Assumption Monastery & Orthodox Religious Center.** Founded in the 1940s by Russian and Chinese refugee nuns, this peaceful religious center was originally a hotel. They built one of its woodsy chapels to replicate the one at Fort Ross. Surrounding the quaint buildings are fountains, a koi pond, and Asian-inspired gardens. If you're lucky, you may spot the friendly resident one-eyed cat. The parish welcomes visitors of all backgrounds. *1519 Washington St.* ☎ *707/942-6244. Hours vary; call ahead. Free, but donations accepted.*

Turn right to get back on Lincoln Avenue, cross a bridge over the river, and enter:

❼ **Lee Youngman Fine Art Gallery,** a store where upbeat staff sell exquisite art. *1316 Lincoln Ave.*

The centerpiece of the Sharpsteen Museum is the diorama built by Ben Sharpsteen, the founder, to depict life in the 1960s in Calistoga.

☎ *707/942-0585. www.leeyoungman galleries.com. Daily 10am–5pm (noon–4pm on Sun).*

At ❽ ★ **Vermeil Wines,** fourth-generation vintners pour you a taste of their heritage. Charbono Frediani's enthusiasm for her family's fields will make you feel right at home. She recommends ordering a couple of tastings to share. Call ahead for availability. *1255 Lincoln Ave.* ☎ *707/341-3054. www.vermeil wines.com. Sun–Thurs 10am–5:30pm (Fri–Sat until 8pm).*

In the same shopping complex is:

❾ ★ **Ca'toga Galleria d'Arte.** A gorgeous space showcasing the works of Venice-born artist Carlo Marchiori. His Renaissance, baroque, and neoclassical styles are evidenced here in the form of porcelain plates, acrylic paintings, original furniture—and a fantastic cosmological ceiling mural that you can marvel at by merely looking up. Look down to see a glittering terrazzo floor that charts the pre-Copernican universe. Find the Latin inscription *Hic Es* ("You are here"), and you'll know you've found Earth. *1206 Cedar St.* ☎ *707/942-3900. www.catoga.com. Thurs–Mon 11am–6pm.*

Calistoga's not exactly a high-stress place, but take time anyway to unwind at either of the town's best coffee shops: **10A** **Calistoga Roastery** for its fresh single-bean varietal coffees. *1426 Lincoln Ave.* ☎ *707/942-5757. $.* Or **10B** **Village Bakery** for sticky buns and creamy gelato, plus sandwiches and tarts. *1353 Lincoln Ave.* ☎ *707/942-1443. $.*

Where to Dine in Calistoga

★★ **All Seasons Bistro** *AMERICAN* This cleanly decorated bistro is very white, save for a red ceiling accented with Art Deco–style fans. As the name might imply, the menu changes seasonally; order from it or ask about Chef Summer Sebastiani's tasting menus. *1400 Lincoln Ave.* ☎ *707/942-9111. Entrees $17–$27. DISC, MC, V. Lunch & dinner Tues–Sun. Map p 98.*

★ **Bosko's** *ITALIAN* This trattoria with rock walls, wood-fired pizza, and fresh homemade pasta has a relaxing atmosphere. Save room for dessert—the tiramisu is stupendous. *1364 Lincoln Ave.* ☎ *707/942-9088. Entrees $13–$24. AE, MC, V. Lunch & dinner daily. Map p 98.*

★ **Brannan's** *NEW AMERICAN* A large Arts and Crafts–style restaurant with a classy fireplace dining room for chilly evenings and alfresco seating for warm days. Big salads, substantial sandwiches, and well-spiced specialties. *1374 Lincoln Ave.* ☎ *707/942-2233. Entrees $10–$34. AE, MC, V. Lunch & dinner daily. Map p 98.*

kids **Checkers** *ITALIAN* Though entrees are mostly Italian—pastas, pizzas, and calzones—the menu

also lists unexpected options like a Thai noodle salad. Start with a hot, garlicky appetizer like spinach and artichoke dip. *1414 Lincoln Ave.* ☎ *707/942-9300. Entrees $14–$20. AE, DISC, MC, V. Lunch & dinner daily. Map p 98.*

★ **Hydro Grill** *AMERICAN* The more casual counterpart of All Seasons Bistro (see above), Hydro Grill has brick walls, lots of mirrors, and a great bar scene. Twenty on-tap

Bosko's trattoria is known for its pizzas.

beers make the Friday and Saturday evening entertainment more fun: Live music encompasses genres from blues to rock 'n' roll to swing. *1403 Lincoln Ave.* ☎ *707/942-9777. Entrees $8–$17. DISC, MC, V. Breakfast, lunch & dinner daily. Map p 98.*

★ kids **Pacifico** *MEXICAN* At this festive spot, try a grilled fajita or one of the many traditional dishes with a pitcher of bright-blue Cabo Waborita. Friday nights, a mariachi band plays; on Saturdays, it's live Latin jazz. *1237 Lincoln Ave.* ☎ *707/942-4400. Entrees $14–$18. MC, V. Lunch & dinner daily. Map p 98.*

★★★ **Solbar** *CALIFORNIA* The Michelin-starred bistro at the eco-friendly Solage Calistoga resort is headed by Brandon Sharp, an alumnus of the French Laundry and Gary Danko. Its culinary repertoire manages to be simultaneously fun and elegant, tied together by local, seasonal ingredients. Choose from light, healthy food on one side of the menu—a warm bulgur pilaf, for example—or hearty soul food on the other—a slow-roasted pork belly comes with pickled shiitake and sticky rice. Dine in the modern interior or outside on the patio, where strung lights and fire-and-water

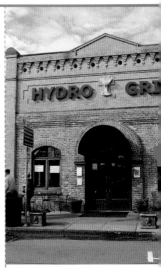

Hydro Grill.

features create a lovely evening setting. *755 Silverado Trail.* ☎ *707/226-0860. Main courses $26–$38. AE, DC, MC, V. Call for hours. Map p 98.*

Sushi Mambo *JAPANESE* A selection of Japanese specialties (udon, tempura, and the like) complement a long sushi list in this small, traditionally decorated restaurant. *1631 Lincoln Ave.* ☎ *707/942-6857. Entrees $14–$19. MC, V. Lunch & dinner Wed–Mon. Map p 98.*

Petaluma

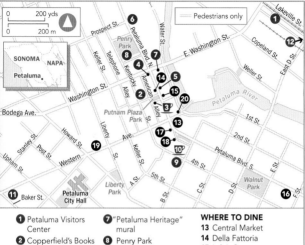

1. Petaluma Visitors Center
2. Copperfield's Books
3. Petaluma Pie Company
4. Seed Bank
5. Chelsea Antiques
6. Military Antiques & Museum
7. "Petaluma Heritage" mural
8. Penry Park
9. Petaluma Historical Library & Museum
10. Acre Coffee
11. Petaluma Creamery Cheese Shop
12. Green String Farm

WHERE TO DINE
13. Central Market
14. Della Fattoria
15. Lala's Creamery
16. Le Bistro
17. Old Chicago Pizza
18. McNear's Saloon & Dining House
19. Tea Room Cafe
20. Water Street Bistro

Petaluma's not on the typical traveler's Napa-Sonoma itinerary—but it should be. This town doesn't put on fancy airs but is rife with hidden treasures, not least of which is its understated devotion to excellent food. Agriculture, especially dairy, is Petaluma's mainstay industry—its Butter and Egg Days festival in April is such a big deal that it draws home many who grew up here, no matter how far away they've moved. This is also as historic as you're going to get in much of the West. Petaluma was chartered in 1858, and since it sits on bedrock, the 1906 earthquake that flattened the rest of this region just couldn't shake Petaluma down. Though it's just 40 miles north of San Francisco, which was devastated, the only recorded damage here was a single broken window in the Carnegie library (now the Petaluma Historical Museum). The people here seem just as sturdy: They're friendly, matter-of-fact folk who say "hello" in the street—not something you find everywhere in California. Antiques shops sit next to tattoo parlors, and die-hard patriots enjoy the welcoming restaurants right alongside New Age spiritualists. This tour blends walking and driving to give you a thorough overview. START: **Petaluma Visitor Center. 210 Lakeville Hwy. Distance: Less than 1-mile (1.6 km) of walking, about 6 miles (10km) of driving.**

❶ Petaluma Visitors Center. If you're into local lore, make this your first stop as you drive into town—the docents staffing this little outpost are knowledgeable and talkative. Its Mission Revival–style building was built in 1914 (at a cost of $7,000) as a train depot. In 2005, after a $3.2 million restoration, the Visitors Center moved in. *210 Lakeville Hwy. (Hwy. 116).* ☎ *877/273-8258. www.visit petaluma.com. Daily 10am–4pm.*

Drive northwest on Lakeville Street to turn left onto E. Washington Street. Drive half a mile, then turn left onto Keller Street. On your right will be a free parking structure. Park here, then walk across the street to:

❷ ★ Copperfield's Books. In our age of disappearing bookshops, Copperfield's is an excellent reminder of why such places are still important. This comfortable, homey store has a useful "local interest" shelf and a wanderlust-inducing travel section. Head downstairs to peruse the rare-books area, where you can find some real collectors' items,

especially if you're interested in art or spirituality. There's also an endearing collection of local memorabilia for sale, including Petaluma High School pennants and letterman patches. *140 Kentucky St.* ☎ *707/762-0563. www.copperfields books.com. Mon–Sat 10am–9pm, Sun 10am–6pm.*

❸ Petaluma Pie Company. In Helen Putnam Plaza, this small store serves sweet and savory pies in traditional flavors like strawberry rhubarb and chicken pot—but also offers a creative selection for adventurous palates, like pear-cardamom or a handheld samosa. Ingredients are mostly organic and sourced from local food producers. Closed Tuesdays. *125 Petaluma Blvd. N.* ☎ *707/766-6743. $.*

❹ ★★★ kids Seed Bank. Owner Jere Gettle was scouting northern California for a West Coast branch of his Missouri shop when he drove by a grand old bank for lease. He loved the high-ceilinged, light-filled space and the 1920s-era detailing, so he took it.

The old train depot is now the Petaluma Visitors Center.

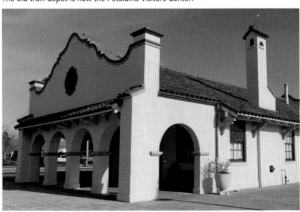

Even non-gardeners marvel at the vastness of the selection here: Nearly 1,800 seed types are for sale in an almost library-like arrangement. The emphasis is on heirloom varieties that are organic and not genetically modified. Also on the shelves: an array of country goods, gardening books and magazines, organic spices, bug and bee houses, soils, pots, and garden tools. A kind, knowledgeable staff stands ready to answer any question. *199 Petaluma Blvd. N. ☎ 707/773-1336. www.rareseeds. com. Mon–Fri 9am–4pm, Sun 9:30am–4pm. Closed Saturdays and major holidays. Extended hours during summer.*

❺ ★ Chelsea Antiques. Browse the country-style Americana in this charming collective featuring the finds of 25 dealers. With items obtained "anywhere from a garage sale to France," as the cashier put it, the well-edited selection includes wood-hewn and iron-wrought furniture, rustic home accents, bunting, even top hats. *148 Petaluma Blvd. N. ☎ 707/763-7686. www.chelseaantiquesca.com. Daily 10am–5:30pm.*

❻ ★★ Military Antiques & Museum. To get to this museum, walk into the storefront of the Petaluma Collective, a cluttered store of collectible kitsch: A quizzical group of vintage robots (and a friendly staff) may greet you at the door. Head downstairs, though, and the wares turn entirely war-themed. You feel as though you're descending into a bunker as a passionate docent leads you into the museum. Prepare to be regaled with stories you've never heard, spanning the Civil War through World War II, and to see evocative scenes patched together with some of the thousands of artifacts given to the

museum by veterans who tell of their wartime experiences, then sign a dedicated wall. The items on display, many of which should probably be in the Smithsonian, include a signed scarf from General Jimmy Doolittle, home-front propaganda, and poignant "trench art" carved onto artillery shells by World War I soldiers between battles—some say these designs spurred the Art Deco era. *300 Petaluma Blvd. N. ☎ 707/763-2220. www.militaryantiquesmuseum.com. Thurs–Sun 10am–5:30pm or by appointment.*

❼ "Petaluma Heritage" mural. Stop for a look at this 100-foot-long (30m) mural, which artist Steve Della Maggiora created in 1998 as a rough timeline of the town. To the far left are the Miwok Native Americans, then General Vallejo and his adobe. Then there are horse wagons, seafaring men (this *is* a river town), a steam train—and, of course, chickens, eggs, and cows. *Petaluma Blvd. at E. Washington St.*

❽ kids Penry Park. This 1¼-acre (.5 hectare) hilltop green space is named for U.S. Army sergeant Richard A. Penry, a Petaluma native who was awarded the Congressional Medal of Honor for the selfless bravery he demonstrated during the Vietnam War. In late 2011, the "Occupy" movement set up camp here. The protesters are gone now, so it's a peaceful place for a picnic lunch amid the fan palms. The park also provides a decent view of Petaluma's typical Victorian homes. *226 Kentucky St. (Petaluma Blvd. at E. Washington St.).*

❾ ★ Petaluma Historical Library & Museum. Housed in a 1903 Greco-Roman-looking building (note the columns) that used to

Fourth of July bell ringing at the Petaluma Historical Library & Museum.

do duty as a Carnegie library, this Smithsonian Institution is still "free to all"—a fact enshrined in mosaic at the entrance. Inside, there's a stained-glass ceiling dome, rotating exhibits downstairs (past topics have included pirates and code-talking Native Americans), and a permanent collection upstairs with exhibits that recall Petaluma's early days. The gift shop is small but good, and the tree out back is 200 years old. Saturdays at 10:30am, meet here for a free docent-led tour of downtown. *20 4th St.* ☎ *707/778-4398. www.petalumamuseum.com. Thurs–Sat 10am–4pm; Sun noon–3pm & by appointment.*

Need caffeine? Head to 🔟² ★ **Acre Coffee.** Open since late 2011, this hip, sophisticated spot serves excellent coffee drinks, including a divine bittersweet mocha. *21 4th St.* ☎ *707/772-5117. $.*

Walk back to your parking spot on Keller Street. Once in your car, turn right on Western Avenue. Take that a half-mile to:

⓫ **Petaluma Creamery Cheese Shop.** This retail store is attached to one of Petaluma's most productive and historic dairies—Petaluma Creamery was founded in 1913. You can get a 45-minute guided tour inside the butter-yellow factory if you've called ahead ($20 for adults, $10 for ages 7–18, free for ages 6 and younger), but if you haven't, sample the signature Spring Hill Jersey Cheese at the nondescript shop, which also sells homemade ice cream, shakes, pizza, and coffee. *711 Western Ave.* ☎ *707/762-9038. www.petalumacreamerycheeseshop. com. Mon–Fri 6am–7pm, Sat–Sun 8am–6pm.*

Drive northeast on Western Avenue, then turn left on Petaluma Boulevard N. Turn right on E. Washington Street, then right again on Lakeville Street. After 2½ miles, turn left on Frates Road. Go 1½ miles, then turn left on Old Adobe Road. On your right, look for:

⑫ ★★ kids Green String Farm. Much more than just a produce stand, this farm—named after a holistic method of sustainable farming—is a culture unto itself. The upbeat staff encourage you to sample anything, talk you through how to grow and cook what they sell, and don't mind if you walk through the peaceful but playful property for a look at the chickens, goats, sheep, and cow. Classic rock plays on vinyl records as customers pick through the seasonal offerings, which include fresh eggs, seedlings, Meyer lemons, fava beans, and all manner of herbs—all pesticide-free. *3571 Old Adobe Rd.* ☎ *707/778-7500. www.greenstring farm.com. Daily 10am–6pm ('til 5pm in winter).*

Where to Dine **in Petaluma**

★★ Central Market *NEW AMERICAN* Farm-to-table cuisine is easy to do when there are plenty of farms not too far from your tables. Central Market has perfected the genre in a beautiful downtown space. The menu's pretty meat-heavy, though, so vegetarians might want to look elsewhere. *42 Petaluma Blvd. N.* ☎ *707/778-9900. Entrees $21–$28. AE, DISC, MC, V. Dinner Tues–Sun. Map p 103.*

★★ Della Fattoria *BAKERY* This brunch spot has walls the color of burnt earth, Italian farmhouse touches, piles of fresh-baked bread (rosemary and Meyer lemon, polenta, ciabatta), and cases of pastries and cream-topped cakes. Entrees are made with amazingly fresh local ingredients. *141 Petaluma Blvd. N.* ☎ *707/763-0161. Entrees $5–$13. AE, DISC, MC, V. Breakfast & lunch daily. Map p 103.*

★ Lala's Creamery *ICE CREAM* This old-fashioned parlor is sure to evoke nostalgia in those who remember checkered floors and golden oldies. Though ice cream creations take the spotlight at cheery Lala's, you can also get crepes (the "salty caramel" and the "cheese and greens" are worth trying), salads, and hot dogs. *134 Petaluma Blvd.* ☎ *707/763-5252. Entrees $4.50–$5.65. MC, V. Lunch & dinner Tues–Sun. Map p 103.*

★★ Le Bistro *FRENCH* This *très français* spot is tiny, dark, romantic, and excellent. Fish dishes are especially good. Reservations are a must. *312 Petaluma Blvd. S.* ☎ *707/762-8292. Entrees $13–$29. AE, MC, V. Dinner Wed–Sun. Map p 103.*

★ kids Old Chicago Pizza *PIZZA* In a historic 1876 building, which was built for America's 100th birthday and used to be a brothel, lives a beloved Petaluma institution. Order a large deep-dish pie—it'll weigh almost five doughy pounds. There's also a nice wine list for a pizza place. *41 Petaluma Blvd. N.* ☎ *707/763-3897. Pizzas $4.10–$27. MC, V. Lunch Mon–Sat; dinner daily. Map p 103.*

McNear's Saloon & Dining House *AMERICAN* A jovial place to grab a beer and a burger and maybe catch a game. This saloon is attached to the **Mystic Theater,** where big musical names play. *23 Petaluma Blvd. N. ☎ 707/765-2121. Entrees $10–$28. AE, MC, V. Lunch & dinner daily; Sunday brunch. Map p 103.*

★ **Tea Room Cafe** *BAKERY* A cute, French-feeling cafe with hearty breakfasts, sandwiches, and fresh-baked pastries. *316 Western Ave. ☎ 707/765-0199. Entrees $7–$12. Cash only. Breakfast & lunch Thurs–Tues. Map p 103.*

★ **Water Street Bistro** *FRENCH* Right on the river, the food at this sunny spot represents what Petaluma dining is all about: fresh, local, seasonal. Options include sandwiches, salads, quiche, and gelato—try the lavender flavor. *100 Petaluma Blvd. N. ☎ 707/763-9563. Entrees $5–$8. Cash only. Breakfast & lunch Wed–Mon. Map p 103.* ●

5 The Great **Outdoors**

Wine Country **by Bike**

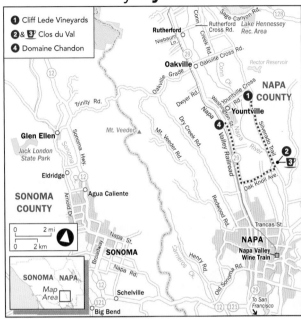

❶ Cliff Lede Vineyards
❷ & ❸ Clos du Val
❹ Domaine Chandon

Majestic scenery and flat terrain combine to make wine country the consummate cyclist destination. Touring on two wheels while inhaling the valley's fresh air is the most exhilarating way to appreciate wine country. This route, appropriate for those in moderate physical condition, cycles through Napa Valley and stops at some of its best wineries. *Tip:* Temper your intake and eat well, because biking under the influence is illegal. If you only want to imbibe at two wineries, picnic but don't taste at Clos du Val. START: **Yountville's Washington Street. Trip Length: Half a day (allow a full day if you like to linger). For where to rent bikes (you can get them delivered to you), see p 200.**

Head north on Washington Street, then turn right on Yount Street, then right again on Yountville Cross Road. After 3 miles (4.8km), on your right will be:

❶ ★★ **Cliff Lede Vineyards.** This is the northernmost winery in the famous Stags Leap District. The tasting room's energetic staffers are happy to tell you all about their rich,

bordeaux-focused varietals. After sipping, notice the works by famous artists (Keith Haring, Jim Dine) on the outdoor terrace, which also offers views of vineyards and the Vaca Mountains. *1473 Yountville Cross Rd., Yountville.* ☎ *707/944-8642. See p 141.*

Turn right out of Cliff Lede's parking lot. After a fifth of a mile (.3km), Yountville Cross Road ends. Turn

Previous page: Bodega Head Beach.

Food and Safety Along the Way

You'll want to eat sometime along this ride. To assemble your own picnic, stop at Yountville's family-owned **Ranch Market Too** (6498 Washington St.; ☎ 707/944-2662) beforehand to buy food (bring a backpack if you do this). Alternatively, book with ★★ **Napa Valley Bike Tours** (NVBT; 6500 Washington St.; ☎ 707/251-8687), a company that, in addition to offering basic bike rentals, will cater lunch at any local winery with picnic grounds, for a fee. Another benefit of going with NVBT: Its experts, who helped us devise this tour, follow you with a van. That way, if you want to buy wine as you taste, you won't have to haul bottles around. Its vans also stock first-aid kits and bicycle-maintenance tools in case of foibles. Best of all, NVBT provides a tour guide so you won't have to worry about looking down to read directions as you ride.

right onto the historic Silverado Trail and pedal the 3.7 miles (6km) to:

❷ ★ Clos du Val. Try this French-influenced winery's signature cabernet, peek at its rose garden, and roll a game at its lovely *pétanque* (French bocce) court. This is also your picnic stop. *5330 Silverado Trail, Napa.* ☎ *707/261-5251. See p 142.*

Enjoy your lunch at **❸ Clos du Val,** which has two picnic areas. For the prettiest surroundings, choose the olive grove.

Continue south on Silverado Trail. Turn right on Oak Knoll, cross Hwy. 29 and the railroad tracks. Turn right on Solano Avenue, and follow it north 4 miles (6.4km) until it ends in an intersection.

Cycle up **❹ ★ Domaine Chandon's** long, vineyard-flanked driveway and across the creek's bridge to the winery's entrance. Because Domaine Chandon was founded by French champagne house Moët & Chandon, the amenities here are luxurious—this is a great place to taste the valley's most renowned bubbly. *1 California Dr., Yountville.* ☎ *888/242-6366. See p 145.*

To get back to this tour's starting point, bike to the end of Domaine Chandon's driveway, then turn left onto California Drive. Cross the railroad tracks, go under a bridge, and ride until California Drive ends. Turn left on Washington Street.

Biking through the vineyards with Napa Valley Bike Tours.

The Best Wine Country **Hike**

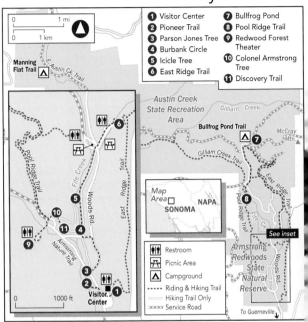

1. Visitor Center
2. Pioneer Trail
3. Parson Jones Tree
4. Burbank Circle
5. Icicle Tree
6. East Ridge Trail
7. Bullfrog Pond
8. Pool Ridge Trail
9. Redwood Forest Theater
10. Colonel Armstrong Tree
11. Discovery Trail

Restroom
Picnic Area
Campground
---- Riding & Hiking Trail
—— Hiking Trail Only
==== Service Road

The **Armstrong Redwoods State Natural Reserve** has the type of natural California scenery you always see in photos: regal, millennia-old redwoods through which only slivers of sunlight slice in. The adjacent Austin Creek State Recreation Area, by contrast, is an open forest with more kinds of trees and wildlife. This loop hike highlights the park's biology and history while taking you into the giant redwoods. It's suitable for those in moderate physical condition. START: **17000 Armstrong Woods Rd., Guerneville.** ☎ 707/869-2015. www.parks.ca.gov. Park for free at the visitor center and walk 2 minutes to the trail head; park entry is $8 per vehicle ($7 for seniors; pedestrians and bicyclists enter for free). Sunrise to sunset. Distance: About 4 miles (6.4km). Trip Length: Half a day. Maps are available at the park entrance (even when staff are not present), so be sure to take one with you.

Travel Tip

Before you head out on this hike, stock up on picnic food and supplies at **Oakville Grocery** (in Healdsburg and Oakville; see p 86).

Park in front of the **1 Visitor Center** and follow the signs to **2 Pioneer Trail,** an accessible mulch path that wends by first-generation redwoods. Notice the green carpeting along the trail. That's not clover, but oxalis—identifiable by its compound leaves with three leaflets and colored flowers. After passing a number of downed trees blown over by strong winds (redwoods have a surprisingly shallow root system), you'll find the still-sturdy ❸ **Parson Jones Tree.** This is a prime example of Coastal Redwood, the tallest of the tree species—and at 310 feet (93m), Parson Jones is the reserve's tallest tree. In shady, cool conditions, a redwood can grow 3 feet (.9m) per year, but once its top is exposed to sunlight, that rate slows to only an inch. This impressive organism, more than 1,300 years old, was named for Rev. William Ladd Jones, who helped save this grove from being logged. He was also the husband of Lizzie Armstrong Jones (see below).

Where the trail splits at the creek, take the right fork and look for ❹ **Burbank Circle,** a perfect ring of centuries-old trees—it's a mystery how they got that way.

Stay on Pioneer Trail, and on your left, you'll see the ❺ **Icicle Tree,** so named because of the massive icicle-like burls that used to hang off it. Burls occur when a tree repeatedly buds over in the same spot. Unfortunately, vandals have sheared the tree of most of its protrusions. Redwood is highly valued for furniture-making, so it can fetch a pretty penny—a sad example of how short-term commercial gain can trump long-term sustainability.

Find a picnic spot and break out the goodies you got from **Oakville Grocery.**

Now that you've got energy, access the ❻ **East Ridge Trail** in the parking lot beyond the picnic area to the right. Foliage becomes more diverse here: You'll notice that cool shadiness shifts to a more open forest highlighted by a mix of redwoods, oaks, firs, and madrones. If it's spring, wildflowers like buttercups, iris,

Ponder the tall trees at Armstrong Redwoods State Natural Reserve.

lupines, and poppies will be showing off their colors. At the paved road, turn right to see ❼ **Bullfrog Pond.** Listen for the pond's singing namesake amphibians.

Walk back down the way you came, but turn right onto ❽ **Pool Ridge Trail,** which ends in a paved loop with a parking area. Veer right here and head down the short path to ❾ **Redwood Forest Theater,** a natural amphitheater that used to regularly seat more than 2,000 people for outdoor concerts and weddings. The theater is used just once a year now, for the Old Grove Festival, which benefits volunteer programs in the parks.

On the other side of the paved loop is the colossal, 1,400-year-old ❿ **Colonel Armstrong Tree.** The preserve's oldest organism stands 308 feet (92m) tall and has a diameter approaching 15 feet (4.5m).

Colonel James Boydston Armstrong was an Ohio-born lumberman who eventually realized that forests are fragile—it was his efforts that kept this reserve preserved. He bought the land in 1875 and fought to make it a state park. Though he died before that happened, his daughter, **Lizzie Armstrong Jones,** saw to it that a county initiative was passed to realize her father's dream.

Finally, take the short ⓫ **Discovery Trail.** It'll merge with the Pioneer Trail to lead you back to your car.

From the **Russian River** to the Pacific Coast

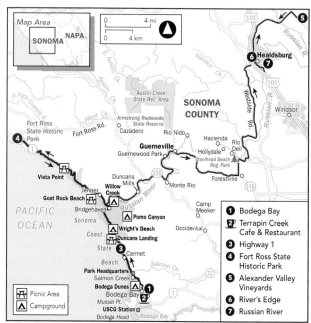

1. Bodega Bay
2. Terrapin Creek Cafe & Restaurant
3. Highway 1
4. Fort Ross State Historic Park
5. Alexander Valley Vineyards
6. River's Edge
7. Russian River

Sonoma's dazzling Pacific coastline and tranquil Russian River are a testament to California's grandeur. This itinerary has you spending the morning at a breathtaking beach and the afternoon floating on a river. You'll also drive the famously rugged, cliff-hugging Pacific Coast Highway 1 ("PCH" to Californians). Start the day early (8:30am or before) to make sure you can fit everything in. *Tip:* Dress in layers for the ever-changing coastal weather, and wear shoes in which you'd be comfortable walking on wet ground. START: **Bodega Bay. Trip Length: 1 day.**

The seaside town of **1** ★★ **Bodega Bay** (www.bodegabay. com) makes for a lovely escape from everyday life. Stroll around for about 10 minutes to get a feel for this fishing village's coastal culture. If you're an Alfred Hitchcock fan, you can head 5 miles (8km) east on Hwy. 1 into Bodega to see **Potter Schoolhouse.** The legendary film director's radar for so-innocent-they're-creepy locations must have been on high alert when he spotted this 1873 structure—he gave it a significant role in *The Birds.* The building is a private residence now, so stroll on by. *17110 Bodega Ln., Bodega Bay.* ☎ *707/876-3257. www.bodegaschool.com.*

2 ★★ **Terrapin Creek Cafe & Restaurant.** The dining room here is a cozy space with a fireplace and handcrafted furnishings—but nice as the interior may be, the real highlight is the view of the bay. The global menu focuses on organic coastal cuisine and seasonal dishes that are elegant takes on comfort-food favorites. As for wine, you won't be able to order anything made west of Highway 101, a result of local pride. *1580 Eastshore Rd., Bodega Bay.* ☎ *707/875-2700. Entrees $26–$32. Dinner Thurs–Mon.*

Exploring the dunes by Goat Rock Beach.

3 ★★★ **kids** **Hwy. 1 along Sonoma Coast State Beach.** This 21-mile (34km) drive shows off some of California's most dramatic coastal lands. Going north on it, you'll pass rugged shale bluffs, coves, headlands, and offshore reefs. More than 300 bird species populate this stretch. If it's spring, look for sprays of wildflowers like blue lupine and verbena. There are plenty of pullouts for photo opportunities, and many of the beaches you'll pass have tide pools teeming with life (they're accessible from

more than a dozen points). Veer left when you reach Goat Rock Road to visit the peninsula's tip, **Whale Point,** so named because the annual grey-whale migration passes here from December to April, and because humpbacks are here year-round. Whale Point is also the site of **Goat Rock Beach,** the Russian River's mouth and where hundreds of harbor seals converge and breed (the pups are here from March to June). *Sonoma Coast State Beach.* ☎ *707/875-3483. www.parks.ca.gov. Call for hours of operation.*

Enjoy the beaches off Highway 1.

4 ★★ **kids** **Fort Ross State Historic Park.** On a wave-cut marine terrace, Fort Ross has steep bluffs, old-growth redwoods, and many spots where you can see the impact of the famous San Andreas Fault, which comes ashore 2 miles (3.2km) south of the fort and cuts through the old Russian orchard—look for sag ponds, escarpments, damaged trees, and off-kilter fences, all remnants of the notorious 1906 earthquake. *19005 Hwy. 1, Jenner.* ☎ *707/847-3286; 707/847-3437 for the museum and bookstore. www.parks.ca.gov. Park grounds open daily sunrise to sunset. The historical buildings, the visitor center,*

Canoeing down the Russian River.

and the bookstore are open Fri–Mon 10am–4:30pm. Park day-use fee: $8 per vehicle ($7 for seniors).

Travel Tip: In Case of Rain . . .

If the day turns out to be rainy, gray, and cold (and kayaking is the last thing you want to do), stop at funky **Guerneville** on your way back from the coast. For a detailed tour, see p 88.

⑤ Alexander Valley Vineyards. Pull off for a quick sip at this award-winning winery. The free four-wine flight comes with a view of Sonoma Valley and a picnic spot on the Russian River. *8644 Hwy.*

128, Healdsburg. ☎ *800/888-7209. See p 134.*

Rent water gear from **⑥ River's Edge** in Healdsburg, whose canoes and double kayaks start at $50 per day per adult ($20 for kids; $10 for dogs)—reservations are strongly recommended. The cost of your rental includes paddles, life vests, and a shuttle ride back to your car. Guided trips are available upon request. *13840 Healdsburg Ave., Healdsburg.* ☎ *707/433-7247. www.riversedgekayakandcanoe.com.*

⑦ ★★★ kids The Russian River. A paddle on this rain-fed river is leisurely for the most part, so it's appropriate for those in moderate physical condition, as well as youngsters—though there are a few hairier sections. Glide through lush Alexander Valley, past vineyards and tree-lined private property. You'll also see unnamed but inviting beaches where you can break out a picnic. Keep an eye out for wildlife: This area is abundant with river otters, turtles, great blue heron, osprey, and egrets. Finish at either Rio Nido (a shorter, 11-mile/18km journey) or Healdsburg Beach (longer at 15 miles/24km)—you'll recognize Rio Nido by the congregation of River's Edge boats, and Healdsburg Beach is a dead end, so it's impossible to miss. River's Edge shuttles you back to your car from either finishing point. *Allow 4–5 hr.*

For dinner options in Healdsburg, flip to p 85. ●

Napa & Sonoma Valley
Accommodations

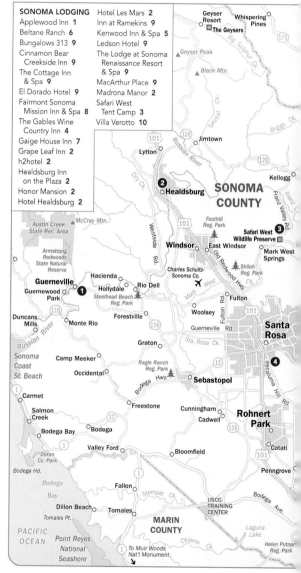

SONOMA LODGING
Applewood Inn **1**
Beltane Ranch **6**
Bungalows 313 **9**
Cinnamon Bear
  Creekside Inn **9**
The Cottage Inn
  & Spa **9**
El Dorado Hotel **9**
Fairmont Sonoma
  Mission Inn & Spa **8**
The Gables Wine
  Country Inn **4**
Gaige House Inn **7**
Grape Leaf Inn **2**
h2hotel **2**
Healdsburg Inn
  on the Plaza **2**
Honor Mansion **2**
Hotel Healdsburg **2**

Hotel Les Mars **2**
Inn at Ramekins **9**
Kenwood Inn & Spa **5**
Ledson Hotel **9**
The Lodge at Sonoma
  Renaissance Resort
  & Spa **9**
MacArthur Place **9**
Madrona Manor **2**
Safari West
  Tent Camp **3**
Villa Verotto **10**

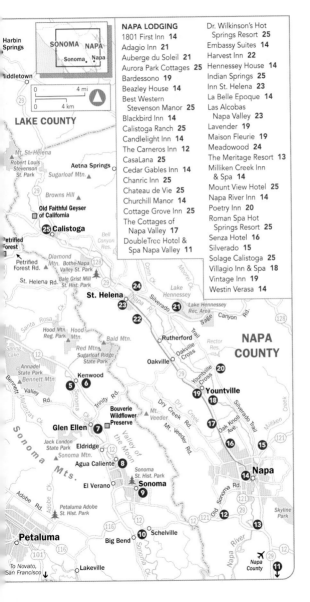

NAPA LODGING
1801 First Inn **14**
Adagio Inn **21**
Auberge du Soleil **21**
Aurora Park Cottages **25**
Bardessono **19**
Beazley House **14**
Best Western
  Stevenson Manor **25**
Blackbird Inn **14**
Calistoga Ranch **25**
Candlelight Inn **14**
The Carneros Inn **12**
CasaLana **25**
Cedar Gables Inn **14**
Chanric Inn **25**
Chateau de Vie **25**
Churchill Manor **14**
Cottage Grove Inn **25**
The Cottages of
  Napa Valley **17**
DoubleTree Hotel &
  Spa Napa Valley **11**

Dr. Wilkinson's Hot
  Springs Resort **25**
Embassy Suites **14**
Harvest Inn **22**
Hennessey House **14**
Indian Springs **25**
Inn St. Helena **23**
La Belle Epoque **14**
Las Alcobas
  Napa Valley **23**
Lavender **19**
Maison Fleurie **19**
Meadowood **24**
The Meritage Resort **13**
Milliken Creek Inn
  & Spa **14**
Mount View Hotel **25**
Napa River Inn **14**
Poetry Inn **20**
Roman Spa Hot
  Springs Resort **25**
Senza Hotel **16**
Silverado **15**
Solage Calistoga **25**
Villagio Inn & Spa **18**
Vintage Inn **19**
Westin Verasa **14**

Napa Lodging A to Z

★★ 1801 First Inn NAPA
Named for its downtown address, this Queen Anne Victorian blends contemporary touches with classic European decor. An in-house chef prepares delicious three-course breakfasts and gourmet hors d'oeuvres for evening wine tastings. *1801 1st St.* ☎ *707/224-3739. www.1801first.com. 8 units. $302–$400. AE, DISC, MC, V. Map p 118.*

★ Adagio Inn ST. HELENA
Rooms in this quiet, Edwardian B&B feature stained-glass windows and reading nooks. Amenities include a decadent breakfast, king beds, and evening wine and cheese. *1417 Kearny St.* ☎ *707/963-2238. www.adagioinn.com. 3 units. $200–$400. MC, V. Map p 118.*

★★★ Auberge du Soleil RUTHERFORD With interior decor that's nearly unsurpassed in the region—it's contemporary Spanish-Mediterranean—Auberge is sophisticated enough to belong to Relais & Châteaux. Oversized beds are sheathed in the softest of linens, and the rooms' other highlights include outdoor terraces and flatscreen TVs. Visit the superb restaurant, the luxurious spa, and the open-air art gallery. *180 Rutherford Hill Rd.* ☎ *707/963-1211. www.aubergedusoleil.com. 50 units. Doubles $675–$5,200. AE, DC, DISC, MC, V. Map p 118.*

★ Aurora Park Cottages CALISTOGA These homey cottages sport outside decks where you can savor a basket of pastries and fruit. Innkeepers are local experts, so ask them to customize a tour plan for you. *1807 Foothill Blvd.* ☎ *707/942-6733. www.aurorapark.com. 6 units. $168–$318. AE, MC, V. Map p 118.*

★★★ Bardessono YOUNTVILLE Bardessono's clean, earthy modernity and fetching artworks just scrape the surface of what makes this pet-friendly hotel so attractive. Its staff is young, energetic, and attentive, whether at the rooftop pool or at **Lucy Restaurant & Bar ★★**, the excellent on-site restaurant (see p 93). This is one of only three hotels in the United States to have earned LEED Platinum certification for its many efforts toward sustainability. Upon arrival, you'll get a glass of wine, then be led through the property's open layout, a design theme that extends into the posh rooms. *6526 Yount St., Yountville.* ☎ *707/204-6000. www.bardessono.com. 62 units. Doubles $504–$945. AE, DC, DISC, MC, V. Map p 118.*

★★ Beazley House NAPA
Open since 1981 and still run by its original owners, this pet-friendly, wood-shingled property stakes its claim as Napa's first B&B. Offerings include country-style rooms (no TV), gardens, and a nightly wine-and-cheese hour in the parlor. Note that guests younger than age 21 aren't permitted, for licensing reasons. *1910 1st St.* ☎ *707/257-1649. www.beazleyhouse.com. 11 units. Doubles $215–$322. MC, V. Map p 118.*

Best Western Stevenson Manor CALISTOGA Close to town center, this value-oriented inn's large rooms feature a fireplace, kitchenette, or balcony. Amenities include breakfast, a pool, a hot tub, a sauna, and a steam room. Check the website for current deals. *1830 Lincoln Ave.* ☎ *707/942-1112. www.stevensonmanor.com. 34 units. Doubles $127–$247. AE, DC, DISC, MC, V. Map p 118.*

★★ Blackbird Inn NAPA A stay at this well-located B&B includes afternoon wine tastings and DVDs to borrow. Craftsman elements give the exterior a lodge feel, while rooms are country-style with spa tubs and fireplaces. *1755 1st St.* 📞 *888/567-9811. www.blackbird innnapa.com. 8 units. $168–$285. AE, DC, DISC, MC, V. Map p 118.*

★★★ Calistoga Ranch CALIS-
TOGA   Operated by the prestigious Auberge brand, this quiet, airy ranch amid the pines combines modern luxury with earthiness. Freestanding, pet-friendly lodges display elegant decor and sport a setup that blurs the line between indoor and outdoor. The restaurant and spa are both impressive. *580 Lommel Rd.* 📞 *707/254-2800. www. calistogaranch.com. 50 units. Doubles $707–$1,700, with cottages up to $4,200. AE, DC, DISC, MC, V. Map p 118.*

★★ Candlelight Inn NAPA   A
Tudor mansion on Napa Creek, this B&B in the redwoods (2 miles/3.2km from downtown) is a perennial favorite. Country-style rooms come with a private balcony, a marble fireplace, or a two-person Jacuzzi tub. Don't snooze through the three-course breakfast. *1045 Easum Dr.* 📞 *707/ 257-3717. www.candlelightinn.com. 10 units. Doubles $192–$359. AE, DISC, MC, V. Map p 118.*

★★ The Carneros Inn NAPA
This cluster of private residences epitomizes clean design. Its 27 acres (11 hectares) encompass vineyards, a spa, an inviting restaurant called **Farm ★** (see p 55), and an infinity pool. In fall 2015, the property introduced five new "Harvest Suites," each with 800 square feet of indoor space, plus a 400-square-foot patio with a fire pit and soaking tub. *4048 Sonoma Hwy. (Hwy. 12).* 📞 *707/299-4900. www.thecarnerosinn.com. 99 units. Doubles $431–$1,040. AE, DC, DISC, MC, V. Map p 118.*

★ CasaLana CALISTOGA   If
you're a gourmand, you'll be enticed by the hands-on cooking classes held here. Even if you're not, you'll be minutes from downtown in a country-style room with a private entrance. *1316 S. Oak St.* 📞 *707/942-0615. www.casalana. com. 2 units. $214–$300. AE, DISC, MC, V. Map p 118.*

★★ Cedar Gables Inn
NAPA   This Shakespeare-inspired 1892 manor, 3 blocks from downtown, mixes Renaissance-era artifacts with rich textures and colors. Rooms have whirlpool baths and fireplaces, and their rates include a three-course breakfast and an evening wine reception. Ask owners

Guest suite at Calistoga Ranch.

The infinity pool overlooking the vineyards at Carneros Inn.

Ken and Susie Pope for a tour of the building's secret staircases. *486 Coombs St.* ☎ *800/309-7969. www. cedargablesinn.com. 9 units. $271– $582. AE, DISC, MC, V. Map p 118.*

★★ **Chanric Inn** CALISTOGA Jim Dollard and Joel Haddad, French natives who lived in Paraguay for more than 2 decades, acquired this 1875 Victorian farmhouse and promptly gave it a complete overhaul. Weaving in modern European and South American influences to reflect their background, they also incorporated a gourmet three-course brunch, lots of original art, French-style gardens, an outdoor pool, and bathrooms featuring luxury linens, and stone showers with marble floors. Stay here and you'll get chocolate truffles at check-in, evening hors d'oeuvres, and a champagne nightcap. *1805 Foothill Blvd.* ☎ *707/942- 4535. www.thechanric.com. 7 units. $441–$579. AE, MC, V. Map p 118.*

★ **Chateau de Vie** CALISTOGA The "house of life" is a B&B on a small working winery (try the cabernet). Highlights include a generous breakfast, refined rooms, a pool, and a view of Mt. St. Helena. *3250 Hwy. 128.* ☎ *877/558-2513. www. cdvnapavalley.com. 4 units. $229– $429. AE, MC, V. Map p 118.*

★★ **Churchill Manor** NAPA This B&B a few blocks from downtown is a beautiful 1889 Victorian mansion. Intricately decorated rooms feature vintage tubs and huge showers. Outside, there's a fountain courtyard, rose gardens, and a large veranda. Borrow a tandem bike before heading out. *485 Brown St.* ☎ *800/799- 7733. www.churchillmanor.com. 10 units. Doubles $226–$340. AE, DISC, MC, V. Map p 118.*

★★ **Cottage Grove Inn** CALISTOGA Calm permeates these cottages set in an elm grove at the end of Calistoga's main strip. Relax by a fireplace or under a skylight in your room's two-person Jacuzzi tub. Furnishings are homey and cozy, and a stay includes breakfast and evening wine. *1711 Lincoln Ave.* ☎ *800/ 799-2284. www.cottagegrove.com. 16 units. Doubles $284–$352. AE, DC, DISC, MC, V. Map p 118.*

★★★ **The Cottages of Napa Valley** NAPA Originally a 1929 motel, this sheltered complex was remodeled to embody country-style chic. A stay here is gratifying in part because of the amenities: a breakfast basket from **Bouchon ★★** (see p 92) and weekend wine receptions. Each comfortable cottage features a king bed, fireplace, kitchenette, Jacuzzi tub, and a front and back patio. *1012 Darms Lane.* ☎ *707/252-7810. www.napa cottages.com. 9 units. $683–$1,025. AE, MC, V. Map p 118.*

Tips for Choosing Lodging

Wine country differs from other tourist destinations in that its lodging options don't consist mainly of huge corporate hotel chains. In fact, many of the region's resorts, hotels, inns, B&Bs, and rentals are family-owned, with surprising personal touches. How to choose where to stay should depend on you: If you're social and interested in an experience that involves meeting your innkeepers and mingling with other guests, go for a B&B. If you prefer anonymity and upscale amenities, choose a resort or a larger hotel. For complete seclusion, or if you're planning something like a small family reunion, a vacation rental is your best bet. Napa and Sonoma offer hundreds of wonderful lodgings, but this book's limited space prevents us from listing all of them—the ones on these pages, however, are either very prominent or highly recommended.

DoubleTree Hotel & Spa Napa Valley AMERICAN CANYON One of the world's eco-friendliest hotels, this DoubleTree is certified LEED Platinum. Enjoy breakfast in bed, the spa, and the heated outdoor pool. Only thing is, it's a bit far from Napa's main attractions. If you stay here, rent a car (preferably a hybrid) and plan your itinerary accordingly. *3600 Broadway St.* ☎ *707/674-2100. www.doubletree.hilton.com. 135 rooms. $110–$212. AE, DC, DISC, MC, V. Map p 118.*

★ **Dr. Wilkinson's Hot Springs Resort** CALISTOGA Calistoga's longest family-owned business (established 1952) still has character. A mud bath here is a must. Equally enjoyable are massages, facials, and mineral pools (see p 99). Easy access to shops and restaurants. *1507 Lincoln Ave.* ☎ *707/942-4102. www.drwilkinson.com. 42 units. Doubles $149–$299. AE, MC, V. Map p 118.*

★ **Embassy Suites** NAPA Effort went into giving this chain a local feel. Touches include a swan pond with a wooden mill, a pool, and a large atrium where breakfast (included in your nightly rate) is

cooked to order and cocktails (also included) are served each evening. *1075 California Blvd.* ☎ *707/253-9540. www.embassysuitesnapahotel.com. 205 units. Doubles $168–$447. AE, DC, DISC, MC, V. Map p 118.*

★★ **Harvest Inn** ST. HELENA This upscale property offers rustic country charm, daily wine tastings, gorgeous gardens, and a worthwhile spa. Breakfast is included, and many suites feature fireplaces, spa tubs, and private terraces. In 2016, celebrity chef Charlie Palmer added the Harvest Lofts, four brand-new guestrooms that became part of the property's recent remodel. *1 Main St.* ☎ *707/963-9463. www.harvestinn.com. 78 units. Doubles $243–$546. AE, DISC, MC, V. Map p 118.*

★ **Hennessey House** NAPA This downtown B&B's rooms are flowery. The main house is an 1889 Victorian, and its six units are less pricey than the four in the Carriage House. A stay includes a sumptuous breakfast, afternoon tea, and evening wine. *1727 Main St.* ☎ *707/226-3774. www.hennesseyhouse.com. 10 units. Doubles $192–$295. AE, DC, DISC, MC, V. Map p 118.*

★★ Indian Springs CALISTOGA Deriving its name from Calistoga's past life as a Native American healing ground, this resort with comfortable bungalows is where you can detoxify in a volcanic-ash mud bath and soak in a naturally heated, thermal-geyser-fed mineral pool. In 2015, 75 homey rooms were added, many of them in a 1930s Mission Revival–style building. *1712 Lincoln Ave.* ☎ *707/942-4913. www.indiansprings calistoga.com. 116 units. Doubles $187–$378. DISC, MC, V. Map p 118.*

★ Inn St. Helena ST. HELENA Once the home of author Ambrose Bierce, this 1872 Victorian's comfortable rooms have canopied beds, fireplaces, and Jacuzzi tubs. A champagne breakfast is included—as for dinner, downtown is an easy walk. *1515 Main St.* ☎ *707/963-3003. www.innsthelena.com. 8 units. $247–$379. MC, V. Map p 118.*

★ La Belle Epoque NAPA This plush B&B and its two-unit sister property across the street, the **Buckley House,** are century-old Queen Annes standing as stately testaments to Napa's rich architectural history. Rooms boast elegant antiques and high-grade linens. Indulge in the candlelit breakfast and the nightly wine-and-cheese reception. *1386 Calistoga Ave.* ☎ *707/257-2161. www.napa boutiqueinn.com. 10 units. $227–$328. AE, DISC, MC, V. Map p 118*

★★ Las Alcobas Napa Valley ST. HELENA Though it wasn't open at press time, this Starwood-run hotel, slated for debut in fall 2016, will have guestrooms and suites featuring outdoor fireplaces on terraces that overlook the Beringer vineyards. It'll also have an outdoor pool, a signature restaurant, and a 3,500-square-foot spa. Las Alcobas will be within easy walking distance of downtown St. Helena, as well as the **Culinary Institute of**

America ★★★ (see p 32). *1915 Main St. www.starwoodhotels.com. 68 units. About $700. AE, DISC, MC, V. Map p 118.*

★ Lavender YOUNTVILLE A homey 1870 B&B with wooden floors and French-style country furnishings, Lavender's small touches include lavender sachets, chocolate upon turndown, and afternoon snacks. Borrowing the inn's bicycles makes exploring fun, though many of the town's attractions are within walking distance. *2020 Webber Ave.* ☎ *800/522-4140. www.lavender napa.com. 8 units. $212–$359. AE, DC, DISC, MC, V. Map p 118.*

★ Maison Fleurie YOUNT-VILLE The "flowering house" certainly is. This garden property offers rooms with country-style decor and stone fireplaces, breakfast each morning, and wine and hors d'oeuvres each afternoon. *6529 Yount St.* ☎ *800/788-0369. www. maisonfleurienapa.com. 13 units. Doubles $167–$316. AE, DC, DISC, MC, V. Map p 118.*

★★★ Meadowood Napa Valley ST. HELENA This exclusive Relais & Châteaux property, also a private club for local leaders, is reminiscent of a grand country estate. Its highly personalized service, all-suite spa, tennis courts, croquet lawns, pools, and golf course put it in a league of its own. Lodging is amid oaks in a private 250-acre (100-hectare) valley. *900 Meadowood Lane.* ☎ *866/963-3646. www.meadowood. com. 85 units. Doubles $545–$1,880. AE, DISC, MC, V. Map p 118.*

★ The Meritage Resort NAPA The Meritage, 4 miles (6.4km) from downtown Napa in the Carneros region, claims the world's only underground-cave spa. Also here: wine caves, vineyards, and expertly run tastings. **Siena** restaurant's Tuscan cuisine accompanies a comprehensive wine list. *875 Bordeaux Way.* ☎ *855/318-1768. www. meritageresort.com. 322 units. Doubles $226–$551. AE, DC, DISC, MC, V. Map p 118.*

★★★ **Milliken Creek Inn & Spa** NAPA This garden property is known for luxury and attention to detail. The earth-toned rooms have canopied king beds, fireplaces, fresh orchids, and private decks with river views. Marble bathrooms feature hydrotherapy tubs and rain showers. Breakfast is gourmet, and vintners host an evening wine-and-cheese reception. Don't forego an aromatherapy massage at the spa. *1815 Silverado Trail.* ☎ *707/255-1197. www.millikencreekinn.com. 12 units. Doubles $317–$684. AE, DC, DISC, MC, V. Map p 118.*

★★ **Mount View Hotel** CALISTOGA Smallish, romantic rooms with European-style antiques are set in a downtown 1917 building. Highlights include a pool, Jacuzzi, and lobby fireplace. Breakfast snacks are delivered each morning, and there's an on-site spa. *1457 Lincoln Ave.* ☎ *707/942-6877. www.mountview hotel.com. 33 units. Doubles $188–$414. AE, DISC, MC, V. Map p 118.*

Meadowood is Napa's most exclusive resort.

★ **Napa River Inn** NAPA In the 1884 Napa Mill complex, this downtown inn, true to its name, overlooks the Napa River. Pet-friendly rooms feature historical, nautical, and country stylings. In-room breakfast service and two restaurants, **Angèle ★★** (see p 72) and **Celadon,** are superb. *500 Main St.* ☎ *707/251-8500. www.napariverinn. com. 66 units. Doubles $217–$411. AE, DC, DISC, MC, V. Map p 118.*

★★★ **Poetry Inn** NAPA Cliff Lede Vineyards (see p 141) has Stags Leap District's only public lodging— and what lodging! Posh rooms sit 500 feet (150m) above the valley. Vineyard views are spectacular, decor is classy, and outdoor showers add to the uniqueness. At breakfast (included in the nightly rate), try the brie-and-strawberry French toast, then enjoy an open-air massage, lounge by the pool, or marvel at the wine cellar's rarities. *6380 Silverado Trail.* ☎ *707/944-0646. www.poetry inn.com. 5 units. $646–$1,430. AE, DC, MC, V. Map p 118.*

Roman Spa Hot Springs Resort CALISTOGA Though this is a spa resort, rooms are modest. The surrounding grounds contain three mineral-water pools (two are on-site) and two Finnish saunas. *1300 Washington St.* ☎ *800/914-8957. www.romanspahotsprings.com. 60 units. Doubles $227–$285. AE, DISC, MC, V. Map p 118.*

★★ **Senza Hotel** NAPA In 2014, Craig and Kathryn Hall, of Hall Wineries (Kathryn is the former U.S. ambassador to Austria), redid the former La Residence hotel, turning it into this bastion of modern luxury. The 2-acre (.8-hectare) property's five main buildings include the eight-room Parker Mansion, built in 1870. Eighteen suites feature king beds and deep soaking tubs, and all guests get treated to the morning breakfast from **Bouchon ★★** (see p 92) and an evening wine-and-cheese hour. Just south of Yountville, this property also has a heated outdoor pool with cabanas, a full spa, and lovely vineyard views. *4066 Howard Ln. ☎ 707/253-0337. www.senzahotel. com. 41 units. $226–$471. AE, DC, DISC, MC, V. Map p 118.*

Silverado NAPA This resort is a country club, so it's great for golf (two courses) but lacks the intimacy of many wine-country inns. Suites have kitchenettes and under-size bathrooms. Decor is low-key—more practical than aesthetic. Highlights include its spa and its restaurant, **The Grill.** *1600 Atlas Peak Rd. ☎ 707/257-0200. www. silveradoresort.com. 280 units. Doubles $177–$400. AE, DC, DISC, MC, V. Map p 118.*

★★ Solage Calistoga CALISTOGA Bright and airy, this luxury resort, open since 2007, stocks a world-class art collection, runs the Michelin-starred **Solbar ★★★** restaurant (see p 102), offers mineral-water pools, and is in the process of getting LEED certified for its green efforts. Rooms are comfortable and come with the use of two cruiser bikes. In 2015, the spa was treated to a $1.2 million expansion. *755 Silverado Trail. www.solage calistoga.com. ☎ 866/942-7442. 89 units. Doubles $414–$814. AE, DISC, MC, V. Map p 118.*

★★ Villagio Inn & Spa YOUNTVILLE This fancy spot has a distinctly Mediterranean feel, from the water features to the Roman-style "ruins." Rooms are luxurious, and a stay comes with a bottle of Beringer and a superb breakfast buffet. Staffers are hospitable, and the spa's river-stone massage is heavenly. *6481 Washington St. ☎ 707/944-8877. www.villagio.com.*

80 units. Doubles $258–$443. AE, DISC, MC, V. Map p 118.

Vintage Inn YOUNTVILLE Villagio's downtown sister property has spacious guestrooms, suites, and villas with generous tubs and balconies. In 2015, this property got treated to a complete renovation—the rooms feel fresh and new. Amenities like free wine and breakfast make guests feel welcome. *Tip:* Ask for a room overlooking Domaine Chandon. *6541 Washington St. ☎ 800/351-1133. www.vintageinn. com. 80 units. Doubles $261–$444. AE, DISC, MC, V. Map p 118.*

★★★ Westin Verasa NAPA Rooms here are so spacious, so extravagant, so chock-full of amenities that you might end up wanting to stay inside. But don't—the hotel sits right on the Napa River and is within walking distance of the town's best landmarks, including **Oxbow Public Market ★** (see p 11) and 12 tasting rooms. It's also the home of **La Toque ★★**, a Michelin-starred dining room (see p 73). *1314 Mckinstry St. ☎ 888/ 657-7169. www.westinnapa.com. 180 suites. Doubles $237–$532. AE, DISC, MC, V. Map p 118.*

Villagio Inn & Spa.

Sonoma Lodging A to Z

★ **Applewood Inn** GUERNE-VILLE   This sweet 1922 Mission Revival–style mansion's rooms are individually decorated. Outside, there's a pool, a hot tub, and an organic herb garden that's plucked often for the on-site restaurant (a stay includes breakfast). It's a 2-minute drive to Main Street but manages to feel forested and remote. *13555 Hwy. 116.* ☎ *707/ 869-9093. www.applewoodinn.com. 19 units. Doubles $220–$345. AE, MC, V. Map p 118.*

★★ **Beltane Ranch** GLEN ELLEN   This B&B in a pastel-yellow 1892 manor has everything a country ranch should: clean, antique-furnished rooms with private entrances (no TV or phone); a big, delicious breakfast; a wraparound porch; hiking trails; a tennis court; and lots of greenery. Enjoy the pretty drive up from the highway and request an upstairs room with a view. *11775 Sonoma Hwy. (Hwy. 12).* ☎ *707/833-4233. www.beltane ranch.com. 6 units. $223–$277. MC, V. Map p 118.*

★ **Bungalows 313** SONOMA   These private, spacious downtown cottages have kitchens, though a tasty breakfast is provided. There's

Beltane Ranch.

also a fountain courtyard and the option of staying in the romantic 1906 brick house. Attention to detail reveals itself in small and large touches like fresh flowers and inviting interiors. *313 1st St. E.* ☎ *707/996-8091. www.bungalows 313.com. 5 units. $267–$355. DISC, MC, V. Map p 118.*

Cinnamon Bear Creekside Inn SONOMA   This 1887 Victorian farmhouse is romantic and comfortable. Rooms feature antique furnishings and memory-foam mattresses sheathed in Frette linens. Other pleasantries include a multi-course breakfast, a hot tub, bikes to borrow, and wine receptions. *19455 Sonoma Hwy. (Hwy. 12).* ☎ *877/935-8197. www.cinnamon bearcreeksideinn.com. 7 units. $110– $275. AE, DISC, MC, V. Map p 118.*

★★ **The Cottage Inn & Spa** SONOMA   This beloved retreat proximal to Sonoma's mission incorporates Cal-Med architecture and gardens. Individually decorated rooms have private entrances, fireplaces, spa tubs, and big, comfy beds. Also included in your price: a pastries-and-fruit breakfast, plus access to a fitness club. *310 1st St. E.* ☎ *707/996-0719. www.cottage innandspa.com. 8 units. $227–$367. DISC, MC, V. Map p 118.*

★★ **El Dorado Hotel** SONOMA   El Dorado's strong points are its chic decor—more town than country—and excellent plaza location. Small but sunny rooms feature four-poster beds, fine linens, and small balconies. Outside, there's a heated lap pool. The hip **El Dorado Kitchen** ★★ (see p 77) is a must-try. *405 1st St. W.* ☎ *707/996-3030. www.eldorado sonoma.com. 27 units. Doubles $143– $396. AE, DC, MC, V. Map p 118.*

★★★ Fairmont Sonoma Mission Inn & Spa SONOMA

Established in 1927, this Sonoma institution just gets better with age. Its rooms are charming, and many have fireplaces. The mineral-water-fed spa is perfect, as is the cuisine at upscale **Santé**. Though it's in a drab area 3 miles (4.8km) from Sonoma, you won't want to leave—free wine tastings add to the desire to stay put. The resort does offer excursions like free hiking and biking tours, plus access to a nearby 18-hole golf course. *100 Boyes Blvd.* ☎ *707/938-9000. www.fairmont.com/sonoma. 228 units. Doubles $206–$658. AE, DC, DISC, MC, V. Map p 118.*

Soak in the elegance of the Gaige House Inn.

★ The Gables Wine Country Inn SANTA ROSA

This cozy B&B looks like a dollhouse from the outside and, on the inside, a Victorian manor. Rooms feature claw-foot tubs and historic appointments. Enjoy the lavender garden and sample wine in the evening. Consider splurging on the quiet creekside cottage, which has a hot tub. *4257 Petaluma Hill Rd.* ☎ *800/422-5376 or 707/585-7777. www.the gablesinn.com. 8 units. $175–$195. AE, DISC, MC, V. Map p 118.*

★★★ Gaige House Inn GLEN ELLEN

Though this creekside inn was built in 1890, it's gone through a major upgrade, which added eight Asian-themed suites with decor rivaling that of five-star hotels. The superb breakfast is served in a light-filled space by friendly attendants. There's also an in-house spa, plus a pool and relaxing hot tubs. *13540 Arnold Dr.* ☎ *800/935-0237. www.gaige.com. 23 units. Doubles $193–$408. AE, DISC, MC, V. Map p 118.*

★★ Grape Leaf Inn HEALDSBURG

Country chic (very chic) with stained-glass touches, this refined B&B in a century-old Queen Anne offers luxury amenities, soothing gardens, a standout four-course breakfast, and cozy rooms with skylights, fireplaces, and spa tubs. The speak-easy tasting room (hidden behind a bookcase!) hosts nightly wine-and-cheese tastings. *539 Johnson St.* ☎ *707/433-8140. www. grapeleafinn.com. 12 units. Doubles $198–$403. MC, V. Map p 118.*

★★ h2hotel HEALDSBURG

This eco-oriented hotel, a sister property to **Hotel Healdsburg** (see below), is the edgier, more youthful option of the two. Its older sibling may be sophisticated but h2 is fun, with quirky design elements and a bar that rocks 'til late. *219 Healdsburg Ave.* ☎ *707/922-5251. www. h2hotel.com. 36 units. Doubles $222–$690. MC, V. Map p 118.*

★ Healdsburg Inn on the Plaza HEALDSBURG

Clean, comfortable rooms have high ceilings, fireplaces, and flourishes hearkening back to 1901, when the inn was built. A stay includes breakfast and afternoon wine. Because the inn is in the middle of town, request a room in the quieter back. *112 Matheson St.* ☎ *800/431-8663. www.healdsburg inn.com. 12 units. Doubles $213–$375. AE, DISC, MC, V. Map p 118.*

★★ Honor Mansion HEALDSBURG

More than $1.5 million went into developing this property, resulting in an indulgent retreat.

Plush suites in an Italianate Victorian building are surrounded by more than 120 rosebushes and a quarter-acre (.1-hectare) vineyard. A talented chef culls herbs from on-site gardens to concoct a great breakfast buffet (included). Also outdoors: a lap pool; a jogging trail; a croquet lawn; a putting green; and tennis, bocce, and basketball courts. *891 Grove St.* ☎ *707/433-4277. www.honor mansion.com. 13 units. Doubles $316–$483. AE, MC, V. Map p 118.*

★★ **Hotel Healdsburg** HEALDS-BURG A modern option amid Healdsburg's more traditional properties, this $21-million hotel offers rooms with hardwood floors, Tibetan rugs, private balconies, deep bath-tubs, and Frette linens. Outside, the pool and green lounging spaces are a draw—and the cuisine is inspired at Charlie Palmer's **Dry Creek Kitchen** ★★★ (see p 86). At the small spa, try the Healdsburg Signature Massage. *25 Matheson St.* ☎ *707/431-2800. www.hotel healdsburg.com. 55 units. Doubles $300–$755. MC, V. Map p 118.*

★★★ **Hotel Les Mars** HEALDS-BURG The ultimate in old-Europe-style luxury. Gracious service awaits, as do elegant touches like Louis XV armoires, lavish four-poster beds, Bain Ultra soaking tubs, and a gourmet three-course breakfast.

Downstairs is a lovely restaurant called **Chalkboard** ★★ (see p 86). *27 North St.* ☎ *707/433-4211. www. hotellesmars.com. 16 units. Doubles $445–$745. AE, MC, V. Map p 118.*

★ **Inn at Ramekins** SONOMA This B&B and culinary school is the perfect stay for foodies. Packages include a bottle of wine and discounts on the cooking classes that take place downstairs. The individually decorated rooms have antique pine furniture and oversized bathrooms. Breakfast features homemade granola and pastries. *450 W. Spain St.* ☎ *707/933-0450. www.ramekins.com. 6 units. $220–$285. AE, DISC, MC, V. Map p 118.*

★★ **Kenwood Inn & Spa** KEN-WOOD Gorgeous mission-style architecture houses rooms with tex-tured decor. Other highlights include fountain courtyards, a tasting room, three Jacuzzis, and a pool. Try a bath or facial at the "vinotherapy" spa. Though it's a bit close to High-way 12, it manages to maintain romance and privacy. Breakfast is included. *10400 Sonoma Hwy. (Hwy. 12).* ☎ *800/353-6966. www. kenwoodinn.com. 30 units. Doubles $465–$674. AE, MC, V. Map p 118.*

★★ **Ledson Hotel** SONOMA This perfectly located hotel built by a fifth-generation

The lobby of the h2hotel.

A guest room at the Kenwood Inn & Spa.

winemaker transports guests to a time when antiques were new. Grand decor and modern amenities come with excellent service. *480 1st St. E.* ☎ *707/996-9779. www. ledsonhotel.com. 6 units. $280–$460. AE, DISC, MC, V. Map p 118.*

★★ The Lodge at Sonoma Renaissance Resort & Spa

SONOMA At this comfortable Marriott-owned resort, an inviting lobby welcomes you before you head to your well-appointed room, suite, or cottage. A treatment at the **Spa at Renaissance Sonoma** invigorates, and a meal at **Carneros Bistro** surpasses even high expectations. *1325 Broadway.* ☎ *707/935-6600. www.thelodgeatsonoma.com. 182 units. Doubles $220–$560. AE, DC, MC, V. Map p 118.*

★★ MacArthur Place SONOMA

On one of Sonoma's main thoroughfares is this country-style inn with very pretty grounds and very comfortable rooms. Breakfast is included, as is a wine-and-cheese reception in the library, where you can borrow a movie or book. Rooms are flowery and, if you upgrade to a suite, spacious. *29 E. MacArthur St.* ☎ *707/938-2929. www.macarthur place.com. 64 units. Doubles $238–$499. MC, V. Map p 118.*

★★ Madrona Manor HEALDS-

BURG Step back into the Victorian era at this gorgeous, sprawling estate that dates back to 1881. Some of its units have fireplaces and balconies with bucolic views for miles. Rooms favor period detail—like vintage books—over modern touches, so you won't find TVs. There's also a heated pool and a healthy garden that feeds the manor's Michelin-starred restaurant. *1001 Westside Rd.* ☎ *707/433-4231. www.madronamanor.com. 27 units. $260–$625. AE, MC, V. Map p 118.*

★★ kids Safari West Tent

Camp SANTA ROSA Central to both valleys is this ultimate family getaway. The 400-acre (160-hectare) preserve, home to hundreds of African animals, offers a cluster of safari tents with hardwood floors. From each accommodation, guests can watch giraffes, zebras, and cheetahs. Breakfast is included, and the safari drive is a must-do (see p 24). *3115 Porter Creek Rd.* ☎ *707/595-9246. www.safariwest.com. 30 units. $263–$334. AE, MC, V. Map p 118.*

★ Villa Verotto CARNEROS Elu-

sive, exclusive, and exquisite, this vineyard estate has a pool, a hot tub, and three smartly decorated bedrooms. The owners of the gated property keep its address confidential until booking to ensure guests' privacy—but it's about 5 miles (8km) from Sonoma Plaza. ☎ *415/225-3027. www.verotto.com. 1 unit. $600–$1,295. MC, V. Map p 118.* ●

Napa Valley Wineries

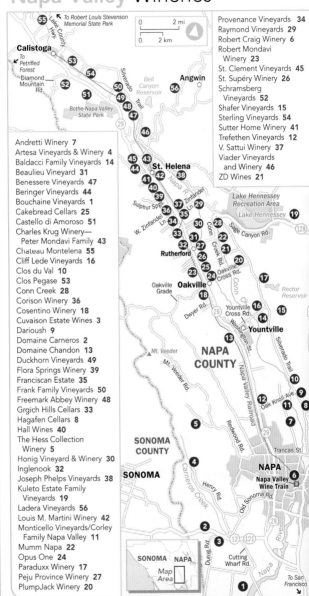

Provenance Vineyards **34**
Raymond Vineyards **29**
Robert Craig Winery **6**
Robert Mondavi
  Winery **23**
St. Clement Vineyards **45**
St. Supéry Winery **26**
Schramsberg
  Vineyards **52**
Shafer Vineyards **15**
Sterling Vineyards **54**
Sutter Home Winery **41**
Trefethen Vineyards **12**
V. Sattui Winery **37**
Viader Vineyards
  and Winery **46**
ZD Wines **21**

Andretti Winery **7**
Artesa Vineyards & Winery **4**
Baldacci Family Vineyards **14**
Beaulieu Vineyard **31**
Benessere Vineyards **47**
Beringer Vineyards **44**
Bouchaine Vineyards **1**
Cakebread Cellars **25**
Castello di Amoroso **51**
Charles Krug Winery—
  Peter Mondavi Family **43**
Chateau Montelena **55**
Cliff Lede Vineyards **16**
Clos du Val **10**
Clos Pegase **53**
Conn Creek **28**
Corison Winery **36**
Cosentino Winery **18**
Cuvaison Estate Wines **3**
Darioush **9**
Domaine Carneros **2**
Domaine Chandon **13**
Duckhorn Vineyards **49**
Flora Springs Winery **39**
Franciscan Estate **35**
Frank Family Vineyards **50**
Freemark Abbey Winery **48**
Grgich Hills Cellars **33**
Hagafen Cellars **8**
Hall Wines **40**
The Hess Collection
  Winery **5**
Honig Vineyard & Winery **30**
Inglenook **32**
Joseph Phelps Vineyards **38**
Kuleto Estate Family
  Vineyards **19**
Ladera Vineyards **56**
Louis M. Martini Winery **42**
Monticello Vineyards/Corley
  Family Napa Valley **11**
Mumm Napa **22**
Opus One **24**
Paraduxx Winery **17**
Peju Province Winery **27**
PlumpJack Winery **20**

Northern Sonoma Wineries

Alexander Valley
Vineyards **15**
Arista Winery **10**
Bella Vineyards **19**
Chalk Hill Estate
Vineyards and Winery **6**
Clos du Bois **17**
De La Montanya Winery
& Vineyards **11**
DeLoach Vineyards **2**
Ferrari-Carano Vineyards
& Winery **20**
Foppiano Vineyards **12**
Gary Farrell Vineyards
& Winery **8**
Geyser Peak Winery **18**
Harvest Moon Estate
& Winery **3**
HKG Estate Wines **9**

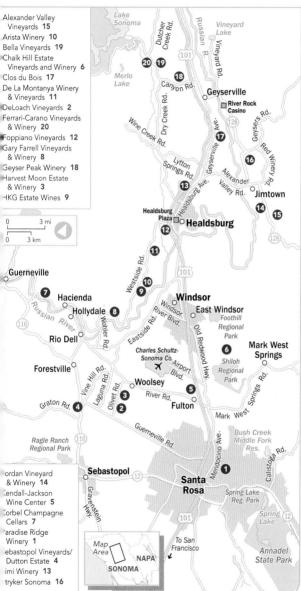

Jordan Vineyard
& Winery **14**
Kendall-Jackson
Wine Center **5**
Korbel Champagne
Cellars **7**
Paradise Ridge
Winery **1**
Sebastopol Vineyards/
Dutton Estate **4**
Simi Winery **13**
Stryker Sonoma **16**

Sonoma Valley Wineries

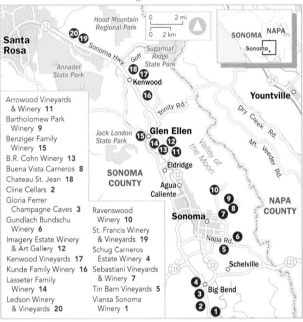

Hood Mountain
Regional Park

0   2 mi
0   2 km

SONOMA   NAPA

Sonoma

Santa Rosa

Sonoma Hwy.

Sugarloaf
Ridge
State Park

Goff

Annadel
State Park

20 **19**

18
17 Kenwood

16

Yountville

Trinity Rd.

Dry Creek Rd.

Mt. Veeder Rd.

Jack London
State Park

15 **12**
14
13 **11**

Glen Ellen

Eldridge

Valley of the Moon

**SONOMA
COUNTY**

Agua
Caliente

10

9
8
7

**NAPA
COUNTY**

Sonoma

6
5

Napa Rd.

Schellville

Big Bend

4
3
2   **1**

121

Arrowood Vineyards
  & Winery **11**
Bartholomew Park
  Winery **9**
Benziger Family
  Winery **15**
B.R. Cohn Winery **13**
Buena Vista Carneros **8**
Chateau St. Jean **18**
Cline Cellars **2**
Gloria Ferrer
  Champagne Caves **3**
Gundlach Bundschu
  Winery **6**
Imagery Estate Winery
  & Art Gallery **12**
Kenwood Vineyards **17**
Kunde Family Winery **16**
Lasseter Family
  Winery **14**
Ledson Winery
  & Vineyards **20**

Ravenswood
  Winery **10**
St. Francis Winery
  & Vineyards **19**
Schug Carneros
  Estate Winery **4**
Sebastiani Vineyards
  & Winery **7**
Tin Barn Vineyards **5**
Viansa Sonoma
  Winery **1**

Wineries A to Z

A note about the winery labels in this book: **ORG** wineries
use organic grapes; **BIO** refers to biodynamic practices; **SUST**
indicates a winery's commitment to sustainability; and **SULF** wines
have no added sulfites.

Alexander Valley Vineyards

SONOMA *SUST* This estate, now
owned by the Wetzel family, was
once the property of Cyrus Alexander (yes, as in Alexander Valley).
The Wetzels bought the land from
the Alexanders and, in 1975, "AVV"
was born. The winery, across from
the Russian River, makes for a perfect picnic spot—views of Sonoma
Valley are superb from here. Try its
award-winning Cyrus (a cab-domi-
nated blend) or its zinfandels,
Redemption Zin and Sin Zin; the

latter was an instant sensation and
is a cult favorite. *8644 Hwy. 128,
Healdsburg.* ☎ *800/888-7209. www.
avvwine.com. Daily 10am–5pm. Free
tours of wine caves 11am & 2pm.
Tastings: $10 (refunded with pur-
chase; free tasting coupon on website). Map p 133.*

Andretti Winery

NAPA Andretti
is a northern Italian–style winery that
was founded by race-car driving
champion Mario Andretti in 1996.
Despite the celebrity cachet, the

staff here couldn't be more down-to-earth. Ask them anything about Napa; they're likely to be able to answer. Tastings take place in a Tuscan villa, adjacent to which is an outdoor patio where visitors take in views of vineyards and mountains while sipping a light, zesty chardonnay or a richer cabernet sauvignon. *4162 Big Ranch Rd., Napa. ☎ 877/ 386-5070. www.andrettiwinery.com. Daily 10:30am–5pm (closed major holidays). Tastings: $15–$45. Map p 132.*

Arista Winery SONOMA *BIO, SUST* Known for its small lots of pinot noir and bone-dry gewürztra-miner, this family-owned boutique winery recently opened a hospitality center. Visitors stroll through beautiful Japanese water gardens and gaze at century-old oaks while tasting wine. Picnic spots are available, and a midweek visit is best to avoid crowds. *7015 Westside Rd., Healdsburg. ☎ 707/473-0606. www. aristawinery.com. Daily 11am–5pm. No tours. Tastings: free for appellation wines, $10 for single-vineyard pinot noirs (fee refunded with wine purchase). Map p 133.*

★ Arrowood Vineyards & Winery SONOMA *ORG, SUST* More than 20 years ago, a married couple founded Arrowood on a hillside overlooking Sonoma. Today, visitors savor samples of the handcrafted cabernets Arrowood is known for in its Hospitality House. The sun-dappled tasting room has a spacious balcony from which sippers can see Sonoma Mountain. *14347 Sonoma Hwy. (Hwy. 12), Glen Ellen. ☎ 800/ 938-5170. www.arrowoodvineyards. com. Daily 10am–4:30pm. Tastings: $15–$25 (refunded with purchase) or by the glass. Wine and cheese pairing is available by appt. for $35. Map p 134.*

★★ Artesa Vineyards & Winery NAPA *SUST* Art and architecture strike first when encountering

this winery; its modern semi-pyramid structure and stake-like sculptures impress, as do arching fountains, a water-centric courtyard, and a stark tasting room. But do the wines live up to the arresting visuals? Yes, especially the chardonnay and pinot noir. Peruse the visitors' center, which documents the region's history. *1345 Henry Rd., Napa. ☎ 707/ 224-1668. www.artesawinery.com. Daily 10am–5pm (last tasting 4:30pm). Tours $30 daily 11am & 2pm. Tastings: $25; specialty tastings and tours: $40–$60. Map p 132.*

Baldacci Family Vineyards NAPA *SUST* Tom and Brenda Baldacci founded their winery in 1998 with the notion of sharing wine with friends and family; hence the reason many of their hand-farmed creations are named after relatives. Try Elizabeth, a pinot noir that shares a name with Tom's mother—but don't miss the winery's signature cabernet. *6236 Silverado Trail, Napa. ☎ 707/944-9261. www.baldacci vineyards.com. Daily 10am–4pm (by appt.). Tastings: $25 (refunded with wine purchase of $100). Map p 132.*

Bartholomew Park Winery SONOMA *ORG* "Bart Park" is more than a winery. It's a full destination with a museum, memorial

Picnic area in the oak grove at Bartholomew Park Winery.

park, picnic grounds, and hiking trails. If you're here solely for tasting, you'll be satisfied with the limited-production single-vineyard wines, particularly the flagship Estate Zinfandel, which, like all of the wines produced here, is made from organically farmed grapes. If you're in a learning mood, check out **Bartholomew Park Museum,** which chronicles the property's whimsical history. But if you're feeling energetic, hit the trails. All 3 miles (4.8km) of them are well-marked and beautiful. On a clear day, you can see San Francisco. *1000 Vineyard Lane, Sonoma.* ☎ *707/939-3026. www.bartpark.com. Daily 11am–4:30pm (closed major holidays). Tours $20 (daily, by appt.). Tastings start at $10. Map p 134.*

★★ Beaulieu Vineyard NAPA

SUST This renowned winery was founded in 1900 by Frenchman and Napa pioneer Georges de Latour. Today, the vintage named in his honor—Georges de Latour Private Reserve Cabernet—is the winery's benchmark and resides in every serious collector's cellar. In the Reserve Room, guests sample this and older selections. For a more pedestrian (and crowded) experience, the understated main tasting room pours four wines from BV's Maestro Collection and other limited-release wines. *Fun fact:* Every American president since FDR has served Beaulieu's wines. *1960 St. Helena Hwy., Rutherford.* ☎ *707/ 967-5233. www.bvwines.com. Daily 10am–5pm (closed major holidays). Tours: $35 historic tour & barrel tasting, daily 11am & 3pm (by appt.). Tastings: $20. Map p 132.*

★★ Bella Vineyards

SONOMA Do yourself a favor—call ahead for a cave tour at Bella. No, not a vineyard tour, a cave tour. Why? Because you'll see mysterious arched doors built into the

Beaulieu's tasting room in Rutherford.

hillside when you pull up to the unassuming, barnlike tasting room. After a few sips of hearty, spicy old-vine zinfandel, you'll ask the staff about the doors. They tell you that behind the doors, flanked by old olive trees, are caves housing barrels and underground function rooms. During the tour, you'll feel cozy thanks to well-placed mood lighting and big, sturdy wood tables filling the winding caverns. You'll be so happy you stopped by this small, family-run winery (named Bella as an ode to the owners' two young daughters) in the heart of Dry Creek Valley that you'll leave plotting a way to schedule your next party underground, in these wine caves. *9711 W. Dry Creek Rd., Healdsburg.* ☎ *866/572-3552 or 707/473-9171. www.bellawinery.com. Daily 11am–4:30pm. Tours: $50 (reservation with 1-week advance notice). Tastings: $10 (no reservation needed); private cave or patio tastings with meal: $35 (reservation required). Map p 133.*

Benessere Vineyards NAPA

SUST *Benessere* is the Italian word for well-being, and that's certainly the feeling one gets here.

This 42-acre (17-hectare) country estate is known for small lots of Italian-inspired wines, many of which come from sangiovese grapes; try Phenomenon—its makers deem it "the pinnacle of winemaking at Benessere." *Tip:* Visit Monday through Wednesday, when the tasting room is least crowded. *1010 Big Tree Rd., St. Helena.* 📞 *707/963-5853. www.benesserevineyards.com. Daily 10am–5pm. Tours available by appt. Tastings: $15 (refunded with three-bottle wine purchase) by appt. Map p 132.*

★★ Benziger Family Winery

SONOMA *BIO, SUST* A highlight here is the 45-minute tractor-drawn tram tour. Sit back as a knowledgeable driver maneuvers through the estate's hilly vineyards and explains how vines get turned into wines. Tours can be reserved in advance or on a first-come, first-served basis, so stop by in the morning to buy afternoon tickets. The winery also has multiple biodynamic gardens, an insectary, picnic areas, and even a flock a sheep. In the tasting room, visitors can taste current and special releases or try a tasting focused solely on pinot noir or library wines. *1883 London Ranch Rd., Glen Ellen.* 📞 *888/490-2739. www.benziger.com. 10am–5pm. Tram tours ($25) daily every 30 min. from 11am–3:30pm except at noon. Tastings: $15–$40. Map p 134.*

★★ Beringer Vineyards NAPA SULF

Whomever knows Napa knows Beringer. Established in 1876 by German brothers Jacob and Frederick Beringer, it's Napa's oldest continually operating winery (the Beringers finagled survival during Prohibition by making sacramental wine). That distinction has earned it a firm spot on the National Register of Historic Places. In 1934, the brothers pioneered the idea of public winery tours and their namesake winery has since perfected their brainchild. Now there are four tour options ranging from a basic introduction to a thorough exploration of Beringer's vintage legacy. In summer, try a seasonal white, but the Knights Valley Cabernet Sauvignon is sublime in any season. *2000 Main St., St. Helena.* 📞 *707/302-7592. www. beringer.com. Daily 10am–6pm (until 5pm in winter). Tours ($30–$45) reservation required. Tastings: $20–$35. Map p 132.*

Tasting at the Benziger Family Winery.

Bouchaine Vineyards NAPA **SUST** Carneros's oldest continuously operated winery presents tastings of its Burgundy-inspired creations in its **Wine Visitor Center.** Try the pinot noir and chardonnay, as well as the more exclusive wines sold only here. After tasting, step onto the terrace, where an endless vineyard view awaits. *1075 Buchli Station Rd., Napa.* ☎ *800/654-9463. www.bouchaine.com. Daily 10:30am–5:30pm (4:30pm Nov–late Jan). Guided tours by appt. Tastings: $20–$30. Map p 132.*

B.R. Cohn Winery SONOMA Founded in 1984 by Bruce Cohn, this estate winery specializes in fine cabernet sauvignon. And with rare, 160-year-old Picholine olive trees all over the property, the winery also produces gourmet oils and vinegars. The tasting room may be small, but the flavors are big. Cohn, incidentally, is the Doobie Brothers' long-time band manager. His other gig inspired the Doobie Red wine series, as well as many musical events at the winery—check the website for the full schedule. *15000 Sonoma Hwy. (Hwy. 12), Glen Ellen.* ☎ *800/330-4064.*

Watch for musical events at B.R. Cohn Winery.

Beringer is Napa's oldest continually operating winery.

www.brcohn.com. Daily 10am–5pm. Tastings: $20. Map p 134.

★★★ Buena Vista Carneros SONOMA Not many wineries can boast that their tasting room is a California Historical Landmark—but then again, Buena Vista is America's oldest continuously operating winery and the birthplace of California's wine industry. Founded in 1857 by Hungarian colonel Agoston Haraszthy, it still has that delightful old-world feel: ivy-covered buildings, antique fountains, and a restored 1862 press house that houses the tasting room. Try the highly rated Estate Vineyard Series, a near-perfect selection of chardonnay and pinot noir. Picnic grounds are gorgeous here. *18000 Old Winery Rd., Sonoma.* ☎ *800/926-1266. www.buenavistacarneros.com. Daily 10am–5pm (closed major holidays). Tastings start at $15. Map p 134.*

Cakebread Cellars NAPA A small, independent winery with handcrafted wines, Cakebread is known for its chardonnay and cabernet. When Jack and Dolores Cakebread founded it with $2,500 in 1973, they wanted to encourage people to incorporate wine and

food into a healthy lifestyle. They've stuck to that goal and now offer a variety of wine and culinary education programs. The tasting area shares space with immense fermenting tanks. *8300 St. Helena Hwy. (Hwy. 29), Rutherford.* ☎ *800/588-0298. www.cakebread.com. Daily 10am–4pm by appt. Tours $25, 10:30am daily (reservations required). Tastings: $15–$25 (by appt.). Map p 132.*

Castello di Amoroso NAPA A breathtaking Tuscan-inspired castle—you'll feel like you stepped into a fairy tale. The winery opened in 2007, the brainchild of well-known vintner Dario Sattui. It offers many Italian-style wines including pinot noir, merlot, and dessert varietals. The 136,000-square-foot castle encompasses 107 rooms, a moat, a drawbridge, a torture chamber(!), a knight's chamber, and a chapel. A food and wine tour and a cheese and wine pairing tour are both available, by reservation only, for $69 (four people maximum; weekends Apr–Oct & Sun in Nov). *4045 St Helena Hwy., Calistoga* ☎ *707/967-6272. www.castellodiamorosa.com. Daily 9:30am–6pm (5pm in winter). Admission: $25–$35 (tastings included; no reservation required), $15 ages 8–20 (juice tasting included). Tours include barrel tasting Mon–Fri*

Barrels at Buena Vista Carneros.

9:30am–4:30pm (5pm in summer) $40–$50; $30 ages 5–20 (by reservation only). Map p 132.

Chalk Hill Estate Vineyards and Winery SONOMA *SUST* Of the estate's 1,300 acres (526 hectares), only 280 (113 hectares) support vineyards. The rest encompass winery buildings and a wilderness preserve—but that doesn't mean the wines aren't great. Selections include rich chardonnay, sauvignon blanc, pinot gris, pinot noir, and estate red. Embark on the culinary tour and tasting, an educational

The Tuscan-inspired castle at Castello di Amoroso.

The carriage house at Charles Krug Winery.

ramble through gardener Brad Agerter's organic culinary garden. *10300 Chalk Hill Rd., Healdsburg.* ☎ *707/657-4837. www.chalkhill. com. Daily 10am–4pm. Tours: $50 estate tour daily by appt. only, 11am; culinary lunch tour $100 by appt. Wed & Thurs at 11am. Tastings $20–$30 (no appt. necessary). Map p 133.*

★ **Charles Krug Winery— Peter Mondavi Family** NAPA **ORG** One of only three Napa wineries deemed a California Historical Landmark (the other two are Beringer and Schramsberg), this is the county's oldest working winery. It was founded in 1861 by Prussian immigrant Charles Krug, the first to make commercial wine in Napa.

The Mondavi family bought the estate in 1943 and has operated it ever since. They opened the valley's first tasting room, which was recently renovated—it's now called the Redwood Cellar Tasting Room, and it's where visitors taste the winery's signature bordeaux varietals. There's also opportunity to try food and wine pairings at the winery's "cucina" on Saturdays and Sundays. *2800 Main St. (Hwy. 29), St. Helena.* ☎ *707/967-2229. www. charleskrug.com. Daily 10:30am–5pm (closed major holidays). Tours $60. Tastings: $20–$95; barrel tastings ($15) Fri–Sun 2–4:30pm (no reservation needed). Map p 132.*

Chateau Montelena.

Wannabe Winemakers

Ever dream of being a vintner? At Judd's Hill MicroCrush (☎ 707/255-2322; www.napamicrocrush.com), you get to make the wine. And not only that: You can also help with picking, sorting, and crushing—you even get to choose your own label. To spend a week learning how to make your own sparkling-wine varietal, head to **Camp Schramsberg** (☎ 800/877-3623; www.schramsberg.com).

★ Chateau Montelena

NAPA   This place really is a château, complete with an immense 1882 stone castle. At the base of Mount St. Helena, it overlooks wildlife-laden Jade Lake and a Chinese garden. The entertaining tour starts with a video introduction, includes the vineyard and cellar, and ends up in the Estate Room for a vintage tasting. On the edifice's highest floor is another cavernous tasting room, where non-tour visitors sample less rare wines. The chardonnay is the most acclaimed, but there's also cabernet and riesling. *Tip:* This winery is hard to find, so call for directions. *1429 Tubbs Lane, Calistoga.* ☎ *707/942-5105. www.montelena.com. Daily 9:30am–4pm (except major holidays and select dates; see website). Vineyard tours: $40, Mon & Wed 10am; tastings: $20–$50. Map p 132.*

★★ Chateau St. Jean SONOMA

At the edge of Sugarloaf State Park, these elegant grounds include European-style gardens with colorful flora and a 19th-century fountain that's a sculpture of St. Jean herself. There's also a gourmet food shop, picnic space, and a welcoming visitor center. Taste winemaker Margo van Staaveren's chardonnay, cabernet, and gewürztraminer before exploring the 1920 château—it's so precisely restored that it made the National Trust for Historic Preservation. If you've ever dismissed merlot as being too passé for you, this is the place at which to fall in love with it again. *8555 Sonoma Hwy. (Hwy. 12), Kenwood.* ☎ *707/257-5784. www.chateaustjean.com. Daily 10am–5pm. Tastings: $35–$75 (appt. required). Map p 134.*

★★ Cliff Lede Vineyards NAPA

This art-rich winery was born when Canadian Cliff Lede bought S. Anderson Vineyard in 2002. The tasting room, in a century-old stone pump house, is where to try Lede's bordeaux-focused varietals and the sparkling wines that still bear the S. Anderson name. The meticulously landscaped rose garden surrounds sculptures by prominent artists,

Chateau St. Jean is available for weddings and other catered gigs.

The outdoor sculpture garden at Cliff Lede in Yountville.

including Keith Haring and Jim Dine. When a new winemaking facility opened in 2005, the former winery turned into a modern-art gallery. Cliff Lede also offers Stags Leap District's only public lodging: the lovely ★★★ **Poetry Inn** (see p 125). *1473 Yountville Cross Rd., Yountville.* ☎ *707/944-8642. www.clifflede vineyards.com. Daily 10am–4pm. Tours subject to change; call for schedules and pricing. Tastings: $30–$75. Map p 132.*

★ **Cline Cellars** SONOMA *SUST, SULF* This family-owned winery in the Carneros district has its tasting room in an 1850s farmhouse. With six ponds and more than 5,000 rose-bushes, it's a beautiful place to sample zinfandel and Rhone-style wines, such as the marsanne-roussanne blend. *24737 Arnold Dr. (Hwy. 121), Sonoma.* ☎ *707/940-4000. www. clinecellars.com. Daily 10am–6pm (closed Christmas). Free tours daily 11am, 1 & 3pm. Tastings: free (or for reserves, $1 per taste). Map p 134.*

★ **Clos du Bois** SONOMA *SUST* Clos du Bois—French for "enclosure in the woods" or "vineyard of drink," depending on the translation—produces France-style varietals. If you're lucky, they'll let you sample the Marlstone wine, one of the most complex flavors around. *Tip:* Bring lunch to enjoy the picnic area with gazebos. *19410 Geyserville Ave., Geyserville.* ☎ *800/222-3189. www.closdubois.com. Daily 10am–4:30pm, last tasting at 4:15 (closed major holidays). Tastings: $15 (no appt. necessary). Map p 133.*

★ **Clos du Val** NAPA Co-founded in 1972 by a Frenchman who scoured the world to find the best possible winery spot, Clos du Val is known for its cabernet, so try it in the rustic tasting room. A one-time fermentation chamber, it has a high, vaulted ceiling and terracotta walls. Double doors in the back allow guests to see steel tanks fermenting the pinot noir this establishment's known for. Outside, there's a rose garden, two picnic areas, and a pétanque court. *5330 Silverado Trail, Napa.* ☎ *707/261-5251. www.closduval.com. Daily 10am–5pm. Customized tours by 24-hour advance appt. (includes tasting). Tastings: start at $25; tour and tasting daily at 10:30am, $35 (appt. required); $75 for romance package (wine, chocolate & roses). Map p 132.*

★★ **Clos Pegase** NAPA Book publisher Jan Shrem bought these vineyards in 1983 and named his winery after Pegasus, the mythological

Sip zin at one of six of Cline Cellars ponds.

winged horse that created a spring that fed divine grapevines. Then, Shrem held an architects' competition. Michael Graves, the winner, designed the winery's stunning structures. They house a world-class fine-art collection, including a huge painting behind the tasting bar, where informed pourers dole out specialties like Mitsuko's Vineyard chardonnay and pinot noir. There's also a remarkable sculpture garden and a vineyard-adjacent picnic facility (call to reserve a table). *1060 Dunaweal Lane, Calistoga. 707/ 942-4981. www.clospegase.com. Daily 10:30am–5pm. Tours (by appt. only) daily 11am, 1pm & 3pm. Tastings: $20– $30. Map p 132.*

Conn Creek NAPA This winery focuses on limited-production cabernets and bordeaux blends. Also try the sauvignon blanc—it's only available here. Taking its name from the stream running alongside the vineyard, Conn Creek has a Mediterranean-style building with a pleasant garden. It's just below Rutherford Hill, in the shadow of the renowned ★★★ Auberge du Soleil resort and spa (see p 120). *8711 Silverado Trail, St. Helena. 707/963-9100. www.conncreek.com. Daily 10:30am– 4:30pm (5pm on Sat). Tastings start at $25, waived with a two-bottle purchase. Map p 132.*

Corison Winery NAPA *ORG* Tastings here are conducted the old-fashioned way: in the barrel cellar. Winemaker Cathy Corison specializes in handcrafted cabernets, and her labels bear ancient symbols. One depicts rain; the other, a sprouting seed. Tours include a visit to the winery's organically farmed Kronos Vineyard. *987 St. Helena Hwy. (Hwy. 29), St. Helena. 707/963-0826. www. corison.com. Daily 10am–5pm. Free tours daily, on the hour, by appt. Tastings: $55 (waived w/$300 purchase). Map p 132.*

Cosentino Winery NAPA Founder Mitch Cosentino and winemaker Marty Peterson offer more than 20 hand-harvested, small-lot wines, including some rich, sweet ones. Though this is fine, artistic wine, the staff is friendly. *7415 St. Helena Hwy. (Hwy. 29), Napa. 707/921-2809. www. cosentinowinery.com. Daily 10am– 6pm. Tastings: $20–$30 (no appt. needed); private tastings $40–$60 (appt. required). Map p 132.*

Cuvaison Estate Wines NAPA This mission-style winery on the Silverado Trail was founded in 1969 by Silicon Valley techies. Since then, Cuvaison, a French word roughly meaning "fermentation of grape skins," has proved that its wines are award-worthy—praise has been especially heaped on the chardonnays and pinots, so try them. From the tasting room, there are great views of northern Napa. Picnic grounds are noteworthy for their 350-year-old oak trees. *1221 Duhig Rd., Napa. 707/ 942-2468. www.cuvaison.com. Daily 10am–5pm last tasting at 4pm. Tours ($35) by appt. in spring and summer. Tastings: $20. Map p 132.*

★★ **Darioush** NAPA "Impressive" is hardly an adequate word to describe this winery. Inspired by the wine culture of Ancient Persia, the winery design honors both its ancient and modern influences. Rows of Greco columns and scalloped rooflines greet visitors outside. Inside, a blend of modern and ancient decor commingles with the effects of the strong bordeaux-style wines Darioush is known for. To splurge, try the fine wines and artisan cheeses experience, which includes a property tour and tasting of limited-release wines expertly paired with hand-crafted cheeses set in the private tasting room of the winery's barrel chai (say "shay"). *4240 Silverado Trail, Napa.*

The pillars of the Darioush Winery.

☎ 707/257-2345. www.darioush.
com. 10:30am–5pm daily. Reservations recommended (required on Saturdays and for groups of 6 or more).
Portfolio tasting: $40. Private wine
experiences: $75–$200. Map p 132.

**De La Montaña Winery &
Vineyards** SONOMA This
upbeat country-style winery has a
tasting room surrounded by beauty:
apple orchards, golden poppies,
and Felta Creek. Most days, owner
Dennis de la Montaña is behind
the counter pouring. Best to try are
the primitivo, pinot noir, viognier,
and zinfandel. And if you want to

stay overnight, the winery's cozy
Little Yellow Cottage sleeps four.
999 Foreman Lane, Healdsburg.
☎ *707/433-3711. www.dlmwine.
com. Daily 11am–5pm (no appt.
needed for groups smaller than six).
No tours. Tastings: $10 (waived with
bottle purchase). Map p 133.*

DeLoach Vineyards SONOMA
BIO Guided tours at this Russian
River winery include the biodynamic
garden and wine samples straight
from the barrel. In DLV's tasting
room, remodeled by sought-after
local architect Howard Backen, sample single-vineyard pinot noir, chardonnay, and zinfandel. Fresh bread
is served with the wine to appease
the moderately hungry. For a bigger
meal, bring lunch and savor it in the
outdoor courtyard with a refreshing
bottle of, say, the winery's sauvignon blanc. Afterward, toss a game
of horseshoes. *1791 Olivet Rd.,
Santa Rosa.* ☎ *707/526-9111. www.
deloachvineyards.com. Daily 10am–
5pm. Tours ($15) daily, by appt. Tast-
ings: $10 (waived w/wine purchase).
Map p 133.*

★ **Domaine Carneros** NAPA
Owned by French champagne
magnate Claude Taittinger, this is

A fall harvest of cabernet sauvignon in Napa Valley.

Summer time on the valley floor of Napa Valley.

the only sparkling-wine producer to exclusively use Carneros grapes. Domaine Carneros also offers a sophisticated welcome: Visitors ascend to the imposing Louis XV–style château via a grand staircase flanked by vineyards. In the tasting room and on the sunny terrace, taste by the flight or by the glass. Make sure to try a light wine called Le Reve—it's a dream. *1240 Duhig Rd., Napa.* ☎ *707/257-0101, ext.150. www.domainecarneros.com. Daily 10am–5:30pm, reservations required. Tours ($40) daily 11am, 1 & 3pm. Tastings: $10–$29 by the glass; $30–$40 for flights. Map p 132.*

★ **Domaine Chandon** NAPA French champagne house Moët et Chandon founded this prominent winery in 1973. Enjoy a bubbly-and-food pairing—the Chandon Blanc de Noirs is highly recommended—while taking in fine art and even better views. *1 California Dr. (at Hwy. 29), Yountville.* ☎ *888/242-6366. www.chandon.com. Daily 10am–5pm. Tour and tasting $40, 10:30am & 3pm daily. Tastings start at $18. Map p 132.*

Duckhorn Vineyards NAPA At Duckhorn's high-end Estate House, taste smooth bordeaux varietals at the O-shaped bar (reservations are required), take the intimate winery

tour, and browse the waterfowl art collection and the handsome gardens. Owners Dan and Margaret Duckhorn are known for their hospitality. *1000 Lodi Lane, St. Helena.* ☎ *888/367-9945. www.duckhorn. com. Daily 10am–4pm. Tastings: $30–$75 by appt. Map p 132.*

★★ **Ferrari-Carano Vineyards and Winery** SONOMA Ferrari-Carano is one of the region's most beautiful wineries. Villa Fiore, its Tuscan-style hospitality center, has a tasting bar overlooking the estate's impressive fountains. Limited releases are seasonally available, but the winery's Italian-influenced classics are more likely to be behind the bar. During the tour, you'll experience behind-the-scenes winemaking, an underground cellar, and an eye-popping ramble through 5 acres (2 hectares) of verdant gardens laced with streams and waterfalls. *8761 Dry Creek Rd., Healdsburg.* ☎ *707/433-6700. www.ferrari-carano.com. Daily 10am–5pm (closed major holidays). Tours (free) Mon–Sat at 10am (reservations required). Tastings: $10–$25 (refundable w/purchase). Map p 133.*

Tasting sparkling wine at Domaine Chandon.

The tasting room at Duckhorn in St. Helena.

Flora Springs Winery NAPA
Forsake the crowds and get off the beaten path at this small, tucked-away estate in the Rutherford appellation. The Komes family specializes in bold reds, so try the meritage blend and the cabernet—but don't miss the smooth sauvignon blanc, either. *677 S. St. Helena Hwy., St. Helena. ☎ 866/967-8032. www.florasprings.com. Daily 10am–5pm. Tastings: $20–$35 (no appt. necessary). Map p 132.*

Foppiano Vineyards SONOMA
SUST The self-guided tour is a highlight at Sonoma County's oldest continually owned family winery (it was founded in 1896). Visitors can walk through the petite sirah, chardonnay, cabernet, and merlot vines and learn about the recycled pumice pile (a sustainable way to feed vines). This low-key winery also has picnic tables. *12707 Old Redwood Hwy., Healdsburg. ☎ 707/433-7272. www.foppiano.com. Daily 11am–5pm. Tours: Self-guided tours (free) all day; guided tours ($10–$20) by appt. Tastings: $10–$20 (refundable w/purchase). Map p 133.*

★ **Franciscan Estate** NAPA This high-end property, with sunny patios and a visitor center that offers a range of tastings, is known for its merlot and cabernet, though its best wine is the Magnificat, a deep, round blend named after Bach's music. To try blending your own wine, book "Mastering Magnificat," one of the estate's educational seminars. *1178 Galleron Rd., St. Helena. ☎ 707/967-3830. www.franciscan.com. Daily 10am–5pm (closed major holidays). Tastings: $15–$50 (no appt. but personalized tastings require reservations). Map p 132.*

Frank Family Vineyards NAPA
Originally known for its sparkling wine, this winery now specializes in still ones: cabernet and chardonnay in particular. But it maintains a separate tasting space for its five versions of *méthode champenoise*

Ferrari-Carano Vineyards and Winery.

bubbly—festive Champagne Rouge is worth trying. The winery's staff is friendly, and the entertaining tour includes all the lore that comes with being old enough for the National Register of Historic Places (it was built in 1884). Outside, a picnic area with vineyard views and centuries-old American elm trees awaits. *1091 Larkmead Lane, Calistoga.* ☎ *800/574-9463. www.frankfamilyvineyards.com. Daily 10am–5pm. No tours. Tastings: $20–$30. Map p 132.*

Freemark Abbey Winery

NAPA   Established in 1886, Freemark Abbey was founded by California's first female winery owner, Josephine Tychson. In 1939, the estate got its name from three partners who bought it: **Charles Freeman, Mark Foster,** and **Abbey Ahern.** The tasting room, once a candle factory, has a fireplace and live piano music on weekends. Winemaker Ted Edwards's Cabernet Bosché is a must-try, as is the limited-production dessert riesling. At press time, there were rumors that an on-site restaurant would open here later in 2016—stay tuned. *3022 St. Helena Hwy. N. (Hwy. 29), St. Helena.* ☎ *800/963-9698. www.freemarkabbey.com. Daily 10am–5pm. Tastings: $20–$50. No tours. Map p 132.*

Gary Farrell Vineyards & Winery

SONOMA   At this boutique producer of premium Russian River Valley pinot noir, sauvignon blanc, and chardonnay, there's a great view from the hilltop tasting room. The tour shows off the state-of-the-art winemaking facility and includes four wine tastes. *10701 Westside Rd., Healdsburg.* ☎ *707/473-2909. www.garyfarrellwinery.com. Mon–Fri 10:30am–4:30pm, Sat & Sun by appt. Tour and tasting: $40, daily at 10:30am, appt. required. Tastings: $20–$30. Map p 133.*

Geyser Peak Winery

SONOMA   Geyser Peak's sunlit tasting room offers free tastes of 10 popular wines—the sauvignon blanc stands out, as does the unusual sparkling shiraz. Staffers are knowledgeable and welcoming. Bring a picnic to enjoy on the flagstone patio; in summer, there's live music on Saturday afternoons. *2306 Magnolia Dr., Healdsburg.* ☎ *707/857-2500. www.geyserpeakwinery.com. Daily 10am–5pm (closed major holidays). No tours. Tastings: $10–$15. Map p 133.*

★ Gloria Ferrer Champagne Caves

SONOMA   The so-called "first lady of Sonoma," Gloria Ferrer is the culmination of seven generations of winemaking. The winery is known for its sparklers, though it also makes chardonnay, pinot noir, merlot, and syrah. Its large hacienda-style tasting room, where wine is served with spiced almonds, opens onto an outdoor terrace overlooking the vineyards. Take the free tour of the fermenting tanks, bottling line, and underground aging caves. *23555 Arnold Dr. (Hwy. 121), Sonoma.* ☎ *707/933-1917. www.gloriaferrer.com. Daily 10am–5pm. Daily guided underground cave tours ($25, including tasting) 11am, 1pm, 3pm. Tastings: $6–$33. Map p 134.*

Grgich Hills Cellar

NAPA *BIO, SUST*   Ever since Croatian immigrant Miljenko "Mike" Grgich founded this winery in 1977, it has won acclaim. The tasting room begins serving wine earlier than most tasting rooms (it opens at 9:30am), so if you're looking for an early start, come here. At the dark-wood bar, taste handcrafted cabernets and chardonnays made from sustainably farmed organic grapes. *1829 St. Helena Hwy. (Hwy. 29), Rutherford.* ☎ *707/963-2784. www.grgich.com. Daily 9:30am–4:30pm. Tours ($35) daily at 2pm (walk-ins okay); specialty tours (with tasting) by*

The Grgich Hills patio tasting room.

reservation ($65–$90). Tastings daily: $20–$40. Map p 132.

★★ Gundlach Bundschu Winery SONOMA *SUST*

Outdoorsy as opposed to stuffy, Gundlach Bundschu's cavernous tasting room is built right into the hillside. In it, winemaker Linda Trotta's creations—mostly reds—are poured for eager guests as they enjoy light snacks. If it's available, try the Kleinberger. An informative tour includes the caves and vineyard, and colorful tales about the winery's illustrious past; it's been around since 1858, after all, and has the distinction of being America's oldest family-owned winery. A variety of excellent picnic grounds overlook the valley. *2000 Denmark St., Sonoma.* ☎ *707/938-5277. www.gunbun.com. Daily 11am–5:30pm (4:30pm in winter; closed major holidays). Tours $30–$50 by appt. Tastings: $10–$20. Map p 134.*

Hagafen Cellars NAPA

In Hebrew, *hagafen* means "the vine," and there are plenty of them at this small, kosher winery—Napa's only one. Banish thoughts of Manischewitz, though. Hagafen's wines might be made according to Jewish law and blessed by an in-house rabbi, but these wines are as premium and flavorful as any on the Silverado Trail—the award party on the tasting room wall attests to that. The most bedecked vintage offered is the white riesling, so don't decline a taste. Hagafen's wines have even been served at the White House. *4160 Silverado Trail, Napa.* ☎ *888/424-2336. www.hagafen.com. Daily 10am–5pm. Free tour Sun–Fri 10:30am by appt. Tastings: $10–$25. Map p 132.*

★★ Hall Wines NAPA

Hall Wines is actually two wineries: one in St. Helena and one in Rutherford. They're both owned by Kathryn Hall, the former U.S. ambassador to Austria, and Craig Hall, her businessman/art-collector husband. The St. Helena location dates to 1885—though it's been thoroughly modernized since. The courtyard works well for picnics, and tours include the original historic building. At the smaller, newer Rutherford location in the eastern hills, visitors see underground caves and modern art—and are treated like VIPs as they taste premium cabernet in a chandeliered tasting room. *www.hallwines.com. St. Helena: 401 St. Helena Hwy. (Hwy. 29), St. Helena.* ☎ *707/967-2626. Daily 10am–5:30pm. Tours by appt. only. Tastings: $15–$75 (walk-in & by appt.). Rutherford: 56 Auberge Rd., Rutherford.* ☎ *707/967-2626. Tour & tasting by appt. only. Map p 132.*

Harvest Moon Estate & Winery SONOMA

Harvest Moon is a little family-owned winery with welcoming servers in the small but nice tasting room. Though the winery focuses on zinfandel, the gewürztraminer is even more taste-worthy. *2192 Olivet Rd., Santa Rosa.* ☎ *707/573-8711. www.harvestmoonwinery.com. Daily 10am–5pm. Tours daily by appt. Tastings: $10 (waived w/purchase). Map p 133.*

★★★ The Hess Collection

Winery NAPA *SUST* This winery might be remote, but the drive up Mt. Veeder is an attraction unto itself. Inside, design is contemporary to match Donald Hess's museum-quality art collection on the upper levels of the 1903 stone winery (formerly Christian Brothers). Downstairs is a dramatic tasting room with a concrete bar, over which patrons taste internationally influenced wines, like the ones in the Small Block Series (don't miss the albarino, syrah rosé, and orange muscat), produced via sustainable farming methods. In the wine store, French oak barrels line the walls. The concierge room provides tourist information and a phone for reservations. *4411 Redwood Rd., Napa.* ☎ *707/255-1144. www.hesscollection.com. Daily 10am–5:30pm (closed major holidays). Free self-guided art tours all day. Tastings: $20. Specialty tasting tours and classes: $35–$85 (reservations required). Map p 132.*

★ HKG Estate Wines SONOMA

The distinctive and old-fashioned hop-kiln structure is a California

Vineyards in St. Helena with Mt. St. Helena in the distance.

Historical Landmark, and was the basis for this winery's former name: Hop Kiln Winery. Built by Italian stonemasons in 1905 as a hop-drying barn, its three stone kilns point skyward, making this winery unmistakable and iconic. Its ranch-like, Western feel permeates the grounds, whether you're savoring wines in the rustic tasting room or picnicking at the old fig garden or by the duck pond. *6050 Westside Rd., Healdsburg.* ☎ *707/433-6491. www.hkgwines.com. Daily 10am–5pm. No tours. Tastings: $7. Map p 133.*

Honig Vineyard & Winery

NAPA *SUST* In addition to its normal winery tours, Honig hosts educational eco-walks through the vineyard to see the winery's sustainable agriculture methods: bat boxes, beehives, row management, and so on. Guides talk about trellising, pruning, growth cycles, and organic pest prevention. It's followed by wine tasting in the tasting room or on the patio. This midsize, family-run winery's award-winning sauvignon blanc and cabernet are handcrafted and blended. *850 Rutherford Rd., Rutherford.* ☎ *800/929-2217. www.honigwine.com. Daily 10am–4:30pm. Tours $30. Tastings start at $10 and are by appt. only. Map p 132.*

★ Imagery Estate Winery & Art Gallery SONOMA This is a

winery for art lovers—each bottle label is a tiny version of an original painting, commissioned specifically for the wine it hugs. Each must somehow include Benziger Estate's Parthenon replica, because Imagery is Benziger's sister winery and its winemaker is Joe Benziger. A curated collection of more than 175 artworks hangs in Imagery's gallery, a testament to the variety of small, uncommon wines (such as malbec, petite sirah, and viognier) produced here. There's a patio, a picnic lawn,

Wine tasting at Inglenook.

and a bocce ball court. *14335 Hwy. 12, Glen Ellen.* ☎ *707/935-4515. www.imagerywinery.com. Daily 10am–4:30pm (Sat–Sun open until 5:30pm). No tours. Tastings: $15. Map p 134.*

★★★ Inglenook NAPA *ORG, SULF*

Formerly Niebaum-Coppola and then the Rubicon Estate, this historic property—now known by its original 1879 moniker—is still owned by the Coppola family of filmmaking fame. Visitors enjoy wine tasting within original 1882 sandstone walls and access to the gardens and ivy-covered château. Founded in 1887 by Finnish seaman Gustave Niebaum, this remarkable winery offers five different tours, all of which highlight the property's understated glitziness. Try the winery's classics, like Blancaneaux, a viognier-roussanne-marsanne blend, or Rubicon, a cabernet sauvignon–dominated claret. *1991 St. Helena Hwy., Rutherford.* ☎ *707/ 968-1100. www.inglenook.com. Daily 10am–5pm. Tours range from free to $50 (call for schedule). Tastings start at $45; reservations strongly recommended. Map p 132.*

★★ Jordan Vineyard & Winery SONOMA

For the ultimate in classic, refined opulence—with a serious and stately tour and tasting to match—visit Jordan's stunning estate. Inspired by southwestern France's grand châteaux, oil magnate Tom Jordan's vine-covered winery was founded in 1972—though his son owns and runs it now. Spanning almost 1,200 acres (485 hectares), it's committed to cabernet sauvignon and chardonnay. During the free tour, you'll see that every detail is attended to—from the winery construction to the way the beautiful stainless-steel tanks line the fermentation room, to the seating under the patio's great oak trees, to the manicured grounds. The tour ends with a tasting in the cellar room. *1474 Alexander Valley Rd., Healdsburg.* ☎ *800/654-1213 or 707/431-5250. www.jordanwinery.com. Mon–Fri 8am–4:30pm, Sat–Sun 9am–3:30pm (reservations required for tours; closed Sun, Dec–Mar). Map p 133.*

Joseph Phelps Vineyards

NAPA *BIO* This state-of-the-art winery is a favorite stop for serious wine lovers. Tastings and seminars (called "Exceptional Wine Experiences") include blending, smelling,

The French chateau–style, ivy-covered tasting room of Jordan Winery in Healdsburg.

or a wine-themed history lesson. For a quicker experience, taste the fabulous flagship wine, Insignia, on the terrace. *200 Taplin Rd. (off the Silverado Trail), St. Helena.* ☎ *800/707-5789. www.jpvwines. com. Mon–Fri 9am–5pm; Sat–Sun 10am–4pm. Tastings start at $75. Mon–Fri 10am–3pm, Sat–Sun 10am–2:30pm, all by appt. only. Map p 132.*

★ **Kendall-Jackson Wine Center** SONOMA The Wine Center's picture-perfect manor is surrounded by gardens, including a culinary and sensory garden and a demonstration vineyard. Picnic grounds are in a 100-year-old walnut grove, but if you're hungry, consider the food-and-wine reserve tasting. At the recently remodeled Healdsburg tasting room, visitors can try any Kendall-Jackson offering, including its best: the Stature and Estate wines. *Wine Center: 5007 Fulton Rd., Fulton.* ☎ *707/571-7500. www.kj.com (tasting coupons on website). Daily 10am–5pm. Garden tours (free) daily 11am, 1 & 3pm. Tastings: $5–$15. Tasting Room: 241 Healdsburg Ave., Healdsburg.* ☎ *707/433-6000. Daily 11am–5pm tasting room; restaurant Wed–Sun 5:30–9pm (Sat & Sun 'til 9:30). Tastings: $10–$20. Map p 133.*

★ **Kenwood Vineyards** SONOMA **SULF, SUST** Though known for its reds, tastings at Kenwood include an array of varietals; the reserve chardonnays are often worth trying. The tasting room is in one of the winery's original 1906 structures—a farmhouse, actually. The interior, of course, has been redone; it's now cozy and welcoming. *9592 Sonoma Hwy. (Hwy. 12), Kenwood.* ☎ *707/833-5891. www. kenwoodvineyards.com. Daily 10am–5pm. Tours by appt. only. Tastings: $10–$30 (no appt. necessary). Map p 134.*

★★ **Korbel Champagne Cellars** SONOMA To see the very pretty grounds of America's oldest *méthode champenoise* champagne producer, take Korbel's tour. It starts at an old railroad station and includes the cellars and its History Museum. There's a rose garden tour (1–3pm; mid-Apr to mid-Oct), during which you'll see more than 1,000 flower varieties. The tasting room is humongous, and the sandwiches from the fancy deli are amazing. Of the wines to taste, the brut is the most popular, but the pinot grigio, a zesty cuvée, is more exclusive. Korbel is on the way to **Armstrong Redwoods State Natural Reserve** (see p 112), so the winery is surrounded by ancient redwoods. *13250 River Rd., Guerneville.*

Pond and vineyards at Kenwood in Sonoma.

☎ 707/824-7000. www.korbel.com. Daily 10am–4:30pm (closed major holidays). Free tours include a tasting and take place hourly 11am–3pm (no reservation needed). Map p 133.

★ Kunde Family Winery

SONOMA **SUST** Owned and run by fourth-generation Kundes, this winery produces estate-grown wines—a surefire bottle to take home is the reserve cabernet sauvignon. The wide tasting room, in a cow-barn replica, overlooks a reflecting pool with a fountain and nicely displays the winery's century-long history on the wall behind the bar. Available to buy are Kunde's popular cabernet chocolate cherries, a great dessert after picnicking on the oak-surrounded grounds. *9825 Sonoma Hwy. (Hwy. 12), Kenwood.* ☎ 707/833-5501. www.kunde.com. Daily 10:30am–4:30pm. Tours $20–$75 (barrel tasting, picnic, hiking & vineyard specialty tours) by appt. Tastings: $20–$40. Map p 134.

Ladera Vineyards NAPA This off-the-beaten-path winery, built in 1886 on Howell Mountain, was originally constructed as a gravity-flow facility. Estate tours begin in the gardens and end with tastings paired with artisan cheeses in the caves. *150 White Cottage Rd. S., Angwin.* ☎ 707/965-2445. www.laderavineyards.com. Tours: $75 daily 11am & 2pm. Tastings: $30 (reservations required) daily 10am–3pm. Map p 132.

★★★ Lasseter Family Winery

SONOMA **ORG** This patch of land has grown grapes since 1894. But a century later, the vineyards and winery were neglected to the point that they needed love and care to matter again. Enter John and Nancy Lasseter—yes, the same John Lasseter that runs Pixar and Disney Animation Studios (he directed or executive produced all

Tasting sparkling wine at Korbel champagne cellars.

their recent smash hits, including *Toy Story, Cars, Up,* and *Frozen*). The Lasseters acquired the property in 2002, but it took them until 2010 to be able to harvest organic grapes for production, and until 2011 to debut the redone winery. The eco-friendly building tips its hat to early California architecture—and though three generations of Lasseters work together to run production here, it's ultimately winemaker Julia Iantosca's skill that turns out the old-world, French-style masterpieces. Taste her fine varietals (alongside artisan cheeses) in the Wine Room, which displays the poster-style works of local artist Dennis Ziemienski, whose rich, colorful pieces are on Lasseter's labels. *1 Vintage Ln., Glen Ellen.* ☎ 707/933-2800. www.lasseterfamilywinery.com. Tastings start at $25; available daily, by appt. only, 10am–4pm. Map p 134.

★ Ledson Winery & Vineyards

SONOMA Known to locals as

"The Castle," Ledson is memorable for its fairy-tale-like architecture, complete with regal gates and a hyper-pruned fountain courtyard. In the Gothic Normandy–style behemoth of a structure, taste hand-crafted wines made from a wide range of small varietal lots at one of multiple bars. Its library and reserve wines are available only at the winery, so tote home the much-praised 2007 Estate Merlot Reserve (if you can afford it, that is: A 6-liter bottle sets you back $420). Hungry? There's picnic space and a gourmet market. *7335 Sonoma Hwy. (Hwy. 12), Kenwood.* ☎ *707/537-3810. www.ledson.com. Daily 10am–5pm. Tastings: $15–$20, no appt. necessary. Map p 134.*

★ Louis M. Martini Winery

NAPA   The winery's circa-1933 name notwithstanding, the drink it's best known for is cabernet sauvignon. Its whites, too, have made a name for themselves. Operated by third-generation Martinis (though it's now owned by Gallo), this tasting room was recently redesigned. Be sure to cap your tasting flight with the winery's 55-year-old tawny port. *254 St. Helena Hwy. (Hwy. 29), St. Helena.* ☎ *800/321-9463 or 707/968-3362. www.louismartini.com. Daily 10am–6pm (closed major holidays). Tours and tastings start at $35; book in advance. Tastings: $25–$40. Map p 132.*

★ Monticello Vineyards/ Corley Family Napa Valley

NAPA   For a just-off-the-beaten-path experience, choose Monticello. In its grand colonial-style Jefferson House (inspired by oenophile Thomas Jefferson), the Corley family hosts comparative seminars and private tastings featuring wines that have been served in the White House. This limited-production winery is known for its cabernet, chardonnay, pinot noir, and merlot. The sheltered picnic grove is a perfect lunch spot. *4242 Big Ranch Rd., Napa.* ☎ *707/253-2802. www. corleyfamilynapavalley.com. Daily 10am–4:30pm. Tastings from $25. Map p 132.*

★★ Mumm Napa

NAPA   Known for its sparkling wines, Mumm's glass-enclosed tasting room and its terrace are the places to sample Brut Prestige, Brut

Mumm's tasting room overlooking the vineyards.

Enjoying the view and cabernet sauvignon in Healdsburg.

Rose, or Santana Supernatural Brut (developed with Carlos Santana) while soaking in expansive valley views. Mumm's photography gallery includes many dramatic Ansel Adams works and rotating exhibits in long, Spanish-style hallways. Tours visit the demonstration vineyard and winery, where guides demystify *méthode champenoise.* 8445 Silverado Trail, Rutherford. ☎ 707/967-7700. www.mummnapa. com. Daily 10am–5:45pm. Tours 10 & 11am, 1 & 3pm. Tastings: $8–$45. Map p 132.

★★ Opus One NAPA *BIO* Opus One is synonymous with luxury—not surprising, given that two huge names founded it: Robert Mondavi (d. 2008) and Baron Philip de Rothschild (d. 1988). Today, Baroness Philippine de Rothschild (Philip's daughter) helps run the place—and what a place. Striking architecture blends Californian and European influences, the salon is plush and opulent, and views from the rooftop deck are unsurpassed. Though the tasting fee is steep, it comes into context when you learn that in 1981, a single case sold for $24,000. Always accessible to the average visitor is the current vintage, usually a preponderance of ripe cabernet

sauvignon blended with smaller quantities of merlot, malbec, petit verdot, and cabernet franc. *7900 St. Helena Hwy., Oakville.* ☎ *707/944-9442. www.opusonewinery.com. Daily 10am–4pm (closed major holidays). Tours are customized and require reservation via phone (no online bookings). Tastings of current vintage $45 per glass, by online reservation. Map p 132.*

Paradise Ridge Winery SONOMA This family-owned boutique winery on a hill devotes itself to art almost as ardently as it does to wine (small lots of cabernet, sauvignon blanc, and chardonnay). Among the oaks is a sculpture grove with abstract metal works. The champagne cellar houses a tribute to Kanaye Nagasawa, who produced the majority of Sonoma County wine in the late 1800s. Come for the spectacular view—you can see Point Reyes from here. *www.prwinery.com. Santa Rosa: 4545 Thomas Lake Harris Dr., Santa Rosa.* ☎ *707/528-9463. Daily 11am–5pm. Kenwood: 8860 Sonoma Hwy., Kenwood.* ☎ *707/282-9020. Daily 11am–6pm. Self-guided tours only. Tastings: $15–$25 (some refunded w/purchase). Map p 133.*

★ **Paraduxx Winery** NAPA
SUST This winery has a sunny, chic sit-down tasting room where personable wine educators pour red wine (a zinfandel-cabernet blend) into stemless glasses. Also provided are local artisan foods to pair with the wine. *7257 Silverado Trail, Napa.* ☎ *866/367-9943. www.paraduxx. com. Daily 10am–4pm. No tours. Tastings: $20–$60 by appt. Map p 132.*

Peju Province Winery NAPA
ORG Beautiful gardens and unique architecture are a big draw here; sculptures and fountains are featured throughout the lush grounds, while a 50-foot (15m) tower houses the tasting room. Ask the musically inclined tasting-room staff to pour samples of Peju's artisan red wines, like the summery carignan, or opt for the food-and-wine pairing, offered only on weekdays. Though this winery stays open later than most, it gets crowded in the late afternoon, especially on weekends. *8466 St. Helena Hwy. (Hwy. 29), Rutherford.* ☎ *800/446-7358. www.peju.com. Daily 10am–6pm (closed major holidays). Tastings: $10 (refunded with purchase); specialty tastings $25–$65 by appt. Map p 132.*

★ **PlumpJack Winery** NAPA
This hip winery, founded in a partnership between oil heir Gordon Getty and politician Gavin Newsom, has always been progressive in its approach to winemaking: It started the trend of using screw caps instead of corks on cabernet sauvignon. The full-bodied, berry-tinged cabernet sauvignons are proof that the system works. The best part? PlumpJack offers reasonably priced bottles to take home. *620 Oakville Cross Rd., Oakville.* ☎ *707/945-1220. www.plumpjack winery.com. Daily 10am–4pm. No tours. Tastings: $15. Map p 132.*

Provenance Vineyards
NAPA Provenance's deep-red building matches the wines it's known for (though winemaker Trevor Durling does make one white, a heck of a sauvignon blanc). The well-lit, cleanly designed tasting room opened in late 2003 and now includes an expansive patio (including fire pit), allowing guests to enjoy their tasting while taking in views of picturesque Rutherford. When in the tasting room, be sure to look down while sipping these handcrafted wines—the floor is made entirely of recycled oak

Mondavi and Rothschild's Opus One Winery.

Barrels at Paraduxx Winery.

barrels. Tours include the cellar and vineyard. *1695 St. Helena Hwy. (Hwy. 29), Rutherford. ☎ 707/968-3633. www.provenancevineyards. com. Daily 10am–5pm (closed major holidays). Tastings: $20. Map p 132.*

★ Ravenswood Winery

SONOMA This family-owned winery's "no wimpy wines" slogan holds true—these bold zins pack a punch. The tasting room is less than a mile from Sonoma Plaza and tours include up-close views of the vines and barrel tasting in the cellar. *18701 Gehricke Rd., Sonoma. ☎ 707/ 933-2332. www.ravenswoodwinery. com. Daily 10am–4:30pm. Tours ($25) daily at 10:30am (reservations required). Tastings: $18. Map p 134.*

Raymond Vineyards NAPA

SUST The Raymonds are fifth-generation winemakers with lineage tracing them to Jacob Beringer. They founded this estate in 1971 between Rutherford and St. Helena. Taste current releases and library vintages of the winery's

cabernet, zinfandel, merlot, and chardonnay. *849 Zinfandel Lane, St. Helena. ☎ 707/963-3141. www. raymondvineyards.com. Daily 10am–4pm. Self-guided tours. Tastings: $25 by appt. Private winery tour and tasting: $50. Map p 132.*

Robert Craig Winery NAPA

Though Robert Craig's winery isn't open to the public, fans of his upscale mountain cabernet can visit the tasting room in downtown Napa. Call ahead to schedule a personalized sit-down tasting and get ready for wines served in restaurants of French Laundry caliber. His cabernet sauvignon offerings tend to have an enveloping mahogany essence. Weekend open houses with barrel tastings happen whenever new vintages are released. *880 Vallejo St., Napa. Tasting Room: 625 Imperial Way. ☎ 707/252-2250. www.robertcraigwine.com. Mon–Sat 10am–4pm & Sun 11am–4pm by appt. No tours. Tastings: $25 (credited toward wine purchase). Map p 132.*

★★ Robert Mondavi Winery

NAPA Robert Mondavi is Napa's most powerful winery in terms of sheer size and strength. This is perhaps because the man himself (Mondavi, that is) pioneered the concept of public tastings; everyone else followed. Still devoted to wine education, this mission-style complex has three tasting rooms and an array of tours, from one focusing on flavor profiling to another ending with a gourmet three-course meal. Try the fumé blanc (Mondavi coined the term) and the reserve cabernet, then enjoy the rotating art exhibit or, if it's summer, a music concert—check the website for the full schedule. *7801 St. Helena Hwy. (Hwy. 29), Oakville. ☎ 888/766-6328. www.robertmondavi.com. Daily 10am–5pm (closed major holidays).*

Call for tour schedule ($20–$50). Walk-in tastings: $5–$30. Map p 132.

St. Clement Vineyards NAPA This winery, once owned by Charles Krug and now part of the Beringer Wine Estates, uses fruit from independent growers to make its reds and whites. The cabernets are the winery's stars. Imbibe at the hospitality center in the New England–style Rosenbaum House, built in 1878. Relax afterward on the veranda or at picnic tables. *2867 St. Helena Hwy. (Hwy. 29), St. Helena.* ☎ *866/877-5939. www. stclement.com. Thurs–Mon 11am–5pm (closed Tues & Wed). Tastings: $35, daily 11am–5pm (reservations recommended). Map p 132.*

★ **St. Francis Winery & Vineyards** SONOMA *SUST* At the foot of Hood Mountain, this mission-style winery offers views as enjoyable as its wine. "The House of Big Reds," as it's known, offers three tasting experiences, the most expensive of which pairs reserve zins, merlots, and cabernets with executive chef Bryan Jones' gourmet small plates. *100 Pythian Rd., Santa Rosa.* ☎ *888/675-WINE [9463], ext. 242. www.stfranciswinery. com. Daily 10am–5pm (closed major*

holidays). Tours available upon reservation. Wine tastings: $15; wine & charcuterie: $35; wine & food pairing: $68. Map p 134.

kids St. Supéry Winery NAPA Known for its meritage whites and reds, the emphasis at St. Supéry, besides wine production, is educating visitors. Don't be put off by the Atkinson House's somewhat nondescript exterior; inside is a beautiful art gallery and informative displays. Near the house, there are family-friendly picnic grounds. *8440 St. Helena Hwy. (Hwy. 29), Rutherford.* ☎ *800/942-0809. www.stsupery. com. Daily 10am–5pm (closed major holidays). Guided winemaker's tour $35, advance notice of 24 hours required. Tastings: $20–$30. Reservations recommended. Map p 132.*

★★ **Schramsberg Vineyards** NAPA California Historical Landmark No. 561 earned the distinction for its founding date (1862) plus its rich history: Robert Louis Stevenson was so inspired by his 1880 visit that he included Schramsberg in *The Silverado Squatters*. Today, the sparkling wines are so venerable that U.S. presidents present them to foreign dignitaries. Tours feature

St. Clement is a great stop for a picnic with vineyard views.

hand-carved champagne caves housing 2 million bottles. At tables in the wood-paneled tasting room, seated visitors taste four Schramsberg sparkling wines, plus one still vintage from Davies Vineyards. *1400 Schramsberg Rd., Calistoga.* ☎ *707/942-4558. www.schramsberg.com. Daily 9:30am–4:30pm. Guided tour & tasting: $60, daily by appt. Map p 132.*

★ Schug Carneros Estate Winery SONOMA

Founded in 1980, this family-owned winery's specialty is French-style pinot noir and chardonnay. Try them in the small tasting room, which is in a German-style timber-frame building. Afterward, picnic at tables near an herb garden, visit the duck pond, or merely take in the view; if it's a clear day, try to spot Mt. Diablo in the distance. *602 Bonneau Rd., Sonoma.* ☎ *800/966-9365. www.schugwinery.com. Daily 10am–5pm. Tours available by appt. Tastings: $10. Map p 134.*

★★ Sebastiani Vineyards & Winery SONOMA

Sonoma's oldest family-owned winery was founded in 1904 by Samuele Sebastiani, though the vineyards have been here since 1825. At the large tasting room, try the winery's specialties: cabernet, merlot, and barbera. The grounds display examples of antique winemaking equipment, including the winery's original press. *Tip:* Sebastiani is 4 blocks from Sonoma Plaza, so park at the winery and walk into town, since parking can be difficult during high season. *389 4th St. E., Sonoma.* ☎ *707/933-3230. www.sebastiani. com. Daily 11am–5pm. Free tours at 11am & 1pm. Tastings: $10–$15; tour, tasting & lunch, or wine & cheese tasting: $35–$75. Map p 134.*

Sebastopol Vineyards/Dutton Estate SONOMA

Taste Sebastopol Vineyards' Russian River Valley chardonnay, pinot noir, and syrah in the Spanish-style hospitality center surrounded by palm trees. Picnic grounds available. *8757 Green Valley Rd. (at Hwy. 116), Sebastopol.* ☎ *707/829-9463. www. sebastopolvineyards.com. Daily 10am–4:30pm. No tours. Tastings: $10–$40. Map p 133.*

★ Shafer Vineyards NAPA SUST

Though you have to make reservations 4 to 6 weeks in advance for this 90-minute visit, it's worth it to see Shafer's cellar, cave, barrel room, and sustainably farmed vineyards and to try six Shafer wines, including the stunning Hillside Select. The bright, intimate tasting room has a fireplace and serene vineyard views. *6154 Silverado Trail, Napa.* ☎ *707/944-2877. www. shafervineyards.com. Retail sales Mon–Fri 9am–noon, 1–4pm. Tours & tasting: $55, Mon–Fri 10am & 2pm by reservation only. Map p 132.*

★ Simi Winery SONOMA

After encountering a UC Davis enology professor at a wine festival, Steve Reeder transferred colleges to learn how to make wine. His creations (chardonnay, cabernet, and sauvignon blanc) are the focal point of Simi's redwood-paneled tasting room. Tours include stone cellars and discussions on how Italian brothers Giuseppe and Pietro founded Simi in 1876—they'd come for the Gold Rush but discovered another California treasure: grapes. For picnics, there's a grove with 70-year-old redwoods. *16275 Healdsburg Ave., Healdsburg.* ☎ *800/746-4880. www.simiwinery. com. Daily 10am–5pm. Tours: $15, daily 11am & 2pm. Tastings: $10 or $3 a la carte. Map p 133.*

★★ Sterling Vineyards SONOMA

The most distinctive part of this winery is the aerial

gondola that takes you there, providing far-reaching views of Napa Valley. Just this alone is worth the $29 to get in ($15 if you're younger than 21). Admission also includes a self-guided tour that includes wine-related art and artifacts (videos and placards provide info). A reserve tour and tasting is $39 and includes a sit-down wine sampling in the upstairs Rotunda. *1111 Dunaweal Lane, Calistoga.* ☎ *707/942-3300. www.sterlingvineyards.com. Mon–Fri 10:30am–4:30pm; Sat–Sun 10am-5pm (closed major holidays). General tour and tasting: $25 (includes gondola ride, self-guided tour, and tasting). Map p 132.*

★ **Stryker Sonoma** SONOMA Friendly, young Stryker Sonoma exudes a fresh, modern vibe. When you arrive at its slatted-wood walkway, walk up to sit at its sleek curved bar, look up at the lofted wood ceiling, order a taste of cabernet sauvignon, and gaze out at the vines through the floor-to-ceiling windows. If you tire of the view (impossible, though), cross the mahogany-stained cement floor and peer through the windows overlooking the barrel room below. *Note:* Stryker sells only out of its tasting room, online, and, per winemaker Tim Hardin, "to a few local restaurants we like." *5110 Hwy. 128, Geyserville.* ☎ *707/433-1944. www. strykersonoma.com. Daily 10:30am– 5pm. Tastings: $10–$40, reservations recommended. Map p 133.*

★ **Sutter Home Winery** NAPA **ORG, SUST** Built in 1874 and founded as a winery in 1890, Sutter Home was bought in 1947 by the Trinchero family, who claim to have invented white zinfandel in 1972. Today, similar blush-colored wines characterize the winery's specialties. The tasting room is in the original 1874 building. The organic

White Zinfandel garden, with its handsome gazebo, nurtures 125 rose species, and century-old palm trees flank the manor. This family winery takes environmental responsibility quite seriously, from its sustainable vineyard and water-conservation practices to its recyclable, low-emission packaging and winery-wide recycling. *277 St. Helena Hwy. (Hwy. 29), St. Helena.* ☎ *707/963-3104, ext. 4208. www. sutterhome.com. Daily 10am–5pm. Free self-guided garden tours all day. Free tastings. Map p 132.*

Tin Barn Vineyards SONOMA Adding to the trend toward wineries self-contained in warehouses is Tin Barn, which is family-owned and eager to show off its facility. Book the hands-on tour, which will take you above massive fermenting tanks and let you sample wines right from the barrel. The no-frills, tin-topped tasting room has a metal-and-wood tasting bar, over which small-lot zinfandel, cabernet, syrah, and sauvignon blanc are

Cabernet sauvignon grapes.

expertly paired with local cheeses. *21692 8th St. E., #340, Sonoma.* ☎ *707/938-5430. www.tinbarn vineyards.com. Fri–Mon noon–5pm. Tastings: $12 (online reservation recommended). Map p 134.*

★ Trefethen Vineyards NAPA

Trefethen was designed and built in 1886 by Scottish seaman Hamden McIntyre, who also designed Far Niente, Rubicon Estate, and the Culinary Institute of America. An old-fashioned wooden gravity-flow winery helped the winery qualify for the National Register of Historic Places. Try its riesling, viognier, and chardonnay. **Note:** At press time, the tasting room at the address below was still closed due to earthquake damage, but spokespeople for the winery assured us that if you call the toll-free number, someone will tell you where to go for a tasting—and that same-day appointments are often available. *1160 Oak Knoll Ave., Napa.* ☎ *866/895-7696. www.trefethen.com. Daily 10am–4:30pm. Tastings: $15–$25. Map p 132.*

★★ V. Sattui Winery NAPA In

1885, Vittorio Sattui established his winery in San Francisco. When Prohibition was enacted, he said, "I'll do nothing against the law" and shut the operation down. In 1976, his descendants reopened the winery in St. Helena. In the large, festive tasting room, a fourth-generation Sattui is likely to pour your wine. V. Sattui's wines aren't sold in shops or restaurants, so stock up here on vintages like the interestingly dry rosés. If you buy food at the gourmet deli (lots of free nibbles to try), you can use the picnic grounds, where giant oaks provide shade and beauty. *1111 White Lane, St. Helena.* ☎ *707/963-7774. www.vsattui.com. Daily 9am–5pm. Tours: $30 for adults, $15 for*

children; Fri–Sun 1pm. Tastings: $15. Map p 132.*

Viader Vineyards and Winery

NAPA **BIO** On 1,300-foot-high (390m) Howell Mountain, Delia Viader's winery affords stunning valley views from its terrace. The tasting fee includes all five of her high-end wines, including hard-to-find "V," a blend of Petit Verdot and cabernet. *1120 Deer Park Rd., Deer Park.* ☎ *707/963-3816. www. viader.com. Daily 10am–4:30pm. Tastings: $50–$100 (by appt.). Daily cave tour at 10am (by appt.). Map p 132.*

★★ Viansa Sonoma Winery

SONOMA Founded in 1989 by Vicki and Sam Sebastiani (the winery's moniker is an amalgam of their first names), this Tuscan-style hilltop estate features signature Sonoma Valley wines, including pinot noir, chardonnay, and cab franc. It also has a deli that sells excellent sandwiches and, sometimes, tours into the underground cellars. An old-world marketplace offers comprehensive wine tastings and plenty of fresh food samples. *25200 Arnold Dr. (Hwy. 121), Sonoma.* ☎ *800/995-4740. www. viansa.com. Daily 10am–5pm. Tastings: $5–$10. Map p 134.*

ZD Wines NAPA ORG Every

day, ZD offers a seated experience ($40) it calls "UnWined," during which visitors choose wines from a long menu—an expert guides you through the options and gives you the vineyard-to-glass history of any of the vintages you're interested in. We recommend trying Abacus, hands down the winery's best cabernet, at the wood-paneled tasting bar. *8383 Silverado Trail, Napa.* ☎ *800/487-7757. www.zdwines.com. Daily 10am–4pm. Tours and tastings start at $40 by appt. Map p 132.*

The Best of San Francisco
in One Day

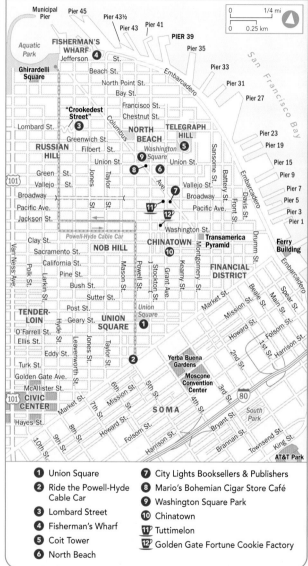

1 Union Square
2 Ride the Powell-Hyde Cable Car
3 Lombard Street
4 Fisherman's Wharf
5 Coit Tower
6 North Beach
7 City Lights Booksellers & Publishers
8 Mario's Bohemian Cigar Store Café
9 Washington Square Park
10 Chinatown
11 Tuttimelon
12 Golden Gate Fortune Cookie Factory

Previous page: San Francisco Golden Gate Bridge from Marshall Beach.

San Francisco has earned its reputation as America's most beautiful city. This first full-day tour introduces you to its four famous neighborhoods: Union Square, Fisherman's Wharf, North Beach, and Chinatown. After getting to Fisherman's Wharf, you can do the rest on foot—but public transportation options are listed just in case. START: BART/Muni: Powell or Montgomery. Bus: 2, 3, 4, or 38 to Powell St.; 30 or 45 to Geary St. Cable car: Powell lines.

❶ ★★ Union Square. Start your tour at this lively urban square, named for a series of uproarious pro-Union demonstrations staged here on the eve of the Civil War. In 2002, a $25-million restoration replaced stretches of lawn with a 245-foot-long (74m) granite floor and scattered greenery, turning it into a welcoming and memorable plaza. All that remains from the old square is the 90-foot (27m) Victory tower, dedicated by Theodore Roosevelt after the Spanish-American War. In winter, the square gets decked out with thousands of twinkling adornments, including a colossal Christmas tree. ⏱ *30 min.; best before 9am. Btw. Post, Geary, Stockton & Powell sts. BART: Powell or Montgomery. Bus: 2, 3, 4, or 38 to Powell St.; 30 or 45 to Geary St. Cable car: Powell lines.*

❷ ★ kids Ride the Powell-Hyde Cable Car. Head to the cable-car turnaround at Powell and Market streets and hop on the Powell-Hyde line. The first of these engineless,

Riding a cable car is one of San Francisco's most memorable activities.

Lombard Street is known as the crooked-est street in the world.

open-air vehicles started running in 1873. As the cable car takes you over Russian Hill, pay attention as you crest Hyde Street at Greenwich Street—you'll catch your first glimpse of the beautiful San Francisco Bay and its storied Alcatraz Island. ⏱ *30 min.; best before 9:30am. Powell & Market sts. $7 per ride.*

❸ ★ Lombard Street. "The crookedest street in the world" is in fact not even the crookedest street in San Francisco (Vermont St. between 20th and 22nd sts. in Potrero Hill is curvier). Zigzags were added in the 1920s because the street's 27-degree pitch was too steep for automobiles. Cars are permitted only to descend, but pedestrians can take the stairs up or down on either side. The street is loveliest in spring, when the hydrangeas bloom. ⏱ *30 min.; best weekday mornings. Lombard St. (btw. Hyde & Leavenworth sts.). Cable car: Powell-Hyde line.*

❹ ★★ Fisherman's Wharf. San Francisco's most visited attraction has history and lots to do. Though the wharf is rife with tacky souvenir shops and overpriced restaurants, it's still a must-see. Consider the following mini-tour, which highlights the wharf's most scenic spots and keeps time near the throngs to a minimum. *Hyde & Beach sts. www.fishermans* *wharf.org. Cable car: Powell-Hyde line to Fisherman's Wharf, Powell-Mason line to Taylor & Bay sts.; F streetcar to Jones & Beach sts. Bus 10, 30, or 47 to Van Ness Ave. & N. Point St.; 19 to Polk & Beach sts.*

4A Victorian Park is where you'll alight from the cable car. Peruse the arts and crafts for sale as you walk toward **4B Ghirardelli Square,** built in 1893 as Domingo Ghirardelli's chocolate factory. When the factory relocated in the 1960s, the building became a National Historic Landmark and now houses charming shops and eateries. The recently renovated **4C Maritime Museum,** a three-story Art Deco structure shaped like an ocean liner, offers a free look at the city's seafaring past. A walk along **4D Municipal Pier** affords excellent views of the Golden Gate Bridge and of **4E Hyde Street Pier,** which berths refurbished antique ships, including a 19th-century square-rigger. **4F The Cannery,** once a fruit-canning facility (hence the name), now houses stores, restaurants, and the National Maritime Visitors Center. At **4G ★ Kids Boudin Bakery,** which has been cranking out sourdough since 1849, order chowder in a bread bowl. Now that you're fortified, go brave the happy crowds at **4H Pier 39.** The cluster of vocal sea lions at the end of the pier are a sight to behold. ⏱ *2–3 hr.; go in the morning to beat the crowds.*

The interior of Coit Tower contains murals painted by local artists as part of a WPA project in the 1930s.

5 Coit Tower. The 210-foot (63m) landmark atop Telegraph Hill was erected in 1933 with $125,000 bequeathed by local character Lillie Hitchcock Coit, who wished to add beauty to the city. Inside the tower's base are murals by several artists who studied under Diego Rivera. Commissioned as part of the New Deal, the murals have a pro-worker motif that caused a stir in their day. The fee to ascend the tower is worth it: A 360-degree city view awaits. While on Telegraph Hill, try to spot (or hear) its large flock of green parrots; no one's quite sure how they got here. ⏱ *45 min. From Fisherman's Wharf, walk or take bus 39 to Coit Tower.* ☎ *415/362-0808. Admission to the top $8 adults, $5 seniors, $5 ages 12–17, $2 ages 5–11, free for kids younger than 5. Daily 10am–6pm (10am–5pm Nov–Apr).*

6 ★★ North Beach. Immigrants from Genoa and Sicily who pioneered the Bay Area's fishing industry settled here in the 1870s, establishing a lively array of Italian restaurants, cafes, bakeries, and bars. In the 1950s, these spots became havens for some of the era's most influential writers and artists. Today, the neighborhood exudes a combination of Mediterranean warmth and bohemian spirit. Step into the famous **7 City Lights Booksellers & Publishers** (at 261 Columbus Ave.; see p 186), a great bookstore that's also an intimate tribute to Beat literature. ⏱ *1–2 hr. Best Mon–Sat from 11am–4pm. Walk from Chinatown.*

Coit Tower, or take bus 39 to Washington Sq. Shops are closed Sun & early mornings.

8 Mario's Bohemian Cigar Store Café. Pick up sandwiches here and enjoy them in **9 Washington Square Park** across the street. *566 Columbus Ave. (at Union St.).* ☎ *415/362-0536. $.*

10 ★ Chinatown. More than 15,000 people live in San Francisco's most densely populated neighborhood. Walk down Grant Street for eclectic knickknacks and imports, and Stockton Street for authentic eateries, fragrant grocery stores, and herb shops. At the end of these teeming streets, try the bubble tea at **11 Tuttimelon** *(601 Broadway;* ☎ *415/398-2996; $).*

At 56 Ross Alley (btw. Washington and Jackson sts.) is **12 ★★ Golden Gate Fortune Cookie Factory,** a hidden treasure where you can sample and buy prophetic confections.

The Best of San Francisco in Two Days

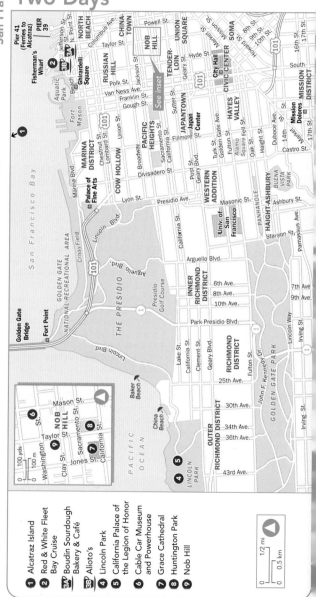

1. Alcatraz Island
2. Red & White Fleet Bay Cruise
3A. Boudin Sourdough Bakery & Café
3B. Alioto's
4. Lincoln Park
5. California Palace of the Legion of Honor
6. Cable Car Museum and Powerhouse
7. Grace Cathedral
8. Huntington Park
9. Nob Hill

If you have 2 days to spend in San Francisco, plan your first day as detailed on p 163. On your second day, start with a major highlight—a visit to Alcatraz. Reserved tickets are required, but if you didn't plan ahead, an alternative bay cruise is listed below. After Alcatraz (or the cruise), visit Lincoln Park, a less visited but still striking corner of the city, and if time permits, relive the glories of 19th-century San Francisco on Nob Hill. **START: Pier 41, Fisherman's Wharf. Cable car: Powell-Mason. Bus: 30. Streetcar: F.**

❶ ★★★ Alcatraz Island.

Beginning in 1934, this island housed a maximum-security prison for the country's most hardened criminals, including Al Capone, "Machine Gun" Kelly, and Robert "The Birdman" Stroud. Given its sheer cliffs, frigid waters, and treacherous currents, Alcatraz was considered inescapable. However, the prison's upkeep cost a fortune; all supplies had to come by boat. After three convicted bank robbers escaped in 1962 using sharpened spoons and a makeshift raft, the prison closed. The island remained unoccupied until 1969, when Native Americans took it over, bringing their civil-rights issues to the forefront. They were removed in 1971, but not before Congress passed more than 50 legislative proposals supporting tribal self-rule. Today, the National Park Service manages Alcatraz. Once there, you'll receive a headset that plays an audio tour that includes riveting tales from former guards and inmates. From October to mid-February, you can tour the island on a walking path. For an eerie evening experience, take the "Alcatraz After Hours" tour. ⏱ *2–3 hr., including ferry ride. Take the first ferry of the day, if possible. Wear a jacket & walking shoes; it's an uphill walk from the ferry landing to the cellblock (motorized carts carry visitors who need them). The ferry sells snacks, but there's no food on the island. Pier 33 at 1398 Embarcadero (at Bay St.), Fisherman's Wharf.* ☎ *415/981-7625. www.nps.gov/alcatraz. Tip: The early-bird 9am tour (which actually departs at 8:45am) is the least crowded. Admission (ferry & audio tour): $31 adult, $29 seniors 62+, $31 kids 12–17, $19 kids 5–11, free for kids 4 & younger,*

Alcatraz Island is in the middle of San Francisco Bay.

$94 family (two adults & two kids ages 5–11). Night tours and combination Alcatraz & Angel Island tours are additional. Ferries run approx. every half-hour, though departure times change frequently, so check www. alcatrazcruises.com before planning your day. Arrive 30 min. before departure in summer (45 min. in winter). Bus: 8X or 47 (then walk a block or 2). Cable car: Powell-Mason line (then walk 6 blocks or transfer to streetcar). Streetcar: F (to Bay St. stop).

➋ ★ kids Red & White Fleet Bay Cruise. If you were unable to pre-reserve Alcatraz tickets, take this 1-hour bay cruise (named after Stanford University's school colors) with audio narration. You'll travel under the Golden Gate Bridge and around Alcatraz. ◷ *1 hr. Pier 43½.* ☎ *415/ 673-2900. www.redandwhite.com. Ferry ride & audio tour: $30 adults, $20 youth 5–17, free for children 4 & younger. Transport: see bullet ➊.*

No San Francisco visit is complete without trying the city's famous bread. If you skipped it yesterday, eat at **3A ★ kids Boudin Sourdough Bakery & Café** today. *160 Jefferson St.* ☎ *415/928-1849. $.* Otherwise, head to **3B Alioto's** for a sit-down Italian meal with a view. *No. 8 Fisherman's Wharf at Taylor St.* ☎ *415/673-0183. $$.*

➍ Lincoln Park. This lovely park in the city's northwest corner has expansive lawns, eucalyptus trees, an 18-hole golf course, and gorgeous ocean views. Walk north to the Land's End trail head for a view of the Marin Headlands—and the world's most famous bridge. It's best in the afternoon, when the fog has burned off and the sun makes the Marin hills appear golden. ◷ *30 min. Clement & 33rd aves.*

Fisherman's Wharf.

Powell-Hyde cable car to Geary St., transfer to bus 38 to Geary Blvd. & 33rd Ave.; then walk or take bus 18 to Legion of Honor. To save time (but not money), you may want to catch a taxi.

➎ ★★ California Palace of the Legion of Honor. Adding to Lincoln Park's splendor is this neoclassical memorial to California soldiers who died in World War I. This replica of Paris's Legion of Honor Palace opened on Armistice Day in 1924. Its fine-art collection spans 4,000 years and includes Monets and Rembrandts, plus tapestries, prints, and drawings from around the globe. The world-class collection of Rodin sculptures includes an original cast of *The Thinker*. ◷ *1 hr. 100 34th Ave. (at Clement St., then into Lincoln Park).* ☎ *415/ 750-3600. www.thinker.org. Admission $10 adults, $7 seniors 65+, $6 youths 13–17, free for kids 12 and younger, free to all first Tues of each month. Tues–Sun 9:30am–5:15pm. Transport: See bullet ➍.*

➏ kids Cable Car Museum and Powerhouse. When British-born engineer Andrew Hallidie saw a horse and its heavy carriage fall backward down a steep San Francisco hill, he vowed to create a mechanical transportation device for the city. By 1873, the first cable car had scaled Clay Street. Cable cars have no engines—instead, they're attached to an electrically powered cable that runs at a constant 9½-mph (15kph) rate through an underground rail. When it's time to stop, the car's conductor, or "gripper," pulls a lever to release the car's grip on the cable. Inside this free, fascinating museum, you'll see the cables that carry the cars. 🕐 *20 min. 1201 Mason St. (at Washington St.).* ☎ *415/474-1887. www. cablecarmuseum.org. Free admission. Daily 10am–5pm; until 6pm Apr– Sept. Closed major holidays. From Lyon & Greenwich sts., take the 45 bus toward Caltrain, then transfer to the Powell-Mason cable car. Or, to save time, take a cab or an Uber from the Legion of Honor.*

❼ ★★ Grace Cathedral. After the Crocker mansion was destroyed by the 1906 earthquake and subsequent fires, the Crockers donated its site to the Episcopal Church. In 1964, Grace Cathedral was complete. Pay special attention to the main doors—stunning replicas of Ghiberti's bronze *Gates of Paradise* on the Baptistery of Florence—and the Singing Tower to the right of the main entrance, with its 44-bell carillon. The cathedral's exterior is made of reinforced concrete beaten to achieve a stone-like effect. Inside, notice the 1840 organ and the impressive stained-glass windows, some of which depict

modern figures such as Thurgood Marshall, Robert Frost (a San Francisco native), and Albert Einstein. 🕐 *25 min. 1100 California St. (at Taylor St.).* ☎ *415/749-6300. www. gracecathedral.org (check website for free docent-led tours). Free admission. Opens daily by 8am; closing hours vary—check website. Bus: 1. Walk or take any cable-car line.*

❽ kids Huntington Park. David Colton, who helped build the Southern Pacific Railroad, had his mansion here until he sold it to a fellow railroad magnate, Collis Huntington, in 1892. The mansion burned as a result of the 1906 quake. Today, the park is a lovely urban oasis. It's still framed by the granite walls that were part of the Colton estate. 🕐 *15 min. Taylor & California sts. Bus: 1. Cable car: All lines.*

❾ Nob Hill. This famous hillcrest neighborhood is named for its wealthy former residents, or "nabobs," as San Francisco elites were then known (today, hipsters take to calling this "snob hill"). Look around to see some of the city's most prestigious hotels and, for a magnificent view of the city (and perhaps a tasty nightcap), head up to the InterContinental's **Top of the Mark** (see p 191), a memorable penthouse lounge. 🕐 *20 min. Taylor & Sacramento sts. Bus: 1 from Clement St. & 33rd Ave. to Taylor & Sacramento sts.*

Legion of Honor museum.

The Best of San Francisco in Three Days

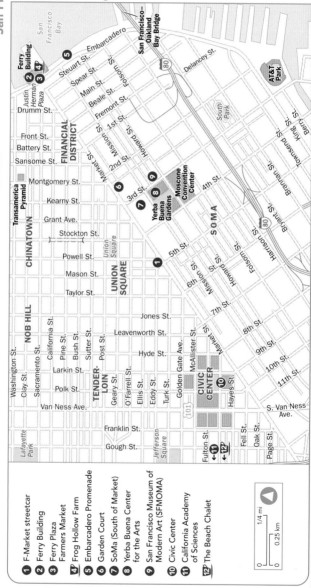

1 F-Market streetcar
2 Ferry Building
3 Ferry Plaza Farmers Market
4 Frog Hollow Farm
5 Embarcadero Promenade
6 Garden Court
7 SoMa (South of Market)
8 Yerba Buena Center for the Arts
9 San Francisco Museum of Modern Art (SFMOMA)
10 Civic Center
11 California Academy of Sciences
12 The Beach Chalet

If you've already made your way through "The Best in Two Days," you'll find that this third full-day tour gives you a taste of the city's epicurean underpinnings, as well as its rich artistic and cultural life. It can be done on foot, though the antique F-Market streetcars are attractions unto themselves. **Note:** Though the Civic Center is just a few blocks from SoMa, the east–west blocks are quite long. START: **From Union Square, hop on the F-Market streetcar at the Powell St. station. Exit at the Ferry Terminal loop.**

① ★ Kids F-Market streetcar. These colorful, character-filled cars rumble up and down Market Street and along the bay's bustling, scenic waterfront. The vintage trolleys were imported from around the world, so take a look to see which city yours is from. ○ *15 min. From Union Square, enter at the Powell St. station; exit at the Ferry Terminal loop. Fare $2.25 adults, 75¢ seniors 65+ & kids 5–17. Free for kids younger than 5. Avoid rush hour (Mon–Fri, before 9:30am & 4:30–6:30pm).*

② ★★ Ferry Building. This 1898 building has a 240-foot (72m) clock tower. Inside, gourmet boutiques sell an impressive array of specialty foods. Make your way to the back of the building for a view of the Bay Bridge—try to visit on a farmers' market day (see below). ○ *1 hr. 1 Ferry Building (at the Embarcadero & Market St.). Minimum hours: Mon–Fri 10am–6pm; Sat 9am–6pm; Sun 11am–5pm (hours for individual businesses may vary). www.ferrybuildingmarket place.com. F or any Market St. street-car to the Ferry Bldg. or Embarcadero; bus 2, 7, 14, 21, 66, or 71 to Steuart & Market sts. Also see p 187.*

③ ★★★ Ferry Plaza Farmers Market. Tuesdays and Saturdays (and from spring to fall, Thursdays and Sundays too), dozens of regional food producers set up booths just outside the Ferry Building. Saturday mornings are busiest, as locals make their regular trek to stock up on fruits and vegetables, fresh-baked

goods, handcrafted cheeses, and ready-to-bloom flowers. Saturdays also bring booths from which city restaurants serve gourmet break-fasts. ○ *1 hr. 1 Ferry Building (at the Embarcadero & Market St.).* ☎ *415/ 291-3276. Tues & Thurs 10am–2pm; Sat 8am–2pm. Also see p 187.*

④ Frog Hollow Farm. Grab coffee and a fruit-filled pastry here before strolling the scenic water-front. *Ferry Building Marketplace.* ☎ *415/445-0990. $.*

⑤ ★ Embarcadero Promenade. This lovely stretch of waterfront extends from AT&T Park to Fisher-man's Wharf. Its wide sidewalk and sweeping bay views make this a perennial favorite for pedestrians and joggers. Notice the Embarcadero Ribbon, a 2½-mile (4km) continuous

View of Coit Tower from Nob Hill.

line of glass encased in concrete. The 13-foot-tall (3.9m) metal pylons and bronze plaques embedded in the sidewalk are imprinted with photographs, drawings, poetry, and historical facts. After sunset, the Embarcadero provides the perfect vantage point from which to enjoy Leo Villareal's *Bay Lights,* a sparkling, shape-shifting art installation on the Bay Bridge that city officials decided, in early 2016, to make permanent. ⏱ *30 min.–1 hr. Return to Market St. to catch the F-Market streetcar to the Montgomery St. station, or walk there along Market St.*

6 Garden Court. The extravagant Palace Hotel astounded San Franciscans and bankrupted its owner, who allegedly committed suicide a day before the 1875 grand opening. Three decades later, the hotel was ravaged by one of the many fires following the 1906 earthquake. It was restored to glory and reopened in 1909, along with the magnificent Garden Court. This impressive atrium's domed ceiling is made from 80,000 glass panes and houses the relaxing **Garden Court Restaurant** (see p 180). After absorbing this court's grandeur, step into the **Pied Piper Bar** for a look at the $2.5-million Maxfield Parrish mural—and maybe to try the "Charlie Chaplin," an enjoyable absinthe-and-rye cocktail. ⏱ *20 min. 2 New Montgomery St. (at Market St.).* ☎ *415/546-5089. Mon–Sat 6:30–10:30am & 11:30am–2pm (Sat brunch until 11am). Sun 7–10am & brunch 10am–1:30pm & Sat tea 2–5pm. Evening service offered daily from 5:30–10pm. BART/Muni: Powell or Montgomery.*

7 ★★ SoMa (South of Market) District. This onetime industrial area south of Market Street has transformed into a major center for museums, galleries, and major league baseball. ⏱ *2–4 hr. to stroll through the neighborhood; visit during daylight hours.*

8 ★ 🄺🄸🄳🅂 Yerba Buena Center for the Arts is SoMa's anchor. It serves as an arts-and-entertainment hub, with cultural programs, oasis-like gardens, bowling lanes, and an ice-skating rink. Pay tribute at the poignant Martin Luther King, Jr. Memorial and its 50-foot (15m) waterfall, ride the Zeum carousel, or catch a new release at the Metreon movie theater. ⏱ *1 hr. 701 Mission St. (esplanade garden on Mission btw. 3rd & 4th St.); Metreon at 101 4th St.; Zeum at 760 Howard St.* ☎ *415/978-2700. www.ybca.org.* ⏱ *1–3 hr. Btw. 3rd & 4th sts., Mission & Folsom sts.*

9 ★★ San Francisco Museum of Modern Art. After a 3-year closure, SFMOMA reopened in spring 2016 to become America's biggest

The Embarcadero and Ferry Building with views of the Bay Bridge.

Garden Court at the Palace Hotel.

modern-art museum—it's now 10 stories tall. Its collection, amassed since the museum first opened in 1935, includes more than 30,000 works by high-caliber artists including Picasso, Matisse, O'Keeffe, Pollock, and Warhol. The first major museum to have recognized photography as an art form, SFMOMA also showcases the works of Ansel Adams, Diane Arbus, Man Ray, and other luminaries. Outside, a new sculpture terrace grows 16,000 native plants. ⏱ *1½ hr. 151 3rd St. (btw. Mission & Howard sts.).* ☎ *415/357-4000. www.sfmoma.org. $18 adults, $12 seniors 62+, free for 18 and under. Check website for hours. Bus: 30, 45. BART/Muni: Montgomery St.*

⓾ ★ Civic Center. Less than a decade after the 1906 earthquake destroyed SF's original City Hall, architect Arthur Brown erected a lavish Beaux Arts–style administrative and cultural center to take its place. Buildings here include extravagant City Hall itself, topped with a 308-foot-tall (92m) dome; the 376,000-square-foot (35,000-sq.-m) main public library; the Asian Art Museum, recently transformed by the architect who did France's Musée d'Orsay; and the War Memorial Opera House, where the 1951 U.S.–Japan peace accord was signed. ⏱ *1 hr. Most Civic Center buildings are bordered by Hayes, Franklin & Hyde sts. & Golden Gate Ave. Farmers' market Sun & Wed 7am–5pm in UN Plaza.*

⓫ ★★★ kids California Academy of Sciences. This science-and-nature museum in Golden Gate Park is an expansive, interactive world of discovery that mesmerizes everyone who visits. Highlights include an incredible array of animal species both terrestrial and marine, captivating planetarium shows, and a four-story rainforest. ⏱ *2–4 hr., weekday afternoons are best, as mornings are full with school tours. 55 Music Concourse Dr.* ☎ *415/379-8000. www.calacademy.org. Admission $35 adults; $30 seniors 65+, youth (12-17), and students; $25 for ages 4–11; free for kids 3 and younger. Mon–Sat 9:30am–5pm, Sun 11am–5pm. Bus: 5, 44. Streetcar: N-Judah.*

⓬ The Beach Chalet. Dinner at this airy Golden Gate Park restaurant and brewery near the ocean is a lively affair made better by good-quality American food. Don't miss the 1930s-era fresco murals in the adjoining Golden Gate Park Visitors Center. *1000 Great Highway at Ocean Beach.* ☎ *415/386-8439. $$. Bus: 5.*

San Francisco Lodging & Dining

DINING ●

21st Amendment **36**
25 Lusk **37**
A16 **5**
Acquerello **44**
Boogaloos **38**
Boulevard **17**
Chez Panisse **1**
Cliff House **41**
Foreign Cinema **38**

Garden Court
Restaurant **34**
Gary Danko **10**
Ghirardelli Soda Fountain
& Chocolate Shop **9**
Greens **6**
Jardinière **39**
Kokkari **14**
L'Osteria del Forno **11**
Mama's **12**
Michael Mina **28**

Mitchell's Ice Cream **38**
One Market **17**
Quince **42**
The Slanted Door **15**

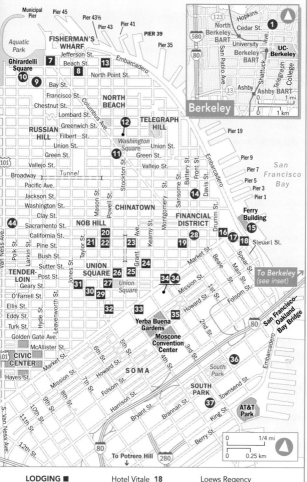

LODGING ■

Adagio **31**
The Argonaut **7**
Casa Madrona **2**
Cavallo Point **3**
Clift Hotel **30**
The Fairmont **20**
Four Seasons **33**
Hotel Abri **32**
Hotel Majestic **43**
Hotel Triton **24**

Hotel Vitale **18**
Hotel Zephyr **13**
Hyatt at Fisherman's
  Wharf **8**
Hyatt Regency
  San Francisco **16**
Inn at the Presidio **4**
InterContinental
  Mark Hopkins **22**
King George Hotel **29**

Loews Regency
  San Francisco **19**
The Palace Hotel **34**
Red Victorian **40**
The Ritz-Carlton **23**
The Scarlet Huntington **21**
Sir Francis Drake **26**
Taj Campton Place **25**
W San Francisco **35**
Westin St. Francis **27**

Lodging A to Z

★ **Adagio** UNION SQUARE Sleek charm for a good price in a central location. Double queen rooms are a great deal for families. *550 Geary St. (btw. Jones & Taylor sts.).* ☎ *800/ 228-8830 or 415/775-5000. www. hoteladagiosf.com. 173 units. Doubles $166–$441. AE, DC, DISC, MC, V. Bus: 2, 3, 4, 38. BART/Muni: Powell St. Map p 174.*

★★ **kids The Argonaut** FISHER-MAN'S WHARF The beautifully restored 1907 brick building in the Maritime National Historical Park has nautical-themed decor, a great location, and bay views. *495 Jefferson St. (corner of Jefferson & Hyde sts.).* ☎ *800/790-1415. www.argonaut hotel.com. 252 units. Doubles $198– $565. AE, DC, MC, V. Bus: 10, 30. Cable car: Powell-Hyde. Map p 174.*

★ **Casa Madrona** SAUSALITO Though it's not in SF proper, the coastal village of Sausalito is a great place to rest your head just across the Golden Gate Bridge. Contemporary-styled Casa Madrona offers comfortable beds and attentive service. *801 Bridgeway.* ☎ *415/332- 0502. www.casamadrona.com. 64 units. Doubles $256–$457. AE, DC, DISC, MC, V. Map p 174.*

★★ **Cavallo Point** SAUSALITO Situated on Fort Baker, a former U.S. Army post with unbeatable views of the bay and the bridge, lodging options here are welcomingly upscale. The eco-friendly hotel's spa is excellent, as is its restaurant, **Murray Circle.** *601 Murray Circle* ☎ *888/651-2003. www.cavallo point.com. 142 units. Doubles $347– $685. AE, DC, MC, V. Map p 174.*

★ **Clift Hotel** UNION SQUARE Hotelier Ian Schrager worked with Philippe Starck to design this über-hip downtown property. Most rooms

Enjoy a drink on the ultramodern terrace of the Clift Hotel.

scream minimalism, and bathrooms are stylish but small. The beautiful and historic **Redwood Room** turns into a stylish after-dark scene (see p 190). *495 Geary St. (at Taylor St.).* ☎ *415/775-4700. www.clifthotel. com. 372 units. Doubles $170–$559. AE, DC, DISC, MC, V. Bus: 2, 3, 4, 27, 38. Map p 174.*

★★★ **The Fairmont** NOB HILL This 1907 landmark makes an immediate impression. An $85-million restoration recaptured architect Julia Morgan's (of Hearst Castle fame) original design. This is where U.S. presidents stay, and where the UN charter was drafted in 1945. For unforgettable views, choose a room in the Tower Building. *950 Mason St. (at California St.).* ☎ *415/772-5000. www.fairmont. com/sanfrancisco. 592 units. Doubles $233–$639. AE, DC, DISC, MC, V. Bus: 1. Cable car: All. Map p 174.*

★★★ Four Seasons SOMA This luxurious hotel's rooms, true to brand, have plush furnishings and large marble bathrooms. Impeccable service and access to the massive **Equinox Sports Club** add even more appeal. *757 Market St. (at 3rd St.).* ☎ *415/633-3000. www.four seasons.com/sanfrancisco. 277 units. Doubles $401–$872. AE, DC, DISC, MC, V. BART/Muni: Montgomery St. Map p 174.*

★ Hotel Abri UNION SQUARE Though it's in the middle of it all, this recently renovated property manages to maintain a homey, relaxed feel. Decor and service are both lovely. *127 Ellis St. (btw. Powell & Cyril Magnin sts.).* ☎ *415/392-8800. www.hotelabrisf.com. 91 units. Doubles $144–$421. AE, DC, DISC, MC, V. Bus: 2, 3, 4. BART/Muni: Powell St. Cable car: Powell lines. Map p 174.*

★★ Hotel Majestic PACIFIC HEIGHTS Furnished with intriguing European antiques, the Majestic provides an escape from modern life's rougher edges. *1500 Sutter St. (btw. Octavia & Gough St.).* ☎ *415/441-1100. www.thehotelmajestic.com. 58 units. Doubles $110–$250. AE, DISC, MC, V. Bus: 2, 3, 4. Map p 174.*

★ Hotel Triton UNION SQUARE This colorful, rock-music-themed

Guest room at the Fairmont Hotel.

hotel—suites are designed by celebrities—offers free Friday-night wine parties with tarot-card readings and chair massages. Rooms at this Kimpton property are small but newly renovated. *342 Grant Ave. (at Bush St.).* ☎ *415/394-0500. www. hoteltriton.com. 140 units. Doubles $127–$417. AE, DC, DISC, MC, V. Bus: 2, 3, 4, 15, 30. BART/Muni: Montgomery St. Map p 174.*

★★ Hotel Vitale SOMA Zen-inspired rooms provide excellent views and a great location right across from the Ferry Building. The top-floor spa is not to be missed. Downstairs, the Italian cuisine at **Americano** restaurant impresses. *8 Mission St. (at Embarcadero).* ☎ *415/278-3700. www.hotelvitale. com. 200 units. Doubles $232–$716 & up. AE, DC, DISC, MC, V. Muni: F, M, N. Map p 174.*

★★ Hotel Zephyr FISHERMAN'S WHARF In 2015, a former Radisson reopened as this hip, stylish property aimed at millennials. It's still waterfront, and it's still got views of the Golden Gate, Alcatraz, and the Bay Bridge (depending on the room), but now there's a much fresher look, plus playful spaces, including a huge outdoor lounge with fire pits and games. *250 Beach St.* ☎ *415/617-6565. www.hotelzephyrsf.com. 361 units. Doubles from $424. AE, DISC, MC, V. Bus: 10, 30. Cable car: Powell-Hyde. Map p 174.*

kids Hyatt at Fisherman's Wharf FISHERMAN'S WHARF Best of the wharf chain hotels. Rooms sport a clean, contemporary look; the beds are luxurious. Downstairs, there's an outdoor pool and a sportsbar-like restaurant. *555 N. Point St. (btw. Jones & Taylor sts.).* ☎ *415/563-1234. www.fishermans wharf.hyatt.com. 316 units. Doubles $180–$479. AE, DC, DISC, MC, V. Bus: 10, 30. Streetcar: F. Map p 174.*

Terrace at the Hotel Vitale.

★ **Hyatt Regency San Francisco** FINANCIAL DISTRICT This hulking hotel has a 17-story atrium, spacious rooms, some fine views, the Embarcadero Center next door, and the Ferry Building just across the street. *5 Embarcadero Center (at Market St. by the Embarcadero).* ☎ *415/788-1234. www.sanfranciscoregency.hyatt.com. 802 units. Doubles $182–$638. AE, DC, DISC, MC, V. BART/Muni: Embarcadero. Map p 174.*

★★ **Inn at the Presidio** PRESIDIO This Georgian Revival building dates to 1903, having served as army officers' quarters until 1994. In 2012, it debuted as a charming inn whose rates include breakfast and a nightly wine-and-cheese reception. *42 Moraga Ave.* ☎ *415/800-7356. www.innatthepresidio.com. 22 units. Doubles $270–$450. AE, DC, MC, V. Map p 174.*

★★★ **InterContinental Mark Hopkins** NOB HILL Plush rooms provide stellar views and the **Top of the Mark** sky-lounge is a stunning place to dine. *1 Nob Hill (at Mason & California sts.).* ☎ *888/424-6835 or 415/392-3434. www.intercontinental markhopkins.com. 380 units. Doubles $133–$524 & up. AE, DC, DISC, MC, V. Bus: 1. Cable car: All. Map p 174.*

King George Hotel UNION SQUARE Popular with European tourists, this 1912 hotel offers modern amenities and handsome (albeit petite) rooms. Have a drink and catch a game on TV in the lobby bar, **Winston's Lounge.** *334 Mason St. (btw. Geary & O'Farrell sts.).* ☎ *415/781-5050. www.kinggeorge.com. 153 units. Doubles $93–$320. AE, DC, DISC, MC, V. Bus: 2, 3, 4, 38. Cable car: Powell lines. BART/Muni: Powell St. Map p 174.*

★★ **Loews Regency San Francisco** FINANCIAL DISTRICT Atop SF's third-tallest building, Loews affords jaw-dropping views. Formerly the Mandarin Oriental, this property is still just as elegant. But now it's hipper too, with "Sky Deck Yoga" on the 40th-floor terrace, chef-guided tours of the Ferry Building, and the stylish **Brasserie S&P** restaurant. *222 Sansome St. (btw. Pine & California sts.).* ☎ *800/622-0404 or 415/276-9888. www.loewshotels.com/regency-san-francisco. 155 units. Doubles $430 & up. AE, DC, DISC, MC, V. BART/Muni: Montgomery St. Cable car: California. Map p 174.*

★★ **The Palace Hotel** SOMA Over-the-top decor encompasses the landmark **Garden Court**

Restaurant (see p 180). Large guest-rooms boast marble bathrooms and 14-foot (4.2m) ceilings. *2 New Montgomery St. (at Market St.).* ☎ *415/512-1111. www.sfpalace.com. 553 units. Doubles $156–$795. AE, DC, DISC, MC, V. BART/Muni: Montgomery St. Map p 174.*

Red Victorian HAIGHT There should be a sign in front of this eccentric Haight-Ashbury B&B that reads: "WELCOME BACK TO 1967." Each guestroom has its own flowery theme, and visitors are expected to participate in community events. *1665 Haight St. (at Belvedere St.).* ☎ *415/864-1978. www.redvic.com. 20 units (6 w/private bathroom). Doubles $105–$200. AE, DISC, MC, V. Bus: 6, 7, 43, 66, 71. Muni: Carl & Cole. Map p 174.*

★★★ The Ritz-Carlton NOB HILL At this palatial property, modern features—flat LCD TVs, 400-thread-count linens, Bulgari toiletries—don't detract from classic ones: regal decor, 18th-century antiques, a spa and fitness center, and an exceptional restaurant, called **Parallel 37**. Above all, this 1909 landmark maintains excellent service. *600 Stockton St. (at California St.).* ☎ *415/296-7465. www.ritzcarlton.com/sanfrancisco. 336 units. Doubles $347–$703. AE, DC, DISC, MC, V. Cable car: All. Map p 174.*

★★★ The Scarlet Huntington NOB HILL A discreet but very upscale choice, especially after a $15 million renovation in 2014. Rooms are sizable and seven suites have kitchens. The spa is magnificent. *1075 California St. (at Powell St.).* ☎ *415/474-5400. www.the scarlethotels.com. 135 units. Doubles $185–$546. AE, DC, MC, V. Bus: 1. Cable car: All. Map p 174.*

Sir Francis Drake UNION SQUARE Despite the grandiose lobby and beefeater-clad doormen, stay here only if you get a great deal. The tiny rooms aren't as well-maintained as the lobby. It's always a party, though, at the 21st-floor **Starlight Room** (see p 190). *450 Powell St. (at Sutter St.).* ☎ *415/392-7755. www.sirfrancisdrake.com. 417 units. Doubles $155–$482. AE, DC, DISC, MC, V. Bus: 2, 3, 4. BART/Muni: Powell St. Cable car: Powell lines. Map p 174.*

★★ Taj Campton Place UNION SQUARE This Indian-owned hotel epitomizes refined opulence. Its restaurant excels at presenting creative entrees worth savoring. Sumptuous guestrooms have bathrooms with Portuguese limestone and deep tubs. *340 Stockton St. (btw. Post & Sutter sts.).* ☎ *415/781-5555. www.tajhotels.com. 110 units. Doubles $282–$524. AE, DC, DISC, MC, V. Bus: 2, 3, 4. BART/Muni: Montgomery St. Cable car: Powell lines. Map p 174.*

★★ W San Francisco SOMA This ultra-hip hotel adjacent to SFMOMA brings you sleek rooms, great views, 24-hour concierge service, free poolside yoga, Bliss Spa, the seasonally inspired **Trace** restaurant, and an active social scene. *181 3rd St. (at Howard St.).* ☎ *415/777-5300. www.wsanfrancisco.com. 404 units. Doubles $185–$715. AE, DC, DISC, MC, V. Bus: 15, 30, 45. BART/Muni: Montgomery St. Map p 174.*

★★ kids Westin St. Francis UNION SQUARE The historic grande dame of SF hotels couldn't be located better: It's right on Union Square. Whichever foreign flag hangs outside the hotel represents the nationality of a dignitary currently staying. *335 Powell St. (at Geary St.).* ☎ *415/397-7000. www.westinstfrancis.com. 1,195 units. $177–$700. AE, DC, DISC, MC, V. Bus: 2, 3, 4, 30, 45. BART/Muni: Powell St. Cable car: Powell lines. Map p 174.*

Dining A to Z

★ 21st Amendment SOMA *BREWPUB* Choose a beer flight or a glass, pair it with straightforward American eats, and if it's a game day, take the short walk to AT&T Park (see p 192). *563 2nd St.* ☎ *415/369-0900. Entrees $13–$17. AE, MC, V. Lunch & dinner daily. Streetcar: N, KT. Map p 174.*

★★ 25 Lusk SOMA *NEW AMERI-CAN* Open since late 2010, this modern restaurant is notable for its design, robust wine program, and creative entrees. *25 Lusk St. (at Townsend St.).* ☎ *415/495-5875. Entrees $28–$40. AE, DC, DISC, MC, V. Dinner daily, brunch Sun. Bus: 8X, 30, 47. Map p 174.*

★★ A16 MARINA *ITALIAN* A chic crowd comes for wood-fired pizza and an exciting wine selection. *2355 Chestnut St. (btw. Scott & Divisadero sts.).* ☎ *415/771-2216. Entrees $13–$32. AE, DC, MC, V. Lunch Wed–Fri. Dinner daily. Bus: 30. Map p 174.*

★★★ Acquerello NOB HILL *ITALIAN* Amid the namesake watercolors in a former chapel, Michelin-starred fare shares space with a 600-wine list. *1722 Sacramento (btw. Van Ness & Polk).* ☎ *415/567-5432. Prix fixe menus (3–5 courses) $95–$140. AE, DC, MC, V. Dinner Tues–Sat. Closed Sun–Mon. Bus: 30. Map p 174.*

★★ Boogaloos MISSION *LATIN* A much-loved brunch cafe with funky mosaic decor and a long wait. *3296 22nd St. (at Valencia St.).* ☎ *415/824-4088. Entrees $6–$13. DISC, MC, V. Breakfast & lunch daily. BART: 24th St. Mission Station. Map p 174.*

★★★ Boulevard SOMA *AMERI-CAN* Industrial Belle Epoque decor enhances a thoughtful menu of seasonal comfort food. *1 Mission St. (at Steuart St.).* ☎ *415/543-6084. Entrees $27–$49. AE, DC, DISC, MC, V. Lunch Mon–Fri. Dinner daily. Bus: 12. BART/Muni: Embarcadero. Map p 174.*

Chez Panisse BERKELEY *CALI-FORNIA* Alice Waters's famous restaurant presents an always-evolving menu that literally defines California cuisine (see p 182). *1517 Shattuck Ave. (btw. Cedar & Vine sts.).* ☎ *510/548-5525. Entrees $75–$125 (prix-fixe). AE, DC, DISC, MC, V. Dinner Mon–Sat; cafe upstairs serves lunch & dinner menu Mon–Sat (reservations recommended for both). BART: Downtown Berkeley. Map p 174.*

★★ Cliff House SUNSET *AMERI-CAN* Breathtaking ocean views and charming early-20th-century decor make the whole experience here—food is almost an afterthought. *1090 Point Lobos Ave. (just west of 48th Ave. Geary Blvd. turns into Point Lobos Ave. after 43rd Ave.).* ☎ *415/386-3330. Entrees $19–$39. AE, DC, DISC, MC, V. Breakfast, lunch & dinner daily. Bus: 18, 38. Map p 174.*

★★ Foreign Cinema MISSION *CALIFORNIA/MEDITERRANEAN* It sounds like a strange pairing, but foreign films and inspired cuisine turn out to be a perfect match. For the full experience, request an outdoor table and order a cocktail off the creative list. *2534 Mission St. (btw. 21st & 22nd sts.).* ☎ *415/648-7600. Entrees $22–$32. AE, DISC, MC, V. Dinner daily, brunch Sat–Sun. Bus: 14, 49. BART: 24th St. Map p 174.*

★ Garden Court Restaurant SOMA *AMERICAN* Elegant service in a lovely, historic setting.

The Cliff House Restaurant on the water.

Palace Hotel, 2 New Montgomery St. (at Market St.). ☎ 415/546-5089. Entrees $19–$38. AE, DC, DISC, MC, V. Breakfast & lunch daily plus Sun brunch & Sat afternoon tea. BART/ Muni: Montgomery St. Map p 174.

★★★ **Gary Danko** FISHER-MAN'S WHARF *CALIFORNIA* This is SF's best restaurant, thanks to its flawless service, outstanding wines, and a chef who knows how to

elevate cuisine to an art form. Reserve at least a month in advance, or try your luck at the bar. 800 N. Point St. (at Hyde St.). ☎ 415/749-2060. Prix-fixe menu (3–5 courses) from $83–$119. AE, DC, DISC, MC, V. Dinner daily. Bus: 30, 47. Cable car: Powell-Hyde. Map p 174.

★ **kids** **Ghirardelli Soda Fountain & Chocolate Shop** FISHER-MAN'S WHARF *ICE CREAM* The ever-present line attests to consistently great sundaes—all chocolate-topped, of course. *Ghirardelli Square, 900 N. Point St. (at Larkin St.).* ☎ 415/474-3938. Desserts $5–$20. AE, DC, DISC, MC, V. Mon–Sun, 9am–11pm (midnight Fri–Sat). Bus: 10, 30. Cable car: Powell-Hyde. Map p 174.

★★ **Greens** MARINA *VEGETARIAN* Excellent flavors and stunning views (especially at night) impress even dedicated omnivores. *Building A, Fort Mason Center (16 Marina Blvd. where Laguna St. turns into Marina Blvd.).* ☎ 415/771-6222.

You don't have to be a vegetarian to enjoy Greens Restaurant.

Entrees $19–$27. AE, DISC, MC, V. Lunch Tues–Fri. Sat–Sun brunch. Dinner daily. Bus: 28, 30. Map p 174.

★ **Jardinière** HAYES VALLEY *FRENCH* Symphony and opera patrons begin (or complete) a night at this upscale Civic Center staple. *300 Grove St. (at Franklin St.).* ☎ *415/861-5555. Entrees $25–$55, AE, DC, DISC, MC, V. Dinner daily. Bus: 21. Map p 174.*

★★ **Kokkari** FINANCIAL DISTRICT *GREEK* Delicious Greek classics in a warm, upscale setting. *200 Jackson St. (at Front St.).* ☎ *415/981-0983. Entrees $24–$53. AE, DC, DISC, MC, V. Lunch Mon–Fri. Dinner daily. Bus: 10, 12. Streetcar: F. Map p 174.*

★★ **L'Osteria del Forno** NORTH BEACH *ITALIAN* An intimate dining room with a small, quintessentially Italian menu. *519 Columbus Ave. (btw. Union & Green sts.).* ☎ *415/982-1124. Entrees $14–$24. No credit cards. Lunch & dinner Wed–Mon. Bus: 15, 30, 41. Cable car: Powell-Mason. Map p 174.*

★★★ **Mama's** NORTH BEACH *BREAKFAST/AMERICAN* Locals line up around the block for Mama's legendary brunch food, so arrive early. *1701 Stockton St. (at Filbert St.).* ☎ *415/362-6421. Entrees $8.95–$15. Cash only. Breakfast & lunch 8am–3pm Tues–Sun. Bus: 12, 30. Cable car: Powell-Mason. Map p 174.*

★★★ **Michael Mina** FINANCIAL DISTRICT *CALIFORNIA* An elegant dining room with expert wait-staff, world-class sommeliers, and startlingly vibrant flavors. *252 California St. (btw. Front & Battery sts.).* ☎ *415/397-9222. Prix-fixe dinner (3 courses) $125, bar dinner menu*

California Cuisine

Chef Alice Waters is the mother of California cuisine. She owns and runs Berkeley's **Chez Panisse** (see p 180), consistently hailed as one of America's best restaurants. Waters revolutionized American food by championing the use of seasonal, local ingredients. Her culinary revelation came to her in France, where she lived near a market street teeming with vendors selling fresh, high-quality produce.

That her grand vision came while she was overseas highlights California cuisine's multicultural, transnational character. It draws from the entire world and, as such, is always evolving. While Waters was inspired by France's culinary tradition, other California chefs draw from Italy, the Middle East, Asia, and South America. But the thread that unites all of California cuisine is this: a strong preference for uncomplicated dishes with superior ingredients that change with the seasons.

The Bay Area's location and immigrant history were central to the emergence of this epicurean style, as were the many family farms and ranches (many of them organic) surrounding San Francisco. Add the Pacific's bounty of fresh seafood, and you've got the perfect place in which to experience California cuisine.

Vietnamese food at the Slanted Door in the Ferry Building.

$20–$50. AE, DC, DISC, MC, V. Lunch Mon–Fri. Dinner daily. Cable car: Powell line. Map p 174.

★ **kids Mitchell's Ice Cream** MISSION *ICE CREAM* Try unexpected flavors like avocado, ginger, and sweet corn. *688 San Jose Ave. (at 29th St.).* ☎ 415/648-2300. $3–$6. Daily 11am–11pm. Bus: 14, 49. Muni: Church & 30th St. Map p 174.

★★ **One Market** SOMA *CALIFORNIA* Bradley Ogden's SF outlet, across from the Ferry Building, is meat-heavy and Michelin-starred. *1 Market St. (at Steuart St.).* ☎ 415/777-5577. Entrees $26–$49. AE, DC, DISC, MC, V. Lunch Mon–Fri. Dinner Mon–Sat. BART/Muni: Embarcadero. Map p 174.

★★ **Quince** NORTH BEACH *ITALIAN* Seasonal dishes in an elegant, discreet setting. *470 Pacific Ave. (at Montgomery St.).* ☎ 415/775-8500. Prix-fixe $220. AE, MC, V. Dinner Mon–Sat. Bus: 12, 30. Map p 174.

★★★ **The Slanted Door** EMBARCADERO *VIETNAMESE* A perpetual crowd awaits Charles Phan's upscale Vietnamese cooking and his modern restaurant's Embarcadero view. Call ahead. *1 Ferry Bldg. #3 (at the Embarcadero & Market St.).* ☎ 415/861-8032. Entrees $12–$48. AE, MC, V. Lunch, afternoon tea & dinner daily. BART/Muni: Embarcadero. Map p 174.

San Francisco Shopping, Nightlife & Arts

NIGHTLIFE & ARTS ■

Beach Blanket Babylon **28**
The Boom Boom Room **11**
Bourbon & Branch **39**
The Buena Vista **24**
Curran Theatre **41**
Dalva **17**
Elbo Room **17**
Fly Bar **13**
The Fillmore **12**
Golden Gate Theater **46**
Greens Sports Bar **27**

Hôtel Biron **20**
Laszlo **17**
Mad Dog in the Fog **19**
Matrix Fillmore **8**
The Mint Karaoke
 Lounge **18**
Moby Dick **16**
Orpheum Theater **47**
Palace of Fine Arts
 Theatre **7**
Press Club **6**
Redwood Room **40**

RN74 **43**
Ruby Skye **42**
SFJAZZ Center **22**
SF Opera **52**
SF Symphony **51**
Starlight Room **1**
Teatro Zinzanni **26**
The Tonga Room &
 Hurricane Bar **38**
The Top of the Mark **37**
Tosca **31**
Vesuvio **30**

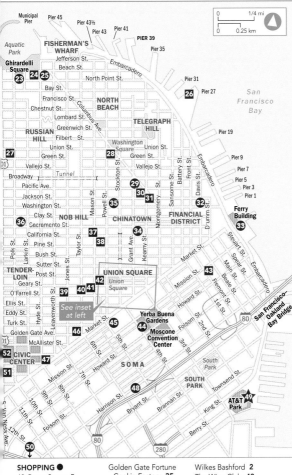

Shopping A to Z

Art

★★ 49 Geary Street UNION SQUARE   You'll find several top galleries here. *49 Geary St. (btw. Grant Ave. & Kearny St.). Streetcar: F. Most galleries closed Sun–Mon. Bus: 16, 17, 50. BART/Muni: Powell St. Map p 184.*

Books

★ kids Chronicle Books UNION SQUARE & SOMA   Since 1967, this publisher has been known for innovative design and whimsical gift creations. *165 Fourth St. ☎ 415/369-6271. (Also at 1846 Union St. ☎ 415/345-8435 and 680 Second St. ☎ 415/537-4200.) www.chroniclebooks.com. AE, DISC, MC, V. Bus: 27, 30. Map p 184.*

★★ City Lights NORTH BEACH   Founded by Beat poet and publisher Lawrence Ferlinghetti in 1953, this landmark shop still stocks avant-garde and alternative lit. *261 Columbus Ave. (at Broadway St.). ☎ 415/362-8193. www.citylights. com. AE, DISC, MC, V. Bus: 15, 30, 41. Map p 184.*

★★ Kinokuniya JAPANTOWN   Even if you don't speak Japanese, this shopping complex fascinates with its foreign selections of books, gifts, tees, and trinkets. *1581 Webster St. (btw. Geary Blvd. & Post St.). ☎ 415/567-7625. www.kinokuniya. com. MC, V. Bus: 1, 5. Map p 184.*

Department Store

★ Nordstrom UNION SQUARE   Nordstrom offers high-quality clothing, an excellent shoe department, and the best customer service in the industry. *865 Market St. (at 5th St.). ☎ 415/243-8500. www.nordstrom.com. AE, DC, DISC, MC, V. Bus: 27, 30, 38, 45. Streetcar: F. Map p 184.*

Electronics

★★ Apple Store UNION SQUARE   This beautiful store houses the trendiest of e-gear. When Steve Jobs died, it became a shrine to his life and work. *1 Stockton St. (at Market St.). ☎ 415/486-4800. www.apple.com. AE, DC, DISC, MC, V. Bus: 30, 38, 45. Streetcar: F. Map p 184.*

Fashion

★★ Maiden Lane UNION SQUARE   Top designers have boutiques on this chic pedestrian alley. Louis Vuitton, Kate Spade, and others are nearby. *Maiden Lane, off Stockton St. Bus: 30, 38, 45. Map p 184.*

★ Patagonia FISHERMAN'S WHARF   This high-quality outfitter's outerwear is a staple in locals' wardrobes. *770 N. Point St. (btw.*

Piedmont Boutique.

Hyde & Leavenworth sts.). ☎ 415/
771-2050. www.patagonia.com. AE,
DC, DISC, MC, V. Bus: 10, 30, 47.
Cable car: Powell-Hyde. Map p 184.

★ **Piedmont Boutique** HAIGHT
Absolutely outrageous vintage
women's garments—sold mostly to
men. The giant fishnet legs over
the entrance epitomize the Haight.
1452 Haight St. (at Ashbury St.).
☎ 415/864-8075. www.piedmont
boutique.com. AE, MC, V. Bus: 21.
Map p 184.

★★★ **Wilkes Bashford** UNION
SQUARE SF's best-known men's
clothing store, selling fine Euro-
pean fashions. 375 Sutter St. (at
Stockton St.). ☎ 415/986-4380.
www.wilkesbashford.com. AE, DC,
DISC, MC, V. Bus: 2, 3, 4, 30, 45.
Map p 184.

Gifts & Souvenirs
★★ **Canton Bazaar** CHINA-
TOWN This center carries Chi-
nese porcelain, jade, antiques, and
hand-carved furniture. 616 Grant
Ave. (btw. California & Sacramento
sts.). ☎ 415/362-5750. AE, DISC,
MC, V. Bus: 1, 15, 30, 45. Map p 184.

Good Vibrations MISSION &
NOB HILL The first and best pro-
woman erotic shop. If you're not
shy, the employees give great
advice. www.goodvibes.com. 603
Valencia St. (at 17th St.). ☎ 415/
503-9522. Bus: 22, 26. Bart to 16th
St. 1620 Polk St. (at Sacramento St.).
☎ 415/345-0400. Bus: 1, 19. Cable
car: California line. AE, DISC, MC, V.
Map p 184.

Housewares & Furnishings
★ **Soko Hardware** JAPAN-
TOWN A great selection of
ceramic plates, tea sets, sake cups,
and more at bargain prices. 1698
Post St. (at Buchanan St.).
☎ 415/931-5510. MC, V. Bus: 2, 3,
4, 38. Map p 184.

Ghirardelli Square.

Music
★★ **Amoeba Music** HAIGHT
The planet's biggest and best independent music store has listening
booths and frequent free live performances. Ask staffers for advice—but
only about something adequately
obscure. 1855 Haight St. (btw.
Shrader & Stanyan sts.). ☎ 415/
831-1200. www.amoeba.com. DISC,
MC, V. Bus: 6, 7, 66, 71. Map p 184.

Shopping Centers
★★★ **Ferry Building Marketplace** FINANCIAL DISTRICT This
is foodie heaven: All sorts of culinary shops and mini-restaurants
tempt with taste. Don't miss Cow-
girl Creamery's Artisan Cheese
Shop, Recchiuti Confections, or
Miette, a delightfully quirky pastry
shop. Go on a Saturday, Tuesday,
or Thursday, when the impressive
farmers' market (see p 171) takes
center stage. 1 Ferry Building (at
the Embarcadero and Market St.).
☎ 415/983-8030. www.ferrybuilding
marketplace.com. Streetcar: F. Map
p 184.

★★ **kids** **Ghirardelli Square**
FISHERMAN'S WHARF   A former chocolate factory offers a priceless view and charming shops. Ghirardelli's flagship store (see p 181) is here—don't leave before ordering a sundae. *900 N. Point St. (at Larkin St.).* ☎ *415/775-5500. www.ghirardellisq.com. Bus: 30, 47. Cable car: Powell-Hyde. Streetcar: F. Map p 184.*

Westfield San Francisco Center SOMA   Anchored by Nordstrom and Bloomingdale's, this attractive mall also houses brand-name chains such as BCBG, Burberry, Coach, Hugo Boss, J. Crew, Kate Spade, and Tiffany & Co. The food court here has got to be one of the world's best. *865 Market St. (at 5th St.).* ☎ *415/495-5656. www.westfield.com/sanfrancisco. Bus: 27, 30, 38, 45. Streetcar: F. Map p 184.*

Specialty Foods & Wines
For Ghirardelli chocolate and the Ferry Building Farmers' Market, see above.

★★ **kids** **Golden Gate Fortune Cookies Factory** CHINATOWN
Buy fortune cookies hot off the press at this tiny Chinatown shop in an alley. Bring your own message to watch it get folded in. *56 Ross Alley (btw. Washington & Jackson sts.).* ☎ *415/781-3956. Cash only. Bus: 8X, 10, 12, 30, 45. Cable car: Powell-Mason. Map p 184.*

★★ **Rainbow Grocery** MISSION   A huge health-food co-op where you can browse through virtually any kind of health food that exists, plus a mind-boggling selection of bulk spices and teas. *1745 Folsom St. (at 13th St.).* ☎ *415/863-0620. www.rainbow.coop. AE, DISC, MC, V. Bus: 12, 47. Map p 184.*

The Wine Club SOMA   The West's largest wine merchant, surprisingly affordable. *953 Harrison St. (btw. 5th & 6th sts.).* ☎ *415/512-9086. www.thewineclub.com. AE, MC, V. Bus: 12, 19, 27. Map p 184.*

Toys
★ **kids** **Ambassador Toys**
FINANCIAL DISTRICT   European dolls, wooden toys, and clever games are among the whimsical playthings sold here. *2 Embarcadero Center (at Sacramento St., btw. Front & Davis sts.).* ☎ *415/345-8697. www.ambassadortoys.com. AE, DISC, MC, V. Bus: 1. Cable car: California line. Streetcar: F. Map p 184.*

Travel Goods
Flight 001 HAYES VALLEY   Shop for hip travel accessories like sleek luggage, "security-friendly" manicure sets, and other midair must-haves. *525 Hayes St. (btw. Laguna & Octavia sts.).* ☎ *415/487-1001. www.flight001.com. AE, DISC, MC, V. Bus: 21, 47, 49. Map p 184.*

Golden Gate Fortune Cookie Factory.

Nightlife & Arts A to Z

Bars, Lounges, Pubs & Clubs

★★ The Boom Boom Room

WESTERN ADDITION A dark, steamy joint that hosts some of America's best blues bands. *1601 Fillmore St. (at Geary Blvd.).* ☎ *415/673-8000. Cover free–$22 (many shows just $5). Bus: 22, 38. Map p 184.*

★★★ Bourbon & Branch

UNION SQUARE You need a password to get into this 1920s-themed speakeasy: Say "books" and you'll be led through a pivoting bookcase to the crowded back-room library. Reserve at least 2 weeks in advance for a seated spot. The talented barmen here concoct SF's best cocktails. Try the cucumber gimlet or anything with whiskey in it. *501 Jones Street (at O'Farrell St.).* ☎ *415/346-1735. Bus: 8X, 30. Map p 184.*

★ The Buena Vista

FISHERMAN'S WHARF It's served more Irish coffees than any other bar in the world. A historic SF tradition. *2765 Hyde St. (at Beach St.).* ☎ *415/474-5044. Bus: 30, 47. Map p 184.*

★★ Dalva

MISSION A dark, intimate cocktail lounge with an eclectic crowd and excellent sangria. *3121 16th St. (btw. Valencia & Albion sts.).* ☎ *415/252-7740. Bus: 26, 49. BART: 16th St. (before dark). Map p 184.*

★★ Elbo Room

MISSION Socialize at the inviting bar or head upstairs for live music (separate cover up to $10). *647 Valencia St. (btw. Clarion Alley & Sycamore St.).* ☎ *415/552-7788. Bus: 26, 49. BART: 16th St. (before dark). Map p 184.*

★★ Fly Bar

NORTH OF THE PANHANDLE A neighborhood

The speakeasy Bourbon & Branch.

lounge with soju and sake drinks, great pizzas, and rotating art. *762 Divisadero St. (at Fulton St.).* ☎ *415/931-4359. Bus: 5, 21, 22, 24. Map p 184.*

★ Greens Sports Bar

RUSSIAN HILL SF's best sports bar boasts 15 TVs and 18 on-tap beers. *2239 Polk St. (at Green St.).* ☎ *415/775-4287. Bus: 19, 47, 49. Cable car: Powell-Hyde. Map p 184.*

Hôtel Biron

HAYES VALLEY This gem of a wine bar is tucked away in an alley right behind Market Street. In addition to its well-edited wine menu, there's an appetizing selection of cheeses. Open daily 'til 2am. *45 Rose St. (at Gough St.).* ☎ *415/703-0403. Bus: 6, 49, 71. Streetcar: F, J, K, M, N. Map p. 184.*

★★ Laszlo

MISSION An industrial-chic bar that serves funky drinks. *2526 Mission St. (btw. 21st & 22nd sts.).* ☎ *415/401-0801. Bus: 14, 49. BART to 24th St. Map p 184.*

Mad Dog in the Fog HAIGHT Catch European soccer games at this quirky British pub. *530 Haight St. (btw. Steiner & Fillmore sts.).* ☎ *415/626-7279. Bus: 22, 67. Map p 184.*

Matrix Fillmore COW HOLLOW The swanky pulse of SF's singles' scene stays open 'til 2am daily. *3138 Fillmore St. (btw. Greenwich & Filbert sts.).* ☎ *415/563-4180. Bus: 22, 30, 45. Map p 184.*

★ **The Mint Karaoke Lounge** MISSION This once-gay song spot now draws patrons of all orientations, who, after a potent cocktail, take to the stage. *1942 Market St. (btw. Guerrero St. & Duboce Ave.).* ☎ *415/626-4726. No cover, but a two-drink minimum. Drinks $4.75–$10. Bus: 6, 22, 71. Streetcar: F, J, K, M, N. Map p 184.*

★ **Moby Dick** CASTRO This gay bar is a 40-year-old Castro institution. *4049 18th St. (btw. Castro & Noe sts.).* ☎ *415/861-1199. Bus: 22, 33. Streetcar: F, J, K, M. Map p 184.*

★ **Press Club** SOMA A sleek wine lounge popular with the after-work crowd that also serves tasty small bites. *20 Yerba Buena Lane (at Market St. btw. 3rd & 4th sts.).* ☎ *415/744-5000. Muni: F. BART: Powell. Map p 184.*

★ **Redwood Room** UNION SQUARE The Clift Hotel's historic lounge epitomizes SF glitz. *Clift Hotel, 495 Geary St. (at Taylor St.).* ☎ *415/929-2372. Bus: 2, 3, 4, 27, 38. Map p 184.*

★★ **RN74** SOMA Michael Mina's wine bar for Francophiles. *301 Mission St (at Beale St.).* ☎ *415/543-7474. Muni: F. BART: Embarcadero. Map p 184.*

Ruby Skye UNION SQUARE A former Victorian movie house is now SF's biggest dance club.

420 Mason St. (btw. Post & Geary sts.). ☎ *415/693-0777. Cover free–$35. Bus: 2, 3, 4, 27, 38. Map p 184.*

★ **The Starlight Room** UNION SQUARE A 1930s-style gathering place with dancing, stellar views, a long appetizer menu, and, on weekends, an orchestra. If you want to see a classic SF drag show, this is the place. *Sir Francis Drake Hotel, 450 Powell St. (btw. Sutter & Post sts.), 21st floor.* ☎ *415/395-8595. Cover varies; call ahead. Bus: 2, 3, 4. Cable car: Powell-Hyde, Powell-Mason. Map p 184.*

★ **The Tonga Room & Hurricane Bar** NOB HILL Umbrella drinks and faux thunderstorms evoke a fun tropical vibe. During happy hour (Wed–Fri 5–7pm), it's $10 for an all-you-can-eat South Pacific buffet. *Fairmont Hotel, 950 Mason St. (at California St.).* ☎ *415/772-5278. Bus: 1. Cable car: All. Map p 184.*

The Tonga Room at the Fairmont.

★★★ The Top of the Mark

NOB HILL A historic venue with SF's best view and an extensive martini menu. Occasional live entertainment. *InterContinental Mark Hopkins, 1 Nob Hill (at Mason & California sts.), 19th floor.* ☎ *415/392-3434. Cover $5–$15 (Wed–Sun). Bus: 1. Cable car: All. Map p 184.*

★★ Tosca NORTH BEACH

This traditional old North Beach institution draws local politicos and celebs. With a dark-wood bar and a jukebox playing only opera, it's a classic. *242 Columbus Ave. (btw. Broadway St. & Pacific Ave.).* ☎ *415/986-9651. Bus: 12, 15, 41. Map p 184.*

★ Vesuvio NORTH BEACH Once

the favored beatnik watering hole, this famous place still draws an artsy crowd. *255 Columbus Ave. (at Jack Kerouac Alley, btw. Broadway St. & Pacific Ave.).* ☎ *415/362-3370. Bus: 12, 15, 41. Map p 184.*

Live Entertainment

★★★ Beach Blanket Babylon

NORTH BEACH For almost 40 years, BBB's outrageously hatted comedians have sung, danced, and spoofed pop culture. A hilarious, must-see revue. *Club Fugazi, 678 Green St. (at Columbus Ave.).* ☎ *415/421-4222. Tickets $25–$150. Bus: 30, 45. Cable car: Powell-Mason. Map p 184.*

★★ Curran Theatre UNION

SQUARE & CIVIC CENTER This beautiful 1,600-seat venue was established in 1922, and got treated to a major renovation in late 2016. Along with the ★ **Orpheum Theater** (1192 Market St.) and the **Golden Gate Theater** (1 Taylor St.), its "Best of Broadway" series brings NYC's biggest hits to SF. *445 Geary St. (btw. Mason & Taylor sts.).* ☎ *888/746-1799.*

Tickets $31–$200. Bus: 2, 3, 4, 38. BART/Muni: Powell St. Map p 184.

★★★ The Fillmore WESTERN

ADDITION The venue that presented bands such as the Grateful Dead and Jefferson Airplane remains SF's best rock venue. *1805 Geary Blvd. (at Fillmore St.).* ☎ *415/346-3000. Tickets $20–$50. Bus: 22, 38. Map p 184.*

★★ Palace of Fine Arts Theatre MARINA This inviting venue

presents a world of cultural performances, from Persian classical music to obscure forms of ethnic dance, as well as thought-provoking lectures and events. *3301 Lyon St. (at Richardson Ave./Lombard St.).* ☎ *415/563-6504. Tickets $20–$99. Bus: 30. Map p 184.*

★★ San Francisco Opera CIVIC

CENTER North America's second largest opera company (second only to the Met) is outstanding. *Tip:* $10 standing-room tickets are sold on the day of the show starting at 10am (cash only; one per person). The season runs from September to December and May to July. The top-notch San Francisco Ballet also performs here. *War Memorial Opera House, 301 Van Ness Ave. (at Grove St.).* ☎ *415/864-3330. Tickets $25–$330. Bus: 5, 21, 47, 49. BART/Muni: Civic Center. Map p 184.*

★★ San Francisco Symphony

CIVIC CENTER Founded in 1911 and conducted by the internationally acclaimed Michael Tilson Thomas. *Davies Symphony Hall, 201 Van Ness Ave. (btw. Grove & Hayes sts.).* ☎ *415/864-6000. Tickets $15–$145. Bus: 5, 21, 47, 49. BART/Muni: Civic Center. Map p 184.*

★★ SFJAZZ Center HAYES

VALLEY This is a newish venue for the city—it debuted in 2013—but the eco-friendly 35,000-square-foot performance space has already

AT&T Park, home of the Giants.

nabbed all sorts of awards for its modern design and diverse musical lineup. Its restaurant, **South,** is headed by Charles Phan, of **Slanted Door** (see p 183) fame. *201 Franklin St. (at Fell St.)* ☎ *866/920-5299. Muni: F, J, 6, 47, 49. BART: Civic Center. Map p 184.*

★★ Teatro Zinzanni EMBAR-CADERO Circus artists, wacky musicians, and a five-course meal come together for a 3-hour extravaganza under a distinctive tent. Tagline: "Love, chaos, and dinner." ***Note:*** "TZ" was closed at press time, due to a municipal issue, but plans to return soon. Call or check the website (www.zinzanni.com/sf) for updates. *Broadway & Embarcadero.*

☎ *415/438-2668. Tickets $100–$165 (3-course brunch starts at $73). Bus: 8X. Streetcar: F. Map p 184.*

Spectator Sports

★★★ kids Giants Baseball SOMA AT&T Park is often called the world's best baseball stadium. It's got dramatic bay views, splashy home runs, lots of stuff for kids, excellent food (get the garlic fries!), and a highly entertaining team and fan base, still giddy from their 2010, 2012, and 2014 World Series wins. *24 Willie Mays Plaza (King & 2nd sts.).* ☎ *415/972-2000. Tickets $8–$275. Bus: 10, 30, 45. Streetcar: N, KT. Map p 184.* ●

The
Savvy Traveler

Before You Go

Tourist Offices

Visit Napa Valley, Napa Valley Welcome Center, 600 Main St., Napa (☎ 855/847-6272 or 707/251-5895; www.visitnapavalley.com).

Yountville Chamber of Commerce, 6484 Washington St., Ste. F (☎ 707/944-0904; www.yountville.com).

Santa Rosa Convention & Visitors' Bureau, 9 Fourth St., Santa Rosa (☎ 800/404-7673 or 707/577-8674; www.visitsantarosa.com).

Healdsburg Chamber of Commerce & Visitors Bureau, 217 Healdsburg Ave., Healdsburg (☎ 707/433-6935; www.healdsburg.com).

Sonoma Valley Visitors Bureau, 453 1st St. E., Sonoma (☎ 866/996-1090 or 707/996-1090; www.sonomavalley.com).

Sonoma County Tourism Bureau, 400 Aviation Blvd., Santa Rosa (☎ 800/576-6662 or 707/522-5800; www.sonomacounty.com).

When to Go

Wine country's beauty is striking at any time of year, but it's most memorable during the **September and October** harvest months, when wineries are in full gear and the landscape is swept with rich autumnal colors. **Spring** is also gorgeous, in part because that's when the mustard flowers bloom, and there'll be less traffic, thinner crowds, and better deals than in the fall. Though **winter** boasts the best rates and fewest people, there's a reason: The days are often chilly and rainy and miles of bare vines lay dormant. The **summer** months bring hot weather and lots of traffic.

Previous page: Vineyards in Rutherford.

Weather

Though the valleys claim a year-round average of 70°F (21°C), if you come with a suitcase packed with T-shirts and shorts during the winter holiday season, you're likely to shiver your way to the nearest department store to stock up on warm clothes and possibly an umbrella. In summer, if you rent a car without air-conditioning, you're liable to want to stop at every swimming pool you pass. And don't let that morning fog and those early cool temperatures fool you—on most days, come noon, the hot sun sends down plenty of rays. Dress in layers and remember that temperatures can drop dramatically at night.

Festivals & Special Events

SPRING: A favorite Sonoma Valley festival is the **Barrel Tasting Weekend,** held in early March. The event, which gives the public a glimpse of Sonoma Valley's finest future releases and features more than 100 wineries, is a celebration that includes demonstrations, pairings, hors d'oeuvres—and all the world-class wine you can drink. Tickets are about $30; buy them in advance (or pay $40 at the door). No children are allowed. *www.wineroad.com.* ☎ 800/723-6336.

Late March to early April brings the **Sonoma Valley Film Festival,** a 5-day extravaganza screening more than 75 new independent films, including features, documentaries, and shorts. Day passes are $75 each, and basic passes to the whole festival are $200 each, but patrons can buy travel packages costing upward of $3,600. *www.sonomafilmfest.org.* ☎ 707/933-2600.

AVERAGE SEASONAL TEMPERATURES IN WINE COUNTRY				
	SPRING (MAR-MAY)	SUMMER (JUNE-AUG)	FALL (SEPT-NOV)	WINTER (DEC-FEB)
Average high (in °F)	78	92	85	72
Average high (in °C)	26	33	29	22
Average low (in °F)	64	81	74	61
Average low (in °C)	18	27	23	16

AVERAGE MONTHLY TEMPERATURES IN SAN FRANCISCO					
	JAN	FEB	MAR	APR	MAY	JUNE
High °F/°C	56/13	59/15	60/16	61/16	63/17	64/18
Low °F/°C	46/8	48/9	49/9	49/9	51/11	53/12
	JULY	AUG	SEPT	OCT	NOV	DEC
High °F/°C	64/18	65/18	69/21	68/20	63/17	57/14
Low °F/°C	53/12	54/12	56/13	55/13	52/11	47/8

In late April, the annual **Vineyard to Vintner (V2V)** day includes seminars, blind tastings, and open houses at many wineries. In the evening, Stags Leap Winery hosts barrel tastings on its Manor House porch, and the event features live music. It's $345 for the whole day including a fancy soiree, $145 for the open houses only. www.stagsleapdistrict.com. ☎ 707/255-1720.

Santa Rosa's **Cinco de Mayo Parade & Festival** happens the first weekend of May. It's the valley's biggest party, featuring authentic Mexican culture at its best, plus vibrant celebrations of other traditions too: mariachis in customary costumes, ballet folklorico, Aztec dancers, Afro-Brazilian flamenco, and lots of musicians and food. Admission is free. www.santarosacincodemayo.com. ☎ 707/548-3475.

SUMMER: The **Napa Valley Wine Auction,** held each June, is the area's most renowned—and exclusive—event. The annual charity affair brings some 2,000 deep-pocketed wine aficionados to Napa Valley to schmooze and spend serious cash. Four-day tickets cost at least $3,000 per person, and they sell out every year. (Less extravagant options are available for $500 and up.) www.auctionnapavalley.org. ☎ 707/963-3388.

Another big June attraction is the 10-day **Healdsburg Jazz Festival.** Venues range from vineyards to restaurants to intimate theaters, and headliners sell out quickly. Admission prices vary, and tickets are available via the website or at the box office. www.healdsburgjazzfestival.org. ☎ 707/433-4633.

Summer is also time for the **Sonoma County Hot Air Balloon Classic,** with a 30-balloon launch, tethered rides, and cartoon-character-shaped dirigibles. www.schabc.org.

In August, Santa Rosa holds **Wings Over Wine Country,** offering a thrilling air show with daredevil stunts and a close-up look at all types of aircraft. Advance tickets cost $18 for adults; kids 10 and under are free. www.wingsoverwinecountry.org. ☎ 707/566-8380.

AUTUMN: Fall into the romance of the **Napa Sonoma Wine Country Film Festival,** a month-long celebration of cinema, cuisine, and wine. Open-air venues screen flicks while film buffs sip, nibble, and socialize. Other activities include symposia, celebrity receptions, and chef demos. Tickets cost $10 to $25 per movie. Daily and weekly passes are also available. www.wcff.us. ☎ 707/935-3456.

The annual **Harvest Fair** takes place in Sonoma County every September. Residents and travelers come to check out the extensive art show, the more than 150 wineries and various microbreweries represented, cooking demos, music bands, the grape-stomping world championship, and a lively marketplace of foods and crafts. Kids enjoy farm animals, beekeepers, and wagon rides. www.harvestfair. org. ☎ 707/545-4200.

Another major Sonoma event—it's taken place each year since 1897—is the **Valley of the Moon Vintage Festival,** held the last weekend in September in Sonoma's historic plaza. This is a real party, complete with live music, dancing, parades, art displays, and, of course, copious wine tasting. www.valleyofthemoonvintage festival.com. ☎ 707/996-2109.

WINTER: Late January or early February heralds the **Sonoma Valley Olive Season Finale Weekend,** a celebration of the ancient fruit. At this culmination of the region's 3-month olive season, activities range from artisan markets to gourmet cooking classes to spa treatments. You could start early in January by taking the Wine Trail for access to 17 wineries' special tastings, or hold out for the VinOlivo February event series that includes 60 wineries and 25 restaurants. www.olivefestival.com. ☎ 866/ 996-1090.

Right before heavy tourist season kicks off, Healdsburg holds the **Winter Wineland** barrel-tasting weekend at more than 140 wineries all along the **Russian River Wine Road.** If you fall in love with a wine you've sampled, secure your share of bottles—at discounted prices—long before they hit the stores, never mind sell out. (It's called buying futures.) $35 for advance 1-day tickets, $45 for the weekend ($10 more at the door). www.wineroad. com. ☎ 800/723-6336.

Useful Websites

- www.visitnapavalley.com
- www.napachamber.com
- www.donapa.com
- www.napavalleyreservations. com
- www.napavintners.com
- www.silveradotrail.com
- www.sonomavalley.com
- www.sonoma.com
- www.sonomavalleywine.com
- www.winecountry.com

Cellphones (Mobiles)

One good wireless rental company is **InTouch USA** (☎ 800/872-7626; www.intouchusa.com). Although Napa and Sonoma don't have stores that rent cellphones, sometimes hotels' business centers, like the one at **Vintners Inn** in Santa Rosa (☎ 707/575-7350), will. Located in San Francisco International Airport, **Triptel Mobile Rental Phones** (☎ 415/474-3330; www.triptel.com) rents cellphones for $15 for a minimum 3-day rental or $75 per week. Phone includes unlimited talk and SMS in the U.S. and unlimited international SMS. Triptel also sells SIM cards for foreign travelers bringing their own phones. International travelers will be happy to know that cellphones (mobiles) with triband GSM capabilities work in the U.S. Remember that you'll be charged for calls received on a UK mobile used abroad. UK visitors can rent a U.S. phone before leaving home.

Contact **Cellhire** (☎ from the UK at 0800 2800 415 or 01904 616 620; www.cellhire.co.uk).

Car Rentals
When booking rental cars online, the best deals are usually on rental-car company websites. Major car-rental companies operating in wine country include **Enterprise** (☎ 707/253-8000; www.enterprise.com), **Budget** (☎ 800/527-0700 or 707/224-7846; www.budget.com), and **Hertz** (800/654-3131 or 707/265-7575; www.hertz.com). UK visitors should check **Holiday Autos**

(www.holidayautos.co.uk). San Francisco International Airport (SFO) and Oakland International Airport (OAK) both have car-rental centers at which the above companies are represented, in addition to discount car-rental companies such as **Fox Rent a Car** (airport location only; 800/225-4369; www.foxrentacar.com). Rates vary depending on season and other factors, but generally, compact cars run about $200 to $350 per week, including taxes and other charges. Most rentals in the U.S. are automatics.

Getting **There**

By Plane
Wine country is easily accessed by the Bay Area's two major airports: San Francisco International (SFO) and Oakland International (OAK), across the Bay Bridge. **San Francisco International Airport** (☎ 650/821-8211; www.flysfo.com) is a 2-hour drive from wine country. **Oakland International Airport** (☎ 510/563-3300; www.oaklandairport.com) is less crowded than SFO and more accessible, but offers fewer carriers. It's a bit more than a 1-hour drive from downtown Napa.

Getting to & from the Airport
Rent a car and drive to wine country (see "Car Rentals," above, for companies and "By Car," below, for driving directions). Because there's no useful public transportation in either valley, it's almost impossible to explore the region without wheels, so you might as well rent right at the airport. If you need to, though, for $29 (one way, cash only) you can ride to many hotels in Napa Valley or Sonoma

from SFO with **Evans Transportation** (☎ 707/255 1559). **Sonoma County Airport Express** (☎ 707/837-8700) offers service from SFO to a few hotels and major hubs in Sonoma (one way $34 for adults; $32 for seniors 62+, military & students; free for children 12 and younger).

By Car
All these routes to wine country are well-marked.

To Napa Valley
FROM SAN FRANCISCO Cross the Golden Gate Bridge and go north on U.S. 101; turn east on Highway 37 (toward Vallejo), then north on Highway 29, the main road through Napa Valley. You can also take Highway 121/12 from Highway 37 and follow the signs.

FROM OAKLAND Head eastbound on I-80 toward Sacramento; a few miles past the Carquinez Bridge ($5 toll) and the city of Vallejo, exit on Highway 12 west, which, after a few miles, intersects with Highway 29 and leads directly into Napa.

To Sonoma Valley

FROM SAN FRANCISCO Cross the Golden Gate Bridge and stay on U.S. 101 north. Exit at Highway 37; after 10 miles, turn north onto Highway 121. After another 10 miles, turn north onto Highway 12 (Broadway), which takes you directly into the town of Sonoma.

FROM OAKLAND Head eastbound on I-80 toward Sacramento. A few miles past the city of Vallejo (and after paying a $5 toll to cross the Carquinez Bridge), exit on Highway 12, which, after a few miles, intersects with Highway 29 at the south end of Napa Valley. Just before entering the town of Napa, you'll come to a major intersection, where Highway 29 meets Highway 12/121. Turn left onto Highway 12/121, which takes you directly into Sonoma Valley.

To Northern Sonoma

FROM SAN FRANCISCO Cross the Golden Gate Bridge and stay on U.S. 101 north. Exit anywhere from Santa Rosa to Healdsburg, depending on your destination.

FROM OAKLAND Head eastbound on I-80 toward Sacramento. A few miles past the city of Vallejo (and after paying a $5 toll to cross the Carquinez Bridge), exit on Highway 12, which, after a few miles, intersects with Highway 29 at the south end of Napa Valley. Just before entering the town of Napa, you'll come to a major intersection, where Highway 29 meets Highway 12/121. Turn left onto Highway 12/121, then turn right onto California 116/Arnold Drive. When the road forks, veer right onto Adobe Road. Turn left on East Washington Street, merge onto U.S. 101 north, and exit at the town of your choice.

By Bus

Wine country's only **Greyhound** (☎ 800/231-2222 or 707/545-6495; www.greyhound.com) terminal is at 3345 S. Santa Rosa Ave. in Santa Rosa and is open weekdays from 1:30 to 5pm and weekends and holidays from 2:30 to 5pm.

Getting **Around**

With hundreds of wineries scattered amid Napa and Sonoma's tens of thousands of acres of vineyards, it's difficult to explore wine country without wheels. See "Before You Go," above, for details about renting a car.

By Car

Driving in wine country is relatively straightforward and enjoyable. All the streets and highways are well-marked and most of them are strikingly beautiful, even when there's traffic. As you drive, keep in mind that one of the preeminent dangers of driving through wine country is

that it's an area highly focused on alcohol consumption. The importance of avoiding drinking and driving can't be stressed strongly enough. Refrain from driving if you feel even a little tipsy (see "By Cab," below, in case you feel inebriated). Beware of others on the road who might have consumed too much in the tasting room.

The only other bungling factor is that some wine-country highways have many different names. For example, Highway 12 is also Highway 121 is also Carneros Highway is also Sonoma-Napa Highway. You'll see examples of this kind of multiple street-naming throughout wine country and it may throw you off. If you get confused, pull over and look at a map (or ask your passenger to guide you). The best online resource for getting directions is Google Maps: www.google.com/maps.

By Cab

(No, not cabernet.) You have to call for a taxi in wine country unless you're boarding one from your hotel. Companies: **Yellow Cab of Napa Valley** (☎ 707/226-3731) and **Black Tie Taxi** (☎ 707/259-1000 or 888/519-8294). In Sonoma, your best bet is **Vern's Taxi Service** (☎ 707/938-8885) and, in northern Sonoma, **Healdsburg Taxi Cab** (☎ 707/433-7088). Rates hover at $2.85 for the first mile and $2.70 for each mile thereafter. **Uber** started operating in Napa and Sonoma in 2014, so if you've got a smartphone, download the app to be able to have a car on call at all times.

On Foot

Many of wine country's treasures within towns can be seen on foot, though you can't easily walk from town to town. See chapter 4 for the area's best walking tours. Though most of these tours traverse flat surfaces, wear comfortable shoes: You'll likely be standing for a long time, especially if you shop and visit tasting rooms.

Crossing Counties

The easiest way to get from Napa to Sonoma Valley and vice versa is through the Carneros District, which serves as the southern end of both valleys, and cross over along the Sonoma Highway (Calif. 12/121). To get from Napa to Sonoma takes about 20 minutes when there's no traffic. Another option: Take the Oakville Grade (also called Trinity Road) over the Mayacamas Range, which links Napa's Oakville to Sonoma's Glen Ellen. It's a steep and winding road, but it can be a time-saver if you're headed to the northern end of either valley. To get to northern Sonoma from points south in Sonoma Valley, follow Highway 12 north to get to Santa Rosa. From there, take U.S. 101 north and exit at the town of your choice. To get to northern Sonoma from downtown Napa, take California 12/121 (Sonoma Hwy.) to Highway 16 to Adobe Road (veer right) to U.S. 101 North. The trip is about an hour and 15 minutes. From northern Napa towns like Calistoga or St. Helena, it's easier to follow Highway 29 north past downtown Calistoga when it becomes Highway 128. Follow Highway 128 for a few blocks and turn left onto Petrified Forest Road. Turn right onto Porter Creek Road and follow it; it becomes Mark West Springs Road, which leads you to U.S. 101 North.

Fast **Facts**

APARTMENT & VILLA RENTALS For short-term rentals, check **www.craigslist.org**. After selecting the "SF bay area" location, click on the "apts/housing" link and put "Napa" into the search bar; you'll likely come up with more than 100 current listings. You'll likely negotiate a rental directly from the unit's owner (or the person subletting). Also check **www.airbnb.com**, **www.nightswapping.com**, **www.sublet.com**, or **www.vrbo.com**. To research house exchanges, check out **Homelink International** (www.homelink.org), which lists more

The Savvy Traveler

than 14,000 rentals in several countries, or try **Homebase Holidays** (www.homebase-hols.com).

AREA CODE Napa and Sonoma counties both use **707.**

ATMs/CASHPOINTS There are ATMs throughout both valleys, though not as many as you'd find in a big city. Unless you go to your bank's ATM, you'll be charged a fee of $1.50 to $3—or more, if you're using an international card. The **Cirrus** (☎ 800/424-7787; www.mastercard.com) and **PLUS** (☎ 800/843-7587; www.visa.com) networks span the globe; look at the back of your bank card to see which network you're on, then call or check online for ATM locations in wine country. Find out your daily withdrawal limit before you depart.

BABYSITTING Most hotel concierges will provide referrals to a babysitting service, which guests must then call on their own. Local companies supplying short-term sitters are **Nannies of the Valley** (☎ 707/251-8035), **Napa Valley Nanny** (☎ 707/226-1474), and, a bit farther south, **Bay Area 2nd Mom, Inc.** (☎ 650/858-2469).

BANKS Most banks are open Monday through Friday from 9am to 5pm. Some are also open until midday Saturday. Many banks also have ATMs for 24-hour banking. **Bank of America** has several branches throughout the area, including one at 1001 Adams St. in St. Helena (☎ 707/967-4080). You'll also find **Wells Fargo** throughout the region, including a branch in Napa at 217 Soscol Ave., inside Raley's supermarket (☎ 707/254-8690). The Sonoma Wells Fargo is at 480 W. Napa St. (☎ 707/996-2360). For a complete listing of Wells Fargo branches, call ☎ 800/869-3557.

B&Bs Reputable booking services include **Bed & Breakfast Inns**

Online (☎ 800/215-7365; www.bbonline.com), **Pamela Lanier's Bed & Breakfasts** (www.lanierbb.com), **BedandBreakfast.com** (www.bedandbreakfast.com), and **Visit Napa Valley** (www.visitnapavalley.com; click on "Hotels & Resorts," then "Bed & Breakfast Inns"). To read the opinions of those who've stayed at a place you're considering, enter its name into the search bar at **TripAdvisor** (www.tripadvisor.com) or **Yelp** (www.yelp.com).

BIKE RENTALS One of the best companies is **Napa Valley Bike Tours** (☎ 707/251-TOUR [8687]; www.napavalleybiketours.com). Daily rentals range from $45 to $74, depending on the type of bike. Kids' bikes are $29 per day, and tandems (synchronized fun) are $90. Napa Valley Bike Tours also provides excellent guided tours, ranging from the $124 classic tour to a $379 hot-air balloon and bike tour. Consider choosing a package that includes lunch—the company's gourmet picnics are fantastic. Other bike-rental companies include **Getaway Adventures** (Sonoma and Napa; ☎ 800/499-2453; www.getawayadventures.com) and **Wine Country Bike Rentals** (Sonoma; ☎ 866/922-4537 or 707/473-0610; www.winecountrybikes.com). Remember that sometimes B&Bs and even hotels will lend bikes for free, so ask if that's the case at your place before renting.

CONSULATES & EMBASSIES All embassies are located in the nation's capital, Washington, D.C. For a directory of embassies in Washington, D.C., go to www.state.gov/s/cpr/rls/dpl. Napa's nearest major city is San Francisco; the following are consulate addresses in San Francisco for a selection of countries: The **Australian Consulate-General** is at 575 Market St., Ste. 1800 (☎ 415/644-3620). The

Consulate General of Canada is at 580 California St., 14th floor (☎ 415/834-3180). The **Consulate General of Ireland** is at 100 Pine St., Ste. 3350 (☎ 415/392-4214). The **British Consulate-General San Francisco** is at 1 Sansome St., Ste. 850 (☎ 415/617-1300). In Southern California is the **New Zealand Consulate-General of Los Angeles** at 2425 Olympic Blvd., Ste. 600E, Santa Monica (☎ 310/566-6555), though honorary consuls have been appointed to serve Sacramento (44733 N. El Macero Dr., El Macero; ☎ 530/756-8013) and San Francisco (☎ 650/342-4443).

CREDIT CARDS Credit cards are a safe way to "carry" money. With them, you can withdraw cash advances from ATMs using your PIN. Let your credit-card company know of your travel plans so they don't freeze your account when you make your big wine purchases.

CUSTOMS Visitors arriving by air, no matter the port of entry, should cultivate patience and resignation before setting foot on U.S. soil. Getting through immigration can sometimes take a very long time, especially on summer weekends. People traveling by air from Canada and certain Caribbean countries can sometimes clear Customs and Immigration at the point of departure, which is much quicker.

DENTISTS If you have dental problems, a nationwide referral service known as **1-800-DENTIST** (☎ 800/336-8478) will provide the name of a nearby dentist or clinic.

DINING Dining in wine country, as in most of California, is generally casual. A jacket is rarely required, except at Napa or Sonoma's most upscale restaurants. **Reservations:** Call the restaurant directly or try **OpenTable** (www.opentable.com), a free online reservations site.

ELECTRICITY Like Canada, the United States uses 110 to120 volts AC (60 cycles), compared to 220 to 240 volts AC (50 cycles) in most of Europe, Australia, and New Zealand. If your small appliances use 220 to 240 volts, you'll need a 110-volt transformer and a plug adapter with two flat parallel pins to operate them here. Downward converters that change 220 to 240 volts to 110 to 120 volts are difficult to find in the U.S., so bring one with you.

EMERGENCIES Dial ☎ **911** for fire, police, and ambulance. No coins are needed from a working public phone. The **Poison Control Center** can be reached at ☎ 800/222-1222 toll-free. If you encounter serious problems, contact **Travelers Aid International** (☎ 202/546-1127; www.travelersaid.org).

GAY & LESBIAN TRAVELERS See www.sanfrancisco.travel/lgbt or www.gaytravel.com for good ideas.

HOLIDAYS Banks, government offices, post offices, and many stores, restaurants, and museums are closed on the following national holidays: January 1 (New Year's Day), the third Monday in January (Martin Luther King, Jr. Day), the third Monday in February (Presidents Day), the last Monday in May (Memorial Day), July 4 (Independence Day), the first Monday in September (Labor Day), the second Monday in October (Columbus Day), November 11 (Veterans Day), the fourth Thursday in November (Thanksgiving), and December 25 (Christmas). Also, the Tuesday following the first Monday in November is Election Day and is a federal government holiday held every four years (next in 2016).

INSURANCE The best way to find an insurance policy is to go to one of two marketplace websites: **InsureMyTrip.com** and **Square-Mouth.com**. Each will lead you to respected companies, and show you the wide range of policies available for your trip.

LIMOUSINE SERVICES   There are many companies chomping at the bit to chauffer your wine tasting in style. Among the best: **Pure Luxury** (4246 Petaluma Blvd. N., Petaluma; ☎ 800/626-5466; www.pureluxury. com), **Beau Wine Tours and Limousine Service** (1754 2nd St., Ste. B., Napa; ☎ 707/257-0887; www. beauwinetours.com), and **Limos of Napa** (☎ 707/334-0411; www. limosofnapa.com).

LIQUOR LAWS   Liquor and grocery stores, as well as some drug stores, are permitted to sell packaged alcoholic beverages between 6am and 2am. Most restaurants, nightclubs, and bars are licensed to serve alcoholic beverages during the same hours. The legal age for purchase and consumption is 21, and proof of age is required.

PHARMACIES   **Rite Aid,** a drugstore and convenience chain, has stores just about everywhere. Call ☎ 800/ 748-3243 or go to www.riteaid.com for the address and phone number of the nearest store.

SAFETY   Don't walk alone at night, stay in well-lighted areas, and carry a minimum of cash and jewels. Though wine country isn't crime-ridden by any means, it's not a 24-hour region. One of the dangers here is drunk driving—avoid it at all costs, and keep watch for other motorists who may have consumed too much wine.

SENIOR TRAVELERS   Many wine-country attractions offer admission discounts for those older than 50; ask if you're not sure. **The Council on Aging Services for Sonoma County Seniors** (30 Kawana Springs Rd., Santa Rosa; ☎ 707/525-0143; www.councilonaging.com) offers services such as entertainment, gentle exercise, arts and crafts,

guest speakers, and current-event discussions. The council's special events for active seniors include nature walks, enrichment workshops, and a special event once a year (usually an art show or derby day in May). Members of **AARP** (601 E St. NW, Washington, D.C. 20049; ☎ 888/687-2277; www.aarp. org) get discounts on hotels, airfares, and car rentals. UK seniors can contact **Saga** (☎ 0800/096-0074; www.saga.co.uk) for a range of products and services, including holidays and insurance. Australians older than 50 should contact the **National Seniors Association** (☎ 1300/76-5050; www.national seniors.com.au).

SMOKING   California has pretty restrictive smoking laws. They prohibit smoking in public buildings (and within 20 ft. of them), restaurants and bars, as well as playgrounds and daycare facilities.

TAXES   California state and local sales tax (9.25%) is added to all purchases except snack foods. The hotel tax, known as the transient occupancy tax, is 9% in Sonoma County and 12% in Napa County. You won't have to pay sales tax if you have your purchases shipped directly out of state.

TELEPHONES   For directory assistance, dial ☎ **411.** See "Cellphones (Mobiles)" p. 196.

TIME   California is in the Pacific Standard time zone: 8 hours behind Greenwich Mean Time (GMT) or 7 hours behind during daylight saving time (Mar–Nov); 3 hours behind Eastern Standard Time (EST).

TIPPING   In hotels, tip bellhops at least $1 per bag and the housekeeping staff $2 to $3 per day (more if you've left a mess); the doorman or concierge $1 to $5 only if he or she has provided you with some specific service (for example, calling a cab or obtaining

203

Wine Country: **A Brief History**

hard-to-get tickets). Tip the valet-parking attendant at least $1 each time your car is retrieved. In restaurants, bars, and nightclubs, waitstaff expect 15% to 20% of the check, bartenders 10% to 15%, checkroom attendants $1 per garment, and valet-parking attendants at least $1 per vehicle. Tip cab drivers 15%, skycaps at airports at least $1 per bag, and hairdressers and barbers 15% to 20%.

TOILETS Public toilets can be hard to find in wine country. Hotels and restaurants are probably the best bet for clean facilities, and they're usually friendly about letting stop-pers-by use them.

TRAVELERS WITH DISABILITIES Many travel agencies offer customized tours and itineraries for travelers with disabilities. Two of them are **Flying Wheels Travel** (☎ 507/451-5005; www.flyingwheelstravel.com) and **Accessible Journeys** (☎ 800/846-4537; www.disabilitytravel.com). From the UK, **Access Travel** (☎ 01942/888844; www.access-travel.co.uk) offers a variety of holidays for persons with disabilities.

Wine Country: **A Brief History**

1542 Wappo Indians inhabit Napa Valley; Portuguese explorer Juan Rodriguez Cabrillo sails up the California coast, the first European to investigate the region.

1780 Franciscan missionaries, establishing the first of what would become the state's 21 missions, plant California's first vineyard near San Diego.

1821 Mexico wins independence from Spain and annexes California.

1824 The *padres* of the 21st mission, San Francisco Solano, plant vines near present-day Sonoma.

1825 California's first commercial vineyards are established in Los Angeles.

1825 George Calvert Yount establishes Napa's first homestead (now Yountville) and is the first to plant vineyards in Napa.

1840 California missions become secular and Mission San Francisco Solano's vines become the region's first commercial vineyard.

1846 The Bear Flag Revolt: Americans capture Sonoma, arresting and imprisoning resident Mexican governor Mariano Guadalupe Vallejo. The Americans declare an independent California Republic.

1846–48 The Mexican-American War rages between the U.S. and Mexico; Mexico loses about half its territory.

1850 Mariano Guadalupe Vallejo is elected to California's first State Senate.

1857 "Count" Agoston Haraszthy plants the first major vineyard of European varieties in Sonoma Valley.

1858 Sonoma's first commercial wines are produced when Charles Krug makes a few gallons for Napa pioneer John Patchett.

1861 Charles Krug goes on to establish Napa's first commercial winery.

1861 Schramsberg is founded.

1875 Sonoma supplants Los Angeles as the state's leading wine region (as measured by acreage).

1875 Beringer is founded.

1885 Napa ousts Sonoma as the state's leading wine region (as measured by acreage). Both valleys' wine industries continue to grow and prosper.

1889 Sonoma has 100 wineries; Napa has more than 140.

1890s Napa loses roughly 75% of its acreage to a plant louse (*phylloxera vastatrix*) epidemic that attacks vineyards.

1919 The 18th Amendment is enacted: "the manufacture, sale, or transportation of intoxicating liquors . . . is hereby prohibited." President Woodrow Wilson vetoes the accompanying Volstead Act but the amendment is made anyway.

1920 Prohibition begins and is enforced. Most of California's wineries shut down, though a few keep operating to produce sacramental and medicinal wine.

1933 The 18th Amendment is repealed by the 21st Amendment, making the Constitution's only provision to be explicitly modified.

1934 Americans pay almost no attention to dry European-style table wines; the bulk of domestically consumed wines are ports and sherries. This lack of interest persists for 35 years.

1937 Napa has only 37 wineries; Sonoma has 91.

1944 Napa Valley Vintners Association is founded with the mission of promoting local wine worldwide.

1960 Napa dwindles to 25 wineries; Sonoma has even fewer (just nine, by one account).

1960 Robert Mondavi leaves Charles Krug winery to start his own. He develops new winemaking techniques and aggressive marketing strategies.

1972 Wineries start burgeoning again in Napa: This year and next, big players appear on the scene, including Chateau Montelena, Stag's Leap Wine Cellars, Clos du Val, Franciscan, Trefethen, Joseph Phelps, and Domaine Chandon. In Sonoma, Kenwood, Chateau St. Jean, and St. Francis open.

1976 At a blind tasting in Paris, French wine experts unwittingly award top honors to Chateau Montelena's chardonnay and Stag's Leap Wine Cellars' cabernet, shocking France and waking the world up to California wines.

EARLY 1980s Vintners in both valleys discover *phylloxera vastatrix* again, requiring replanting of most of their acreage. Wine sales level off.

1981 The first annual Auction Napa Valley takes place, starting a tradition that has raised more than $60 million for charity and helped establish Napa as a prestigious region capable of drawing considerable wealth.

1981 Sonoma Valley is designated an American Viticulture Area (AVA).

1982 Napa Valley is designated an AVA. Since then, more than a dozen other AVAs have been designated.

1990 Replanting continues and new labels steadily emerge. Restyled red wines become particularly popular.

1992 Sonoma Valley Vintners & Growers Alliance is formed to promote Sonoma wines and grapes.

2016 Napa Valley and Sonoma Valley each boast more than 400 wineries.

A Quick Guide to **Wine Varietals**

Major Grape Varietals

Below is a list of some of California wine country's most prevalent grape types.

Cabernet sauvignon This transplant from Bordeaux has become California's best-known varietal. The small, deep-colored, thick-skinned berry is a complex grape, yielding medium- to full-bodied red wines that are highly tannic when young and usually require a long aging period to achieve their greatest potential. Cabernet is often blended with other related red varietals, such as merlot and cabernet franc (see below), into full-flavored red table wines. These blends, if sanctioned by the Meritage Association, are often called Meritage wines. Cabernet is often matched with red-meat dishes and strong cheeses. If you're looking to invest in several cases of wine, cabernet sauvignon is always a good long-term bet.

Chardonnay The most widely planted grape variety in wine country produces exceptional medium- to full-bodied dry white wines. In fact, it was a California chardonnay that revolutionized the world of wine when it won the legendary 1976 Paris tasting test. You'll find a range of chardonnays in wine country, from delicate, crisp wines that are clear and light in color to buttery, fruity, and oaky (no other wine benefits more from the oak aging process) wines that tend to have deeper golden hues as they increase in richness. This highly complex and aromatic grape is one of the few that doesn't require blending; it's also the principal grape for making sparkling wine. Chardonnay goes well with a variety of dishes, including seafood, poultry, pork, veal, and pastas made with cream or butter.

Merlot Traditionally used as a blending wine to smooth out other grapes' rough edges, merlot has gained popularity in California since the early 1970s—enough so that wineries such as Sonoma's St. Francis are best known for producing masterful merlots. Though it got a bad rap in the 2004 film *Sideways*, it's still America's most popular red (at least by sales figures). The merlot grape is a relative of cabernet sauvignon, but it's fruitier and softer, with a pleasant black-cherry bouquet. Merlots tend to be simpler and less tannic than most cabernets, and they're drinkable at an earlier age, though these wines, too, gain complexity with age. Serve this medium- to full-bodied red with any dish you'd normally pair with a cabernet—it's great with pizza.

Pinot noir It took California vintners decades to make relatively few great wines from pinot noir grapes, which are difficult to grow and vinify. Even in their native Burgundy, the wines are excellent only a few years out of every decade. Recent attempts to grow the finicky grape in the Carneros District's cooler climes have shown promising results. During banner harvest years, California's pinot grapes produce complex, light- to medium-bodied red wines with such low tannins and silky textures that they're comparable to the world's finest reds. Pinots are fuller and softer than cabernets and can be drinkable at 2 to 5 years of age, though the best improve with additional aging. Pinot noir is versatile at the dinner table but goes best with lamb, duck, turkey, game birds, semisoft cheeses, even fish.

Riesling   Also called Johannisberg riesling or white riesling, this is the grape from which most of Germany's great wines are produced. It was introduced to California in the mid–19th century by immigrant vintners and is now used mainly to make floral and fruity white wines of light to medium body, ranging from dry to very sweet. It's also often used to make late-harvest dessert wine. Well-made rieslings, of which California has produced few, have a vivid fruitiness and lively balancing acidity, as well as the potential to age for many years. Suggested food pairings include crab, pork, sweet-and-sour foods, Asian cuisine, and anything with a strong citrus flavor.

Sauvignon blanc   Also labeled as fumé blanc, these grapes are used to make crisp, dry whites of medium to light body that vary in flavor from slightly grassy to tart or fruity. The grape grows well in Napa and Sonoma and has grown in popularity due to its distinctive character and pleasant acidity, recently becoming a contender to the almighty chardonnay. Because of their acidity, sauvignon blancs pair well with shellfish, seafood, and salads.

Zinfandel   Often called the "mystery" grape because its origins are uncertain, zinfandel first appeared on California labels in the late 1800s. So it's come to be known as California's grape, and in fact, most of the world's zinfandel acreage is in northern California: Some of the best zin grapes grow in cool coastal locations and on century-old vines in California's more eastern Gold Country. Zinfandel is by far wine country's most versatile grape, popular as blush wine (the ever-quaffable white zinfandel: a light, fruity wine usually served chilled); as dark, spicy, and fruity red wines; even as a port. Premium zins, like those crafted by Sonoma's Ravenswood winery (see p 156), are rich and peppery with a lush texture and nuances of raspberries, licorice, and spice. Food-wise, it's a free-for-all, though premium zins go well with beef, lamb, hearty pastas, pizza, and stews.

Lesser-Known Grape Varietals

Cabernet franc   A French black grape that's often blended with—and overshadowed by—the more widely planted cabernet sauvignon, cabernet franc was recently discovered to be one of the grape species that gave rise to cabernet sauvignon. The grape grows best in cool, damp conditions and tends to be lighter in color and tannins than its sauvignon cousin, so it matures earlier in the bottle. These wines have a deep purple color with an herbaceous aroma.

Chenin blanc   Planted mainly in France, chenin blanc runs the gamut from cheap, dry whites with little discernible character to some of the world's subtlest, fragrant, and most complex wines. In wine country, the grape is mostly used to create fruity, light- to medium-bodied and slightly sweet wines. Chenin blanc lags far behind chardonnay and sauvignon blanc in popularity, though in good years, it develops a lovely and complex bouquet, especially when aged in oak. It's often served with pork and poultry, Asian dishes with soy-based sauces, mild cheeses, and vegetable and fruit salads.

Gewürztraminer   This grape (pronounce the "w" like a "v") produces whites with strong floral aromas and lychee-nut-like flavor. Slightly sweet yet spicy, it's somewhat similar in style to the Johannisberg riesling and is occasionally used to make late-harvest, dessert-style wine. The grape grows well in California's cooler coastal regions, especially in Mendocino County to the north. The varietal is appreciated for its ability to complement Asian foods: Its sweet character stands up to flavors that would diminish a drier wine's nuances.

Petite sirah   Widely grown throughout California's warmer regions, petite sirah's origins are a mystery. The grape, which produces rich, high-tannin reds, serves mainly as the backbone for Central Valley "jug" wines. Very old vines still exist in cooler northern regions, where these grapes are made into robust, well-balanced reds.

Pinot blanc   A mutation of pinot gris, the pinot blanc grape is prevalent in France's Alsace region, where it makes for dry, crisp white wines. In California, pinot blanc produces a fruity wine similar to chardonnay's simpler versions. It's also blended with champagne-style sparkling wines, thanks to its acid content and clean flavor.

Sangiovese   This is Italy's favorite grape: It makes everything from chianti and Brunello di Montalcino to "Super Tuscan" blends. Now it's also making a name for itself in California. Its style varies depending on where it's grown, but it's commonly described as anything from "fruity," "smooth," "spicy," "good acidity," and "medium-bodied" to "structured" and "full-bodied."

Syrah   This red varietal is best known for producing France's noble and age-worthy Rhône Valley reds such as côte-rôtie and hermitage. Syrah vines produce dark, blackish berries with thick skins, resulting in typically dark, rich, dense, medium- to full-bodied wines with distinctive pepper, spice, and fruit flavors.

Index

See also Accommodations and Restaurant indexes, below.